NEWCOMER'S HANDBOOK ®

FOR MOVING TO

London

FIRST BOOKS

3000 Market Street NE, Suite 527
Salem, OR 97301 USA
503-588-2224
www.firstbooks.com

1st edition

Author: Janetta Willis
Series Editor: Bernadette Duperron
Publisher: Jeremy Solomon
Design: Erin Johnson
Maps provided by DesignMaps.com

ISBN 0-912301-47-3
ISSN 1525 4968

Printed in the USA on recycled paper.

Published by First Books, 3000 Market Street NE, Suite 527, Salem, OR 97301 USA.

What readers are saying about Newcomer's Handbooks:

I recently got a copy of your Newcomer's Handbook for Chicago, and wanted to let you know how invaluable it was for my move. I must have consulted it a dozen times a day preparing for my move. It helped me find my way around town, find a place to live, and so many other things. My only suggestion is a more detailed map of the area. It's just a small gripe however, as your book helped me so much. Thanks.

—Mike L.
Chicago, Illinois

Excellent reading (Newcomer's Handbook for San Francisco and the Bay Area). Haven't checked out the information yet, but it seems balanced and trustworthy. One of the very best guides if you are considering moving/relocation. Way above the usual tourist crap.

—Gunnar E.
Stockholm, Sweden

I was very impressed with the latest edition of the Newcomer's Handbook for Los Angeles. It is well organized, concise and up-to date. I would recommend this book to anyone considering a move to Los Angeles.

—Jannette L.
Attorney Recruiting Administrator for a large Los Angeles law firm

I recently moved to Atlanta from San Francisco, and LOVE the Newcomer's Handbook for Atlanta. It has been an invaluable resource – it's helped me find everything from a neighborhood in which to live to the local hardware store. I look something up in it everyday, and know I will continue to use it to find things long after I'm no longer a newcomer. And if I ever decide to move again, your book will be the first thing I buy for my next destination.

—Courtney R.
Atlanta, Georgia

In looking to move to the Boston area, a potential employer in that area gave me a copy of the Newcomer's Handbook for Boston. It's a great book that's very comprehensive, outlining good and bad points about each neighborhood in the Boston area. Very helpful in helping me decide where to move.

—no name given (online submit form)

TABLE OF CONTENTS

CONTENTS

L ONDON IS ONE OF THE MOST EXCITING PLACES ON THE PLANET IN which to live and work. Its origins as a grand capital city began with the Roman period 2000 years ago, and the tradition of intense commercial and social activity continues unabated. The first thing to impress upon the newcomer is London's vital statistics: it sprawls across an area thirty miles in diameter, with a population in excess of seven million. It has an ancient centre redolent with history and constantly invigorated by new development. In London there is urban grandeur, picturesque Dickensian pockets, suburban steadiness and inner-city blight all in close proximity and varying proportions. "When a man is tired of London he is tired of life; for there is in London all that life can afford," Samuel Johnson famously declared back in the 18th century, and his epigram seems more true today than ever. Whether you're looking for the spirit of the swinging sixties, a centre of learning, a high-tech business environment or just red buses, you will find London is all it's cracked up to be, plus some. It is its multiplicity of details and possibilities that makes London so many things to so many different people.

London's communities are plentiful, diverse and ever-evolving. During its history London has been the first port of call for many invading armies, the Romans, the Angles and Saxons, and the Normans; it has also assimilated many different waves of immigration. It is difficult to pinpoint typical Londoners, but they are as likely to be new arrivals as to be indigenous. There are sizeable communities of different diaspora—Asian, Afro-Caribbean, Italian, Irish, Jewish, Chinese, Turkish—resulting in a local population where one in five is from an ethnic minority group. Add to this a large influx of European Union nationals taking advantage of the right to move and work freely within the European Community, and a big lesbian and gay presence, and you have a thoroughly diverse picture. Although the streets are most definitely not paved with gold (inevitably perhaps there *is* a road here called Treadgold Street), the economy remains buoyant, with many new developments, enterprise zones and transport links attracting new business to even previously run-down areas. The hoop-la surrounding the year 2000 sparked many regeneration plans throughout the London boroughs. Unfortunately, despite the grand projects and celebrations inspired by the millennium, problems remain; deteriorating housing and unemployment are always issues, and it's estimated that 24% of London's population live below the poverty line. The number of people sleeping on the streets can be a shock to newcomers, especially those not used to urban life.

> **THE FIRST PROBLEM YOU ARE LIKELY TO EXPERIENCE UPON YOUR ARRIVAL IS ORIENTATING YOURSELF TO LONDON'S LABYRINTHINE STREETS. GETTING LOST IS A RITE OF PASSAGE FOR NEW LONDONERS.**

In 2000 the Economist Intelligence Unit's cost of living survey placed London as the seventh most expensive city in the world. What's perhaps more interesting/frightening, is that London rated 14th just three years before! Many aspects of life in London are pricey, most notably housing and public transport. Countrywide, London's cost of living is acknowledged to be higher than in any other part of the UK and many salaries come with "London weighting," which means you receive more money than you would for a comparable job elsewhere. There are, however, many ways to dine and be entertained inexpensively in the city. It costs nothing to enjoy London's historic architecture or stroll around its world famous parks. Whatever your background, interests or budget, London is sure to have something for you.

The first problem you are likely to experience upon your arrival is orientating yourself to London's labyrinthine streets. Getting lost is a rite of passage for new Londoners. Be sure to carry with you a street map, either the *Geographers' London A-Z* or *Nicolson's Streetfinder* (available at any newsagent or bookshop). Sticking to main routes to start with, you soon will develop a nose for shortcuts. Public transport in London centres on the London Underground, or "the Tube" as it is known—an underground passenger rail system similar to the New York subway or Paris Metro. The Tube consists of different lines (with names such as the Piccadilly, Jubilee, Central, etc.), which link stations all over the capital. The Tube network is made intelligible by its well-designed map, which can be obtained from Tube stations, or you'll find it reproduced on the back of the *A-Z*.

The severity of British weather is greatly exaggerated (although our ability to talk about it endlessly is not!). Despite Britain's reputation for rain, the southeast of England experienced a shortage of rain during several years in the 1990s, which resulted in hosepipe bans and increasing worry about dwindling water supplies. Contrast this with the endless rain and flooding which, were a feature of the winter of 2000/2001. Summer here gets noticeably hotter than it did just a decade ago, and you may find public transport and many buildings not very well-equipped to deal with higher temperatures. The combined affects of warm weather and pollution at times make for poor air quality in the capital. British winters can be harsh but London and the southeast rarely bear the brunt, with more than a couple of days of snow per year unusual. The key is to be prepared for anything. Due to its northerly position, daylight hours are long in summer, roughly 5 a.m. to 9:30 p.m., and very short in winter, only lasting from about 8 a.m. to 4 p.m.

To assist you with UK phrases and London jargon, you will find, at the end of the introduction to the borough profiles, a glossary that lists general and housing related terms.

HISTORY

The streets of London are steeped in history; a sense of this is vital to understanding the physical and cultural shape of London today. The city has a long and fascinating past which can be glimpsed in the array of period architecture and in place-names. All sorts of historic events and people loom large—blue plaques attached to buildings draw attention to the capital's famous residents from Mozart to Hendrix.

With the 1998 discovery of the remains of the earliest known bridge across the Thames which dates back to 700 BC, there is evidence that London has been inhabited since prehistoric times. But London's history really gets going after the Roman invasion of AD 43. The Romans quickly established a port and a settlement on the north bank of the river Thames. The Thames, a tidal river reaching from the sea into the heart of the English countryside in Gloucestershire, served as the gateway for commercial traffic. Roman Londinium was superseded by the Saxon town of Londenwic before the establishment of the walled city of the middle ages. It is here that Chaucer composed his poetry in medieval times, and Shakespeare, in Elizabethan times, staged his plays alongside cockfighting and bear baiting in the theatres of Southwark, on the south bank of the river.

Throughout London's history literary figures have inhabited and documented its streets. In the seventeenth century Samuel Pepys wrote his diary which included descriptions of the destruction wreaked by the great fire of London in 1666 and the horrors of the plague. The re-building after the fire with contributions from famous architects such as Christopher Wren and Inigo Jones originally envisioned a re-fashioning of London's streets on a grand scale. But despite such progressive thinking, the pre-fire medieval street patterns of narrow passageways remained largely intact. Today, the square mile of the City of London is the financial centre of the country, and is where the London Stock Exchange is situated. It is known colloquially as "the City" and is where you are far more likely to work than to live. (The weight of archaeological deposits at this centre is so extensive that the natural land surface lies as much as six metres below.) Westminster, home to Parliament and the seat of government, was originally an adjacent city, explaining why that borough is still known as the City of Westminster. London began expanding in earnest beyond these boundaries in the late 18th and early 19th centuries when the Industrial Revolution led to the first canals being cut, new bridges constructed across the Thames, and four new docks. In time this development led to the growth of the slums of the East End which housed the new workers. Manufacturing industry in London continued to grow and thrive well into the 20th century but is now very much in decline. Whereas in the rest of the country manufacturing still employs one in five workers, in London the figure is one in ten and shrinking. London's big employers are now the burgeoning service and financial sectors.

Expansion during the course of the 19th century gradually enveloped outlying villages, hamlets and towns. Added to this was the building of new suburbs, which, by the 20th century, were also integrated into Greater London. It is still possible to trace the old villages of London; often place names will have semi-rural connotations and it sometimes helps to remember these origins when faced with the bewildering multiplicity of localities and place-names in Greater London. The Greater London area is now split into the City of London and 32 boroughs, each of which has its own elected local authority called a "council" responsible for local services and social housing.

THE WEIGHT OF ARCHAEOLOGICAL DEPOSITS AT THIS CENTRE IS SO EXTENSIVE THAT THE NATURAL LAND SURFACE LIES AS MUCH AS SIX METRES BELOW.

Over the years there have been many different mutations of local government. The scale and pace of development in the mid-19th century led to the formation of the London County Council (LCC) in 1889. The LCC was responsible for many public housing developments of the early 20th century and the re-building which took place after the Second World War, during which bombing raids destroyed large tracts of buildings. It also erected the first blue plaques commemorating London's connections with famous people. In the 1960s the Greater London Council (GLC) replaced the LCC, and this survived until the early 1980s when it was abolished amid bitter political opposition. Since then the fragmentary nature of government in the capital has led to a debilitating lack of an overall vision for the capital (though this is nothing new in the history of London).

However, this all has changed. As of 2000 London has a unitary body, the Greater London Assembly (GLA) and elected mayor. The system, based on the New York City model, gives a voice to Londoners and promotes city-wide initiatives to tackle such pressing issues as transport and pollution.

UNITED KINGDOM, GREAT BRITAIN, ENGLAND

London is the capital of England, of Great Britain and the United Kingdom. The United Kingdom in turn is part of the European Community and subject to laws and regulations made by the European Parliament in Strasbourg. The term Great Britain refers to mainland Britain and so encompasses Scotland and Wales as well as England. The Scots and the Welsh have their own cultures and their long-standing desire to be recognised as distinct from England has recently resulted in the establishment of a Scottish Parliament and a Welsh Assembly. The term United Kingdom (UK) includes Northern Ireland as well, and the residents of Northern Ireland are British citizens. However, some different conditions exist there, due to it being a disputed territory. The brief historical causes are that after a long and bitter struggle for independence from Britain, the Republic of Ireland (Eire) was formed in 1921. Since then the Republic has laid claim to that part of Ireland (Ulster or Northern Ireland), which Britain retained under pressure from the loyalist Protestant community settled there. Nationalists, mostly Catholics, make up a minority in Northern Ireland and have been the subject of long-standing discrimination. From the early 1970s a minority of nationalists in the North were involved in an ongoing terrorist war (principally carried out by the IRA) against the British government, and against loyalist paramilitary organisations. At moments of tension London was frequently targeted, and security alerts, mostly false alarms but occasionally accompanied by real bombs, were regular occurrences. However with the advent of the 1998 Good Friday Agreement, and with a new parliament in place, a peaceful solution to what has proved to be the most intractable problem in contemporary British politics seems closer than ever before.

Britain has a constitutional monarchy. This means that Parliament—the British House of Commons (made up of elected members of parliament, MPs) and the House of Lords (the second chamber, made up of appointed peers)—makes the laws, but the nation's figurehead is the Queen. The monarchy's support has been dropping fast over the last decade or so, and this has been even more the case since the death of the enormously popular Princess of Wales, who had many links with London communities. The monarchy is an institution in decline, and there is no certainty it will survive to see out the end of another century.

The multicultural nature of London means it is, in many ways, quite different from the rest of the country. Those outside of the capital often complain of media bias towards the southeast of England and insular London in particular. The English countryside, although so near, is a world away, and London is arguably closer to many of the cities of continental Europe, in spirit if not in miles, than it is to Scotland, Wales or Ireland.

As with most large cities, living in London can make one feel quite anonymous. Londoners are not known for their friendliness, but you are likely to find that community spirit is alive and well on a local level. We hope this first edition of the *Newcomer's Handbook, for London* will help you quickly acclimate to your new surroundings and let you begin to enjoy all that London has to offer. Best of luck!

I F YOU ARE COMING TO BRITAIN FOR LONGER THAN SIX MONTHS you must apply for a work permit or entry clearance before coming into the country. Immigration rules are a complicated matter. The following information is intended as a general guide only and clarification of individual cases should be sought from the relevant authorities.

WORK PERMITS

For those travelling to the UK with the intention of living and working here, work permits are required for most forms of employment. Permits must be secured in advance of arrival, and your prospective employer has to be the one to make the application. (Processing of applications will take *at least* eight weeks.) Permits are issued for specialised and senior positions and generally not for manual or clerical positions. For further information, contact the British diplomatic mission in your country. Dependants of permit holders must secure permission to enter the UK in advance of arrival in the form of entry clearance from a British diplomatic mission. Work-permit holders and their dependants must register with the British police on arrival.

People already admitted to the UK on a temporary basis, students or trainees for example, can sometimes apply for work permits if the position they are filling requires specialised skills or qualifications.

Work-permit holders are not allowed to change jobs without the permission of the Department of Employment. After four years in the UK you can apply for settlement which, if granted, bestows the right to stay indefinitely.

Contact **Work Permits UK, Department of Education and Employment**, Level West 5, Moorfoot, Sheffield, S1 4PQ, 0114 259 4074; fax: 0114 259 3728; www.dfee.gov.uk/ols, for more details.

ENTRY CLEARANCE CERTIFICATES

Some categories of employment do not require a permit. These include those seeking to establish a business, ministers of religion, journalists, sole representatives of overseas firms, employees of overseas governments, airline ground staff, doctors and dentists. In these cases an entry clearance certificate must be obtained from the nearest British diplomatic mission before departure for the UK. In addition, retired persons of independent means and investors may apply for entry clearance.

STUDENTS

In order to enter the UK as a student you must be accepted as a full-time attendee at a publicly funded institution, or a recognised private institution, and must be able to meet, in full, the costs of your course fees and the living expenses of yourself and any dependants. Students in full-time education who are citizens of the USA can apply for a Blue Card, which is a special work permit allowing employment in the UK for up to six months. The Blue Card must be obtained before leaving home. For further information and an application form contact BUNAC (British University of North America Club), P.O. Box 430, Southbury, CT 06488, 800-GO-BUNAC, www.bunac.org.

For non-US students, see the following section.

NEWCOMERS FROM COMMONWEALTH COUNTRIES

Citizens, including students, between the ages of 17 and 27 of Commonwealth countries, including Canada, Australia, New Zealand and South Africa, or British Dependent Territories, have the option of applying for entry clearance to stay in the UK as "working holidaymakers" for a period of up to two years. The rules: in order to qualify as a working holidaymaker the work you take up must be of a casual or part-time nature. In reality the range of acceptable work is quite wide and can include things like teaching and nursing, if there is a particular shortage. If you have UK ancestry, defined as one or more grandparent born in this country, the rules are far less stringent. Ancestry entry clearance enables you to live and work unrestricted in the UK for up to four years and then apply for permanent residence. Neither working holidaymakers nor those with ancestry clearance are eligible to claim any state benefits, and will be asked to prove that they will be able to support themselves whilst here. As with all entry clearance, applications must be made in advance of arrival, and in the country in which you are living, to the British Embassy, or particular British Diplomatic Mission designated to process entry clearance applications. Advice about where to apply can be gained from any British diplomatic post.

NEWCOMERS FROM THE EUROPEAN UNION

Citizens of the member countries of the European Union have free access to enter the UK, take up work, study and claim state benefits.

ENGLISH SPEAKING EMBASSIES

- **American Citizen Services at The Embassy of the United States**, 24 Grosvenor Square, London W1A, 020 7499 9000; will give general information and lists of American attorneys and relocation services.
- **Australian High Commission**, Australia House, The Strand, London WC2B, 020 7379 4334; www.australia.org.uk
- **Canadian High Commission**, Macdonald House, 1 Grosvenor Square, W1X, 020 7258 6600
- **Irish Embassy**, 17 Grosvenor Place, SW1X, 020 7235 2171
- **New Zealand High Commission**, 80 Haymarket, SW1Y, 020 7930 8422
- **South African High Commission**, South Africa House, Trafalgar Square, WC2N, 020 7930 4488

IMMIGRATION ADVICE

Applications and enquiries should be made to the **Immigration and Nationality Directorate** of the Home Office, Lunar House, Wellesley Road, Croydon CR9, phone 087 0606 7766 (to speak to someone) or 020 8649 7878 for extensive recorded information. Their Public Enquiry Bureau is open Monday-Friday, 9 a.m. to 4 p.m. to personal callers. Or contact them by post at The Correspondence Unit, Migration & Visa Department, Foreign & Commonwealth Office, 1 Palace Street, London SW1E 5HE. There is a web site too: www.homeoffice.gov.uk.

UK Immigration Advisory Service (UKIAS) is a voluntary organisation, funded by the Home Office but operated independently. They can offer advice on all aspects of immigration free of charge. They are located at 190 Great Dover Street, London SE1 4YB (nearest Tube: Borough on the Northern line), phone: 020 7357 6917. You can also pay someone to take up your case; look for immigration consultants under "Legal Services" in the *Yellow Pages*.

PARTNERS OF BRITISH CITIZENS

Married partners of British citizens have the right to remain in the country whatever their prior immigration status, but may be investigated by immigration officers to check if the marriage is genuine. Long-term partners in same-sex relationships of at least four years may also be granted leave to remain with their British partner—this is also the case for unmarried heterosexual couples. Favourable decisions are also made on compassionate grounds, for instance if one or both partners is HIV positive, even if other criteria are not met. For further advice on how the UK immigration laws and rules affect same-sex couples contact **Stonewall Immigration Group**, 46-48 Grosvenor Gardens, London SW1W, 020 7881 9440.

THE HISTORIC CITY OF LONDON, REFERRED TO AS "THE CITY," comprises the square mile centrally located on the north bank of the Thames. This is the financial heart of London, where the Stock Exchange is situated and where most financial and business activity takes place, and is the starting point for this guide. Around this nucleus are 32 London boroughs fanning outward to make up Greater London. For the purposes of this book they are divided into inner and outer London boroughs, but as transport links improve and business spreads to new areas, such distinctions become less relevant. The following profiles, beginning with the City and Westminster, describe the inner circle of boroughs going around clockwise from Kensington and Chelsea to Hammersmith and Fulham. One more circuit is made around the outer boroughs, counterclockwise this time, from Haringey round to Waltham Forest; the remaining ten boroughs are covered briefly. The current boroughs were "created" in 1965 by the amalgamation of smaller ones, sometimes resulting in arbitrary groupings of very different neighbourhoods falling under one administration. Undoubtedly some boroughs have more of a London sensibility than others; for instance, in some ways Waltham Forest is a typical East End locality, whereas Croydon is much like a separate town, and Ealing has a very suburban feel. With boroughs located further out, you may find higher quality housing and more value for your money, but these advantages should be weighed against the time and money you may then have to spend commuting. The profiles that follow are designed to give you an overall picture of the different elements that make up each borough.

In London there are many different weekly papers serving local areas. Perusing these, in addition to the daily London-wide *Evening Standard*, will give you an impression of local community issues and crime levels. Crime is a problem everywhere in the city and no neighbourhoods are immune, though inevitably some are worse than others. Fortunately, random violent crime remains fairly rare, and incidents involving guns are even less frequent. London's homicide rate is fairly low measured against that of comparable world cities. Local radio and local television news programmes are also good resources when getting to know the capital. *In any emergency situation dial 999 for police, fire or ambulance services.*

The haphazard and uncoordinated fashion in which London has developed, with outlying towns, villages, and parishes gradually being subsumed into boroughs of London, makes **defining neighbourhood boundaries** sometimes problematic. When skimming classified ads for housing be aware that the location of properties may be described in various ways: by the borough name, or by an older more localised name, or by the postcode which represents it, or even by the name of the nearest Tube station. **Postcodes** have quite elaborate meanings and decoding them is a skill you can only acquire with familiarity. Those postcodes containing a single 1: W1, SW1, N1, etc. tend to denote the most central areas. But apart from this, postcodes do not always correspond to what you might expect their geographical position to be. For some reason there are places that are north of the Thames with an SW postcode. To add to the confusion, there are parts of boroughs and some whole outer boroughs of London that do not have a London address. If a postcode starts with something other that N, E, S, or W then it is not in the London postal area and its address will include a county name such as Essex, Middlesex, Kent, or Surrey rather than London. For postcode specifics refer to the London Centre and Greater London maps, pp. 17-19 and 70-71.

The **London Underground**, or Tube, divides London into six circular fare zones beginning with the central area or Zone 1. Zone 1 is what people class as central London and encompasses the centres of commerce and nightlife, i.e. mostly the City and Westminster. To live in Zone 1 is fairly unusual and the most common pattern is for people to live in Zones 2, 3 or 4 and to work in Zone 1. Maps illustrating zones are available from Tube stations. All the boroughs described as "inner London" here are primarily in Zones 1 and 2, and those in outer London are mostly Zone 3 and beyond. Please refer to the **Transport** chapter for more Tube specifics.

There are two **telephone codes** for London—loosely, an 020 7 number is inner London, and 020 8 is outer. When phoning another London number from a landline within the city, you do not need to dial the 020 prefix.

Where you work or study will probably play a central role in your decision about where you choose to live. Transport links, local amenities, and quality of accommodation also will influence your decision. Types of accommodation, the choice to buy or rent, and recent trends in London's property market are discussed in more detail in the **Finding a Place to Live** chapter. Privately rented accommodation is available either as self-contained flats or houses, or as a room in a shared flat or house ("flatshare" or "houseshare"—usually the cheapest option). Short-term furnished accommodations for wealthy visitors in the smartest bits of town are always available to rent. A rough guide to rental prices for furnished flats or house-shares goes as follows: a low rent for a room in a flat or houseshare is any-thing up to £80 per week; mid-range rentals run from £80 to £120 (most come in at this level); a high rent flat is anything above that. For a self-con-tained one bedroom flat, a low rent is defined as anything below £130 per week, a medium rent between £130 and £200, and a high rent above that.

Council owned property accounts for between 17% and 50% of the total property in any one borough. It is allocated on a basis of waiting lists and need, and generally is not available to newcomers. Council estates are usually identifiable as collections of tower blocks or low-rise blocks of flats or estates of houses, built in the 1950s and '60s. They often have reputations for squalid living conditions and high levels of crime. Many have been or are in the process of being revamped, including landscaping and the installa-tion of adequate security. Still the larger estates in particular are probably best avoided unless you are really sure of what you're letting yourself in for.

Available property comes in various architectural forms. Much mar-velous Georgian, Victorian and Edwardian architecture survives in London as streets of terraced, semidetached or detached houses. There is a premi-um on property which can boast original period features. In the Georgian and early Victorian periods houses often were laid out around small com-munal central spaces (London's characteristic "squares") with crescents and streets laid out around. Today this pattern survives most clearly in parts of town such as Bloomsbury (Camden), Belgravia (Westminster), Notting Hill (Kensington and Chelsea) and parts of Islington, although you will find examples all over. With the demand for living space so high in London many properties have been divided into flats and bedsits. This sometimes means a very high density of people live in a building originally designed for one family, with the attendant problems you might expect. Streets of brick Victorian or turn-of-the-century terraces of varying quality make up the bulk of private property in London. You'll notice that similar houses or flats will have quite different prices according to their location. Purpose-built flats, especially the newest, may offer better sound insulation and greater security, with entryphones, double glazed windows and off-street parking. The numerous luxury residential developments that dominated the property market in the 1990s began with Docklands (Tower Hamlets), and have been part of the gentrification of previously overlooked and large-ly uninhabited corners of the inner city. The trend for "loft living" has led to areas like Clerkenwell (Islington) and Hoxton (Hackney) becoming very fashionable with the young professional classes. The common pattern for gentrification in previously industrial areas is for property developers to convert disused industrial buildings, often dating from the 1920s and '30s, into luxury flats or lofts. You'll find these advertised as "warehouse conver-sions," "loft apartments" or "penthouses."

GLOSSARY

GENERAL TERMS

A-Z—this London street map also includes a map of the Tube network; it is officially known as the *Geographers' London A-Z*.

Borough—any of the 32 constituent divisions of Greater London, excluding the City of London; "local authority" or "council" refers to the administration of services in a borough, which is overseen by elected councillors.

The City—the City of London, referred to as "the City," comprises the square mile centrally located on the north bank of the Thames, where most financial and business activity takes place. If "city" has a capital letter it refers to the square mile, if not then the entity referred to is London as a whole.

Docklands—the area of the East End (in Tower Hamlets) around what used to be London's dockyards. It was made an enterprise zone in 1981 and subject to wholesale re-building. The area is now characterised by modern office and apartment blocks and its most well known symbol is 1 Canada Square, Canary Wharf, the largest skyscraper in Britain.

Green Belt—a protected zone of parks, forest and farmland surrounding Greater London.

High Street—usually the historic hub and main street of any local area, where you are most likely to find concentrations of shops, transport links and municipal offices. High street shops are chains such as Next, Gap, Boots, Woolworths, WH Smith, Body Shop, Marks & Spencer.

Leisure Centre—local, authority-run sports amenity, usually with indoor swimming pool, gym and racquet sports facilities. They vary in quality but are always much cheaper to use than private health clubs.

Minicom—refers to phone numbers using the national telephone relay system available for the deaf, hard of hearing, and speech impaired.

Postcode—like the American zip code. Refer to the maps on pp. 17-19 and 70-71. Postcodes are indicated in gray.

Rail—local and national train services. In Britain train companies compete to win franchises to run different sections of the network making for a confusing, decentralised system.

Tube—a.k.a. the London Underground, this is the subway train system which runs in tunnels under London. For more detail on both rail and Tube see the **Transport** chapter.

Zones—the Tube divides London into a series of fare zones that radiate outward in rings, beginning with the central area or Zone 1. The number of zones you pass through on your journey dictates its price.

HOUSING TERMS

Bedsit—a furnished sitting room also containing a bed and sometimes kitchen facilities. The bathroom is shared. Bedsits were the most common form of budget accommodation in the 1970s and are associated with student living. Bedsit is a term that now tends to imply a certain old-fashioned cheapness, and has largely been replaced by the word "studio."

Council Estate/Council Housing—housing provided by a local authority at a subsidised rent for residents in economic need. Such housing often takes the form of estates, which are collections of low-rise or high-rise blocks of flats and houses.

Detached—a house that is not structurally connected to any other. Often detached houses have large gardens and garages.

Conversion—where flats have been created out of what was originally one house.

Flatshare/Houseshare—private rented accommodation where a bedroom is your own but the kitchen, living room, and bathroom are shared. Landlords may live on the premises or elsewhere.

In-fill—newer buildings constructed in gaps between older rows of buildings, caused for instance by World War II bombing.

Listed building—a building that is officially registered as one having special architectural merit or historical interest and is protected from rebuilding or demolition.

Maisonette—a type of flat originally designed as such, i.e. is not converted. A maisonette usually occupies two floors of a larger house and has its own entrance.

Mansion Blocks—blocks of private, purpose-built flats, usually portered, and generally dating from the late 19th or early 20th centuries. They tend to be quite grand and often are located in the most desirable parts of town.

Mews—a yard or street, often entered through an archway, lined with buildings originally used as stables or servants quarters, but which have since been converted into little houses. Mews houses, despite having only one or two bedrooms, are usually very desirable.

Purpose-built—made to serve a particular purpose, for instance flats built as such rather than converted from houses.

Semidetached—a house which is joined to another identical one by a common wall. "Semis," as they are known, are the typical idiom of the 1920s and '30s suburban developments of outer London.

Square—an arrangement of rows of houses to overlook a central area (usually, but not always, square in shape). A popular London style of the Georgian and Victorian periods, garden squares have a railed off garden in the central area. In the most exclusive squares public access is denied to the garden and only residents have keys.

Studio—a small, self-contained living space where the bedroom, living room and usually kitchen are all in one room. A bathroom is usually part of the space, but may be shared.

Terrace—a row of joined houses. Terraces were the most common form of London residential development through the 18th and 19th centuries.

Tower Block/High Rise Block—a multi-storey block of flats. Tower blocks were built, usually as local authority housing, from the 1950s onwards, as a way of maximising space and replacing old slum areas of London. Believing they had discovered the solution to urban housing problems, town planners hastily constructed hundreds of tower blocks in London, which were then rejected by residents who found them anonymous, impractical, and even dangerous places to live. The most ill designed and structurally unsound have been demolished and others are being gradually improved. Although the dream of creating "communities in the sky" generally is believed to have failed, tower blocks, especially those in central areas and which command terrific views, are currently undergoing a bit of a re-assessment.

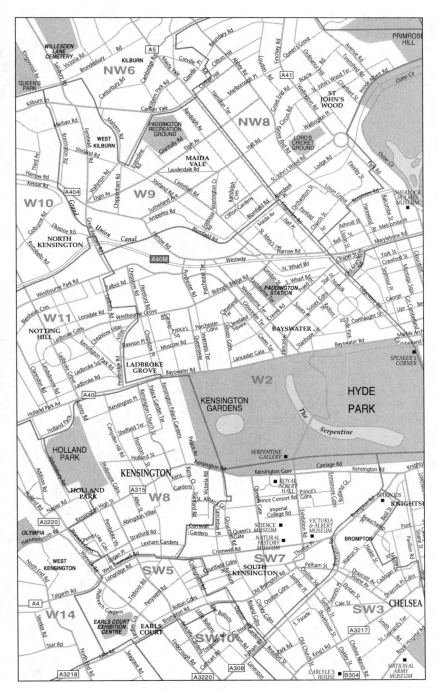

LONDON CENTRE (PLATE 1)

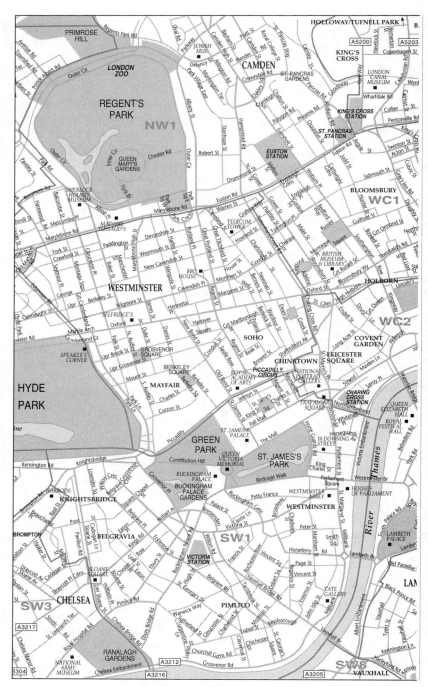

LONDON CENTRE (PLATE 2)

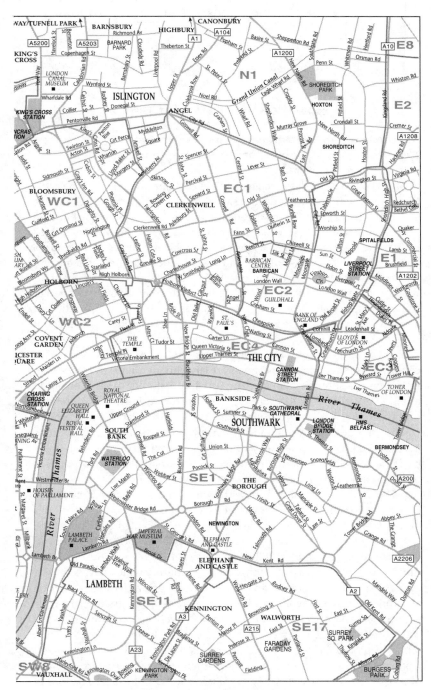

LONDON CENTRE (PLATE 3)

INNER LONDON

THE CITY OF LONDON

Boundaries and contiguous boroughs: **North**: Islington/Hackney;
East: Tower Hamlets; **South**: Thames; **West**: Westminster

In 1671 London's leading architect of the day Christopher Wren built the
Monument, commemorating the site of the start of London's Great Fire
which had broken out five years earlier in a baker's shop in nearby Pudding
Lane. From the top of this white Doric column's 62 metres, you are offered
a bird's eye view of the City, and you can imagine the course of the original
Roman wall which marked the boundaries of Londinium—an area encompassing only 330 acres. While the rest of London has expanded ever outwards, the City has remained a small region and today it is often referred to
as "the square mile." The City of London is run by the Corporation of
London which functions in a way quite different from London's other councils. The Corporation is an archaic and anomalous body that is older than
Parliament and comes from privileges granted by the Crown in the 13th
century. It is independent and non-partisan, although not terribly democ-
ratic. The Corporation manages the usual local authority services but in
addition is responsible for policing the City, for business and residential
properties, and it also owns much park and common land in and around
London. It is up to the Corporation to maintain the character of the historic
parts of the City—its churches and particular streets, some of which date
back to Elizabethan and even medieval times—whilst allowing for modern
developments and promoting the business interests of the City.

The variety of architecture, with buildings from different centuries
pressed up against each other, is one of the most striking aspects of this
part of London. Interesting architectural features include fragments of the
Roman wall, an array of churches built by Christopher Wren, grand
Victorian bank buildings, and Richard Rogers' 1980s Lloyds Building. The
City has suffered several cataclysms during its history which have led to its
re-shaping. During medieval and Tudor times it was a densely populated
and thriving place of work and life. Commercial life centred on the river
with traders and merchants coming from all over the world to make and
break their fortunes. Writers such as Chaucer, Shakespeare, and Marlowe
found inspiration in the bustling mercantile life around them. However,
cramped and unsanitary living conditions led to the devastating outbreak
of plague in 1665, which wiped out a large section of the population. In
the following year the Great Fire of London swept through, ridding the City
of the plague but flattening more than 13,200 timber-built buildings. At

the time of rebuilding Wren put forward a grand plan to redesign the City along continental lines, with wide boulevards and gridded street patterns. But, in the hurry to get the job done, this plan was rejected—although brick was used instead of wood for the new buildings. So the chaotic, medieval nature of the City, a maze of alleys and courts, has persisted to the present day. As London recovered from these disastrous events it continued to grow in cultural and commercial importance, eventually becoming the centre of the British Empire, under the reign of Queen Victoria. In the 20th century, the blitz took its toll, destroying many churches and commercial buildings. Unfortunately, post-war reconstruction brought a great number of hastily built and insensitively designed office blocks, which are at odds with the narrow streets and historic nature of the City.

Today Wren's surviving churches are the most striking legacy of the 17th and 18th centuries (23 out of 51 are extant), the most famous being the distinctive domed St. Paul's Cathedral, dating from 1711. The Tower of London, begun in 1066 and then altered and added to over the centuries, lies outside the boundary of the City, on the southeastern corner, but its iconic presence looms over the City. It is a fortress originally intended to strike fear and awe into the hearts of the people, but over the centuries it has served variously as a prison, a place of execution, and a palace. Today, along with St. Paul's, it is one of London's top tourist attractions. Inside the Tower you can see the Crown Jewels and explore the Tower's chequered history.

The gates, which once punctuated the Roman and medieval walls of the City, are remembered in street names: Aldgate, Ludgate, Moorgate, Aldersgate, Bishopsgate, Broadgate, and Newgate. The earliest commerce is also traceable in names such as Milk Street, Fish Street Hill, and Bread Street. Jewry Street and Old Jewry mark the Jewish ghettos of the early Middle Ages. The City is the repository for many of London's quirkier place-names too; one grisly example is Houndsditch, so called after the number of dead dogs which could be seen floating in the Fleet ditch (a tributary of the Thames which is now a sewer) in medieval times.

Over the last two centuries, the City's growth as a commercial zone has led to its decline as a residential area. It now has comparatively few residents, approximately 5,000 today, compared to some 128,000 in 1801. Instead, tens of thousands of people travel here every day, to Europe's financial centre, to work. The rapid development and growth of nearby Docklands threatens the City's place as the heart of business in London, and Frankfurt is in turn mounting a European challenge to London's financial dominance, but generally, the City is as busy and important as ever. Most residents here live in the **Barbican**, located in the northwestern corner. Comprised of a large-scale and self-contained complex of flats, shops, and cultural amenities, built in stages between 1959 and 1979, the Barbican also claims to be the largest arts and conference centre in Europe.

Its attractions include the Museum of London (a good place to visit for more about the history of London), a glasshouse, and the Royal Shakespeare Company. Architectural opinion has tended to savage the Barbican, criticising its crisscrossing concrete walkways and angular buildings, but wander through it on a summer's day and its peacefulness may take you by surprise. It's a car-free oasis of calm in the midst of one of the world's busiest commercial hubs. Other buildings in the City are occasionally converted to residential usage but this is still a rare occurrence. However, if companies do start de-camping en masse to the slick high-tech environment of Docklands, residential opportunities may become more common. As it stands, there is no sense of a residential community in the City, outside of the Barbican. Weekends here offer an interesting time to explore the architecture and history of the City, as much of it is eerily deserted. Beware though, many pubs and restaurants will be closed.

Web site: www.cityoflondon.gov.uk

Postcodes: EC1, EC2, EC3, EC4

Council Office: Corporation of London, Guildhall, London EC2P, 020 7606 3030

Main Post Offices: 35 Broadgate Circle, Broadgate, EC2M; 33 Cannon Street, EC4M; 40 Fleet Street, EC4Y; 72 Fore Street, EC2Y; 16 New Bridge Street, EC4V; Seething Lane, EC3N; Customer Helpline: 0345 223344

Police Station: City of London Police: Bishopsgate, EC2; Snow Hill, EC1; Wood Street, EC2; all, 020 7601 2222

Accident and Emergency Departments: St. Bartholomew's Hospital, West Smithfield, EC1A; The Royal London Hospital, Whitechapel Road, E1; both, 020 7377 7000

Public Libraries: Barbican, Barbican Centre, Silk Street, EC2Y, 020 7638 0569; Camomile Street, 12-20 Camomile Street, EC3A, 020 7247 8895; City Business Library, 1 Brewers Hall Gardens, EC2V, 020 7332 1812; Shoe Lane, Hill House, 1 Little New Street, EC4A, 020 7583 7178

Cultural Resources: Barbican Centre, Silk Street, EC2: Barbican Cinema, 020 7382 7000; Royal Shakespeare Company at the Barbican, 020 7638 8891; The Bridewell Theatre, Bride Lane, Fleet Street, EC4, 020 7936 3456

Leisure Centre: Finsbury Leisure Centre, Norman Street, EC1V, 020 7253 2346

TRANSPORT

Tube: **Central line**: Chancery Lane, St. Paul's, Bank, Liverpool Street; **Circle line**: Blackfriars, Mansion House, Cannon Street, Monument, Tower Hill, Aldgate, Liverpool Street, Moorgate, Barbican, Farringdon; **District line**: Blackfriars, Mansion House, Cannon Street, Monument,

Tower Hill, Aldgate East; **Hammersmith & City line**: Aldgate East, Liverpool Street, Moorgate, Barbican, Farringdon; **Metropolitan line**: Aldgate, Liverpool Street, Moorgate, Barbican, Farringdon; **Waterloo & City line**: Bank

Docklands Light Railway: Tower Gateway, Bank

Rail: **Connex South Eastern**: Cannon Street, Blackfriars; **Great Eastern Railway**: Liverpool Street; **LTS Rail**: Fenchurch Street; **Thameslink**: Blackfriars, City Thameslink, Farringdon, Barbican, Moorgate; **WAGN Railway**: Moorgate, Liverpool Street

WESTMINSTER

Boundaries and contiguous boroughs: **North**: Camden; **East**: Islington, The City; **South**: Thames; **West**: Kensington and Chelsea

COVENT GARDEN
SOHO/CHINATOWN/LEICESTER SQUARE
MAYFAIR
BELGRAVIA
PIMLICO/WESTMINSTER
BAYSWATER
MAIDA VALE/LITTLE VENICE
ST. JOHN'S WOOD

Originally an island, historically Westminster was a separate city built outside the boundaries of the City of London. So, although it now functions in exactly the same way as London's other boroughs, it retains the grand title The City of Westminster. If you have ever visited London as a tourist, you no doubt spent most of your time in Westminster, even if you didn't realise it! Here you will find the capital's most famous landmarks: Big Ben and the Houses of Parliament, Westminster Cathedral, Trafalgar Square, Piccadilly Circus, and Buckingham Palace, as well as four royal parks. The borough represents the heart of town and government, and encompasses the centres of nightlife known colloquially as the "West End"—Theatreland, Soho, and Covent Garden. The area has been home to a vast array of important figures from the spheres of politics, the arts, and the sciences, from Mozart, Handel and Isaac Newton, to Samuel Pepys, Samuel Johnson and Fanny Burney, to Benjamin Franklin, Benjamin Disraeli and William Gladstone. The places where they lived, studied, worked and died are commemorated by blue plaques. Westminster's neighbourhoods are still sought after by the rich and famous. In these eight square miles are many of the popular images of London, where most tourist activity is to be found. Underlying this you can still discern the old system of parishes that made up the area. The names of these historic areas are now enormously prestigious address- es: Mayfair, Belgravia, Knightsbridge and St. John's Wood. Because Westminster lies at the heart of London, opportunities to live here perma- nently (there are a high number of luxury flats available for short-term lets) are fairly limited, but if you've got pots of cash and are determined to be at the centre of things then it'll be worth persevering.

The south end of the borough is bounded by the Thames. North of Charing Cross station, which is in the southeast corner of this area, is **Covent Garden**, which, dating back to the early 17th century, is the old- est planned square in the capital. Covent Garden was a highly fashionable residential area before becoming the site of a large fruit, vegetable, and flower market at the end of that century. The 18th century saw its well- heeled residents move west and the area gained certain notoriety, as much for its brothels and gambling dens as for its fresh fruit and vegetables. The covered marketplace, which exists today, was built during the 19th centu- ry as an attempt to impose order on the unruly nature of the place. In the 20th century the market was finally moved to a new home in Nine Elms, south of the river, and the Covent Gardens was developed into a tourist dis- trict. Today the London Transport Museum, street entertainers, clothing retailers, and folks selling jewellery, cosmetics, and arts and crafts from stalls, draw the crowds. There are a few clusters of new and old develop- ments of flats scattered among the tourist sights, theatres, and shops of Covent Garden. Around the Strand, at the southern end of the district, is where you will find many large theatres and hotels. In the 17th century this was a seething haunt of criminals, and the novelist Henry Fielding, who worked here as a magistrate trying to clean up the neighbourhood, bor- rowed from the colourful street life for his comic novels.

West of Covent Garden is **Soho**, one of London's most complex and infamous neighbourhoods. Its name dates from 17th century when the area was comprised of fields and "So-ho" was a hunting cry. In this century Soho has been the well-known stomping ground of bohemian and avant-garde artists, musicians and writers, complete with trendy coffeehouses, bars, and jazz clubs. The *bon viveur* spirit survives in Soho's small resident population of older artists and journalists, many of whom frequent such local landmarks as the French House pub, the Groucho Club and the Gay Hussar restaurant. In the 1960s and '70s Soho's reputation was that of a red-light district with a large number of unlicensed strip joints and bookstores, often operating with the connivance of corrupt police officers. Since a cleanup in the 1980s there are fewer of such premises though they are still a feature of the area. Present day Soho is probably best known as the centre of London's gay community with lively bars, shops, and cafes. It's also the centre of Britain's television and film industries, with many media-related companies housed here. Indeed, it was in a small backroom in Frith Street in 1926 that John Logie Baird first demonstrated the television set he'd constructed out of tea chests, a hat box, darning needles and biscuit tins! In the last century Soho was one of the cheaper parts of central London in which to live; Karl Marx spent some time here when he was down on his luck. There are remnants of an established community around Berwick Street Market, but it's fading fast due to the increased commercial activity and prohibitive prices. Scattered about are a few houses but properties here usually takes the form of small luxury flats. There is a primary school in the area, and a vocal residents' association that wages a constant battle against the seedier aspects of Soho life, including drug abuse and prostitution. Adjacent to Soho, on the other side of Shaftesbury Avenue, are **Leicester Square** with its concentration of tourists, cinemas, and bars, and **Chinatown**, which is the traditional home of London's Chinese community. Here you'll find innumerable Chinese-owned and operated businesses, restaurants, and shops packed into a tiny area around Gerrard Street.

Oxford Street straddles Soho and **Mayfair**, an exclusive area where there are many upmarket hotels and luxury flats occupied by very rich residents from all over the globe. Having few of the trappings of everyday life, it can seem almost soulless. Oxford Street, London's most legendary shopping mecca, leads to Marble Arch and the entrance to Hyde Park, a massive green space popular with tourists, and which is separated from Kensington Gardens by the Serpentine lake. Kensington Gardens is home to Kensington Palace, the erstwhile residence of the late Princess Diana, where there is now a commemorative garden. Kensington Gardens takes you to the western edge of the borough and marks the boundary with Kensington and Chelsea.

Below Hyde Park is **Belgravia**, again a very exclusive locale with a preponderance of elegant stuccoed period houses, luxury flats and mews cottages. There is a mixture of diplomatic residences, hotels, and overseas student accommodation as well as the private residences of the wealthy. To give you an idea of the prestige of this area, back in the mid-1990s Andrew Lloyd Webber sold his house on Eaton Square for £11 million! Things become a bit scruffy around Victoria Station with grimy, busy streets lined with cheap hotels, office blocks, and burger bars. East of Buckingham Palace Road is **Pimlico**, which extends down to the Thames and borders on the neighbourhood of **Westminster** in the east. Both these areas are, to varying degrees, dominated by the proximity of the Houses of Parliament and other governmental buildings, with a large percentage of pied-a-terre type accommodation in converted Regency stucco houses and mansion flats. There is also the odd brick Georgian terrace such as Downing Street in Westminster, which is home to the Prime Minister. Pimlico has some council estates, and was historically a less well-off area, but it pretty much holds it own now.

In the other direction, north of Hyde Park, is **Bayswater**, bounded by the busy Edgware Road (A5) in the east, and the even busier Westway (A40) in the north. Due to its proximity to Paddington Station, which is in the northeast corner of the area, and its major roads, there are, again, a lot of hotels and short-let flats. The area runs from grand squares, to the seedy, down-at-heel bed and breakfast hotels.

The A40 dual carriageway (incorporating Marylebone Road) bisects Westminster. Immediately north of it is **Maida Vale**, which is a far more residential area compared to the rest of Westminster. Maida Vale has increased in desirability in the wake of the new fast rail link from Paddington Station to Heathrow airport—bringing the area up with the previously more exclusive St. John's Wood. **Little Venice** refers to the area around Blomfield Road and Maida Avenue, which picturesquely overlooks a stretch of the Grand Union Canal. The houses on these streets command huge prices. The rest of Maida Vale is spaciously laid out with a preponderance of flats in mansion blocks and luxury conversions of large and small period houses. Properties that back onto private communal gardens are quite popular. Property developers and investors take a keen interest in the area, and there is always available rented property aimed at the higher end of the market. Clifton Road is where to go for neighbourhood shopping. As with the rest of the borough, bus and Tube links into the West End are convenient (or, you could walk from here).

East of Maida Vale (A5) is **St. John's Wood**, which has the genteel Lord's Cricket Ground at its centre. St. John's Wood is often regarded as London's first suburb. Many of its grand semidetached and detached houses were built in the early Victorian era, contrasting with the packed-in nature of much other 19th century construction. Today these large houses often belong to rock stars and media celebrities. The streets are smart, broad, and tidy, with the exception of the flowering of fans' graffiti around Abbey Road Studios, made famous by The Beatles. The area attracts many international buyers and renters, and is popular with Americans. Newsagents here have banners for *Newsweek* and the *Herald Tribune* rather than for English newspapers. The American School is on Loudoun Road, and the London Central Mosque and several synagogues can be found here too. Streets of attractive houses from many different periods are complemented by impressive mansion blocks of flats. These often enormous blocks, dating from the 1920s and '30s, line the main thoroughfares of St. John's Wood, and provide the area with a huge supply of penthouses and luxury flats. It is only in the occasional council-run tower block that homes of more modest means are represented. There are good shopping facilities; St. John's Wood High Street is manageable in scale and has a mix of cafes, restaurants, fancy clothes stores, specialty food shops, and high street chains. Nearby Regent's Park and Primrose Hill are further assets, and in the northeastern corner of St. John's Wood is Regent's Park marking the boundary with Camden. St. John's Wood residents benefit from the atmosphere of a content and loyal local community and an active residents' association—rare for a neighbourhood with such a high percentage of renters. (There are some that find the wealth and poise of the area stifling.) Adding to its many attractions are the superb road and Tube links with the West End, and some quick little bus routes. The Jubilee Line Extension provides the St. John's Wood Tube station with a direct route to Docklands.

Web site: www.westminster.gov.uk

Postcodes: W1, W2, W9, WC2, SW1, NW8

Council Office: Westminster City Hall, 64 Victoria Street, SW1E, 020 7641 6000

Main Post Offices: 111 Baker Street, W1M; 1 Broadway, SW1H; 15 Broadwick Street, W1V; 28 Circus Road, NW8; 4 Eccleston Street, SW1W; 354 Edgware Road, W2; 54 Great Portland Street, W1N; 56 Haymarket, SW1Y; 18 Kingsway, WC2B; 10 Lancelot Place, SW7; 121 Lupus Street, SW1V; 19 Newman Street, W1P; 128 Praed Street, W2; 167 Vauxhall Bridge Road, SW1V; 110 Victoria Street, SW1E; 125 Westminster Bridge Road, SE1; 24 William IV Street, WC2N; Customer Helpline, 0345 223344

Police Stations: 202-206 Buckingham Palace Road, SW1, 020 7730 1212; Agar Street, WC2, 020 7240 1212; 2-4 Harrow Road, W2, 020 7402 1212; 20 Newcourt Street, NW8, 020 7722 4447; 7 Savile Road, W1, 020 7437 1212

Accident and Emergency Department: St. Mary's Hospital, Praed Street, W2, 020 7725 6666

Public Libraries: Charing Cross, 4 Charing Cross Road, WC2H, 020 7641 2058; Church Street, 69 Church Street, NW8, 020 7641 1479; Maida Vale, Sutherland Avenue, W9, 020 7641 3659; Marylebone, 109 Marylebone Road, NW1, 020 7641 1037; Mayfair, 25 South Audley Street, W1Y, 020 7641 1391; Paddington, Porchester Road, W2, 020 7641 3705; Pimlico, 20 Rampayne Street, SW1V, 020 7641 2983; Queen's Park, 666 Harrow Road, W10, 020 7641 3575; St. James's, 62 Victoria Street, SW1E, 020 7641 2989; St. John's Wood, 20-24 Circus Road, NW8, 020 7641 1487; Victoria, 158-160 Buckingham Palace Road, SW1W, 020 7641 2187; Westminster Reference Library, 35 St. Martin's Street, WC2H, 020 7641 2036

Cultural Resources: Institute of Contemporary Arts, The Mall, SW1, 020 7930 3647; Metro Cinema, Rupert Street, W1, 020 7734 1506; Prince Charles, Leicester Place, WC2, 020 7437 8181; Donmar Warehouse, Earlham Street, WC2, 020 7369 1732; more than 30 West End theatres and 15 cinemas (see local and national press for details).

Leisure Centres: Porchester Centre, Queensway, W2, 020 7792 2919; Queen Mother Sports Centre, 223 Vauxhall Bridge Road, SW1V, 020 7630 5522; Westbourne Green Sports Complex, Torquay Street, W2, 020 7641 3707

TRANSPORT

Tube: **Bakerloo line**: Maida Vale, Warwick Avenue, Paddington, Edgware Road, Marylebone, Baker Street; **Central line**: Bond Street, Oxford Circus, Tottenham Court Road; **District & Circle lines**: Victoria, St. James's Park, Westminster, Embankment; **Jubilee line**: St. John's Wood, Baker Street, Bond Street, Green Park, Westminster **Northern line**: Embankment, Charing Cross, Leicester Square, Tottenham Court Road **Piccadilly line**: Hyde Park Corner, Green Park, Piccadilly Circus, Leicester Square, Covent Garden; **Victoria line**: Pimlico, Victoria, Green Park, Oxford Circus

Rail: **Chiltern Railways**: Marylebone; **Connex South Central**: Victoria, Charing Cross; **Heathrow Express**: Paddington; **Thames Trains**: Paddington

KENSINGTON AND CHELSEA

Boundaries and contiguous boroughs: **North**: Brent; **East**: Westminster; **South**: Thames; **West**: Hammersmith and Fulham

KNIGHTSBRIDGE
CHELSEA
EARL'S COURT
SOUTH KENSINGTON
KENSINGTON
HOLLAND PARK
NOTTING HILL
NORTH KENSINGTON/LADBROKE GROVE

The once separate areas of Kensington and Chelsea were linked in 1965 to form one of London's royal boroughs. A long-standing connection with the monarchy dates back to 1689 when William III lived in Kensington Palace. The title of Royal Borough was conferred in 1901 by Edward VII to commemorate the birthplace of his mother, Queen Victoria. The King's Road, an important landmark in London life over the 20th century, traverses the Royal Borough from the eastern boundary with Westminster to the western boundary with the borough of Hammersmith and Fulham. The King's Road takes its starting point as Sloane Square, home to the Royal Court Theatre, a venue that has been at the cutting edge of British theatre for over 40 years. Over the last few decades the King's Road has seen much of London's notorious counter-cultures and street life—from beatniks and artists to mods and punks. Today however, echoing the same gentrification and escalating house prices of many previously mixed parts of London, the King's Road has become a classy shopping street and exclusive residential area where there is no longer any room for the bohemian. The borough as a whole has a high proportion of flats serving its single-person households, 80% of them without children, and residents tend to be wealthy, often from abroad. All parts of the borough are served by main roads and by good Tube links on the Piccadilly and District lines, but the high number of residents with cars makes parking a perennial problem. Note also that Kensington and Chelsea have the highest overall property prices in London (and in Britain for that matter). Living here you are paying for location, prestige and the decadent possibilities of shopping for your dinner in Harrod's Food Hall.

Knightsbridge also belongs to the Royal Borough although a section of it below Hyde Park is officially in Westminster. Here we find what has been traditionally thought of as the poshest bit of London. It is popular still with established money, successful business people—from the Middle East, Europe, North America—and international playboy types. Harrods is on the Brompton Road with plenty of other select stores on the same road and on Sloane Street. Much residential property, the flats and the large stucco Italianate terraces which aren't embassies or offices, is owned by companies, or by investors who rent it out as short-term luxury accommodation. The main roads in the area, Kensington Gore/Knightsbridge to the north, Sloane Street and Brompton Road (A4) running southwards, are very busy and attract a lot of tourists. Away from the main thoroughfares there are a few smaller roads and cul-de-sacs with attractive Victorian mews houses. These were originally stables or servants' quarters which have been converted into bijou cottage style homes, usually with just one or two bedrooms.

Chelsea, which covers the area south of the Brompton Road, has fewer business and embassy premises than Knightsbridge or nearby Belgravia (see Westminster). Chelsea has an enticing mix of property, including grand stuccoed houses, flat-fronted Georgian-style terraces, late Victorian mansion blocks, and new developments. Much of Chelsea has been owned in the past (and some of it still is) by large landowners—hence the predominance of certain estate names such as Cadogan and Stanley. Around Sloane Square the major streets are lined by mansion blocks—the traditional residencies of wealthy bachelors about town. The complex of streets around Pont Street are known for their gabled, 19th century, red-brick houses harking back to 17th century Flemish architecture, which contrast dramatically with the white stucco sweeps found in Belgravia. On the southern side of Royal Hospital Road is the Royal Hospital itself, designed by Christopher Wren and established in the 17th century to provide care for disabled soldiers. Its residents today are known as the Chelsea Pensioners and are recognisable by their distinctive red uniforms. Royal Hospital Road leads you down to Chelsea Embankment/Cheyne Walk, a busy road that overlooks the river. The tranquil Chelsea Physic Garden occupies a space at the junction of the two roads. Surrounding the main streets are quaint side streets and mews with lovely assortments of characteristic London terraces and squares dating from the 18th and 19th centuries. (There are reams of literary connections here—Oscar Wilde lived on Tite Street, and Thomas Carlyle's home was on Cheyne Row.) The "Old Chelsea" part of the neighbourhood extends back from Cheyne Walk to the King's Road and prices are at their highest here. On Cheyne Walk are large Victorian mansion blocks interspersed with rather grim looking new-build flats, which nonetheless command views over the river and the pretty Albert Bridge. At the southwestern corner of the borough Cheyne Walk becomes Finborough Road (A3220), and climbs northwards, away from the river, before changing its name to Warwick Avenue, forming the western boundary of the borough. Here at the western end of Chelsea, property is of a more uneven standard with more council and housing association property mixed in with the posh stuff. There is also the slightly off-putting presence of an industrial area around Lot's Road.

Occupying a triangle in the centre of the Kensington and Chelsea borough, between the Old Brompton and Cromwell roads, is **Earl's Court**. The area is named after the court house of the De Vere family who were given the Earldom of Oxford in 1155. The court house site is now occupied by Earl's Court International Exhibition Centre. Art deco in style, it opened in 1937. Earl's Court used to be a source of cheap accommodation with many small flats and bedsits in the rented sector converted from tall Victorian terraces. Nowadays many of these have been spruced up and are marketed as luxury pads. There are also many Bed and Breakfasts and hotels. In the 1970s Earl's Court was the heart of gay London and the capital's longest standing gay bar, The Coleherne, is still here. Although the centre of this action has moved on to Soho, there is still a resident population of gay men.

South Kensington, bordering Knightsbridge in the west and the Fulham Road to the south, is famous for its "big three" museums, all within a stone's throw of each other: the Natural History Museum, The Science Museum and The Victoria and Albert Museum. All were built on the Cromwell and Exhibition roads in the mid-19th century (see **Cultural Life**). Today there are an increasing number of international organisations and venues in the area, such as the Goethe Institute, and a French school and Institute, making for a very cosmopolitan crowd in the streets around the Tube. Naturally there are a lot of tourist accommodation in the area, especially on the Cromwell Road, but again there are also mansion blocks and flats above shops. The more residential areas are to be found west of here and include a number of garden squares, a few Georgian terraces, and assorted old and new-build terraces.

In **Kensington** proper the streets and squares tend to be very genteel, with Holland Park and Kensington Gardens adding to an impression of space and luxury. The homes around this area are all part of London's most consistently wealthy enclave with Hyde Park at its heart. Earls Terrace, an 1811 Regency-era street that recently has been lovingly restored to its former glory, has luxury four-bedroom houses priced around the £4 million mark, attracting some serious international money. Shopping here centres on High Street Kensington, which has mainstream shops of every variety including a supermarket. In contrast there are also contemporary high fashion outlets like Hyper-Hyper and Red or Dead. **Holland Park** covers the streets which are west of Campden Hill Road and east of Holland Road (A3220), and marks the borough boundary. Holland Park has lush leafy streets and massive houses, which are either grand, single-family residences or subdivided into good-sized flats.

North of Notting Hill Gate/Holland Park Avenue (A40) is **Notting Hill**. Probably since the mid-1990s this has been considered the most fashionable place to live in west London. This is partly because an elaborate Victorian street plan offers many large stuccoed houses along curvy, tree-lined streets, many of which overlook leafy communal gardens. The nearer you get to the top of the hill, the higher the prices and the better quality the housing. The best of these streets radiate outwards from Stanley and Lansdown Crescent and are a match for anything Holland Park or Belgravia might have to offer. In addition to the patches of council housing, the appeal of Notting Hill for the young and trendy has to do with its long-standing Afro-Caribbean community, and its beguiling and youthful mix of people. This cultural cachet has attracted pop stars and writers as residents. As with other areas that have seen a dramatic upswing in popularity, property investors here have been active in ensuring a supply of rented accommodation. Around Notting Hill Gate (the road) there are a number of high street stores, two cinemas, and an ever-proliferating range of wine-bars and restaurants. Pembridge Road has some interesting little housewares and clothes shops, as well as numerous places in which to sip a cappuccino. Notting Hill is famous too for its annual carnival, the largest street festival in Europe, which attracts thousands of revellers every August Bank Holiday. Portobello Road Market is also a major tourist draw. Visitors flock here on the weekends to buy everything from antiques to reggae records. The variations to be seen along the Portobello Road as it winds its way north through the area and into North Kensington are a neat summary of the contrasts that exist in this corner of London.

North Kensington (not to be confused with Kensington proper!) comprises the areas around the elevated section of Westway (A40) motorway, Ladbroke Grove Tube station, and further north. This neighbourhood has been less favoured in terms of property, with fewer grand homes and a higher proportion of council housing, and there are above average rates of unemployment and poverty. However, streets like the All Saints Road, famous for 1960s race riots and drug dealing, are now benefiting from the forces of both gentrification and government regeneration money. The Golborne Road has a cheerful array of local shops, cafes and groceries. The Trellick Tower, a tower block instantly recognisable by the side bar that houses the lift and staircase, and which was the tallest in Britain when it was built in 1973, has become a fashionable place to live. Terraced streets and new developments in this up-and-coming market are particularly attractive to those unable to afford the pricier Kensington proper.

Web site: www.rbkc.gov.uk

Postcodes: SW3, SW5, SW7, SW10, W8, W10, W11, W14

Council Offices: Town Hall, Hornton Street, W8, 020 7937 5464

Main Post Offices: 232 & 351 King's Road, SW3; 185 Earls Court Road, SW5; 25 Exhibition Road, SW7; 118 Gloucester Place, SW7; 10 Lancelot Place, SW7; 41 Old Brompton Road, SW7; 369 Fulham Road, SW10; Kensington Church Street, W8; 257 Kensington High Road, W8; 224 Westbourne Grove, W11; Customer Helpline 0345 223344

Police Stations: 2 Lucan Place, SW3, 020 7589 1212; 72 Earl's Court Road, W8, 020 7376 1212; 101 Ladbroke Grove, W11, 020 7221 1212

Accident and Emergency Departments: Charing Cross Hospital, Fulham Palace Road, W6, 020 8846 1234; St Mary's Hospital, Praed Street, W2, 020 7725 6666; Chelsea & Westminster Hospital, 369 Fulham Road, SW10, 020 8746 8000

Public Libraries: Central, Hornton Street, W8, 020 7937 2542; Brompton, 210 Old Brompton Road, SW5, 020 7373 3111; Chelsea, Kings Road, SW3, 020 7352 6056; Kensal, 20 Golborne Road, W10, 020 8969 7736; North Kensington, 108 Ladbroke Grove, W11, 020 7727 6583; Notting Hill, 1 Pembridge Square, W2, 020 7229 6583

Cultural Resources: Leighton House Museum & Art Gallery, 12 Holland Park Road, W14, 020 7602 3316; Holland Park Theatre, Holland House, Holland Park, W8, 020 7602 7856; Man in the Moon Theatre, 392 King's Road, SW3, 020 7351 2876/5701; Royal Court Theatre, Sloane Square, SW3, 020 7565 5000

Leisure Centres: Kensington Sports Centre, Walmer Road, W11, 020 7727 9923; Chelsea Sports Centre, Chelsea Manor Street, SW3, 020 7352 6985

TRANSPORT
Time to City: 15 to 30 minutes; **Time to West End**: 10 to 20 minutes
Tube: **Central**: Holland Park, Notting Hill Gate; **Circle line**: Gloucester
    Road, South Kensington, Sloane Square, High Street Kensington,
    Bayswater, West Brompton, Kensington Olympia, Notting Hill Gate;
    District line: Earl's Court, Gloucester Road, South Kensington, Sloane
    Square, High Street Kensington, Bayswater, West Brompton,
    Kensington Olympia, Notting Hill Gate; **Piccadilly line**: Earl's Court,
    Gloucester Road, South Kensington, Knightsbridge
Rail: **Silverlink & Connex South Central**: Kensington Olympia

CAMDEN

Boundaries and contiguous boroughs: **North**: Barnet/Haringey;
East: Islington; **South**: Westminster; **West**: Brent

CAMDEN TOWN
KENTISH TOWN/DARTMOUTH PARK/CHALK FARM
PRIMROSE HILL
BELSIZE PARK/SWISS COTTAGE
HAMPSTEAD/GOSPEL OAK
WEST HAMPSTEAD
HIGHGATE
KING'S CROSS
BLOOMSBURY/HOLBORN

On the eastern and northern sides of Regent's Park lies the London
Borough of Camden. This northerly part of town was heathland until 1812
when the Prince Regent appointed the architect John Nash to lay out a
park. The result is a beautifully landscaped area complete with harmonious
and palatial white buildings, all part of Nash's ambitious plan. Going east
along Parkway brings you away from the white stuccoed splendour of
Nash's terraces to Camden Town Tube, the hub at which five roads con-
verge. From here you can go northwest to Chalk Farm and Hampstead,
north to Kentish Town, or south to Bloomsbury, where lies an amazing
array of neighbourhoods incorporating some of the most desirable, picturesque and historic residential areas in the capital.
    Camden Town is known for its dynamic youth culture and nightlife.
It is the spiritual home of Britpop and every night of the week hopeful
young bands bang away at their guitars in the pubs on the High Street and
Parkway. The heart of the area is Camden Market, a teeming hive of street
markets and shops, and a major weekend tourist destination. Everything

the trendy and the alternative might desire can be found here. The original market at Camden Lock, next to the canal, is constantly extending as other sites pop up across the road and further along Chalk Farm Road. The popularity of the markets on the weekends can make it difficult to even get near the stalls, especially on sunny days. On weekdays Camden Town becomes a less frenetic prospect. Many of the streets around the Tube are full of elegant narrow townhouses, some converted into flats and all very marketable real estate. Camden Town Tube offers access to the City and the West End via the two branches of the Northern line, and there are buses running in many directions. The population of Camden is mixed, with the market and music venues attracting travellers, students, and revellers, as well as the inevitable drug dealers. Due to the proximity of hostels for the homeless, in particular the 1,000 bed Arlington House, there are also quite a high number of street people. Nonetheless its vibrancy and central location make Camden Town's prospects secure, and is particularly enticing to the young, both the professionals who rent smart flats in converted townhouses, and the more down-at-heel who live in squats or dilapidated shared houses. On the southern end of Camden High Street you'll find a good selection of shops such as Boots, Marks & Spencer, and Woolworth's, plus takeaways, restaurants and large pubs. Groceries can be purchased at the innovatively designed Sainsbury's, located at the Camden Town end of the Kentish Town Road.

Directly north of Camden Town, along the Kentish Town Road, is **Kentish Town**, traditionally a quiet, less glamorous outpost of Camden and surrounding areas. However, Kentish Town is now reaching new heights of popularity due to the overall reliable standard of its terraces, which are a mix of flat conversions and houses. These recently have been supplemented by smart new loft-style developments on the Prince of Wales Road. The area is popular with professionals who have found themselves priced out of neighbouring Hampstead. Public transport in the area is quite adequate; Kentish Town Tube station is on the Northern line and commuters also have the option of using the Thameslink rail services that pass through here on their way to the City. Kentish Town West station is on the North London line. The shops on the northern end of the Kentish Town Road will supply you with basics and are improving all the time. For the kids there is the added attraction of the Kentish Town City Farm at Cressfield Close, off Grafton Road (see **Sport and Recreation**). **Dartmouth Park** is the patch of hilly streets that reach up to the northeastern corner of Hampstead Heath, where you'll find good family homes in the large terraced houses. **Chalk Farm** is made up of the small area of modest terraced streets that straddle Chalk Farm Road, extending west to **Primrose Hill**. Primrose Hill is a hilltop extension of Regent's Park, and a marvellous viewing spot. The small residential area directly around the park and neatly bounded by the railway line is named after it, and is a desirable enclave of large family houses set on quiet, well-maintained streets.

Belsize Park, north of Primrose Hill and west of Haverstock Hill (A502), is a well placed neighbourhood, with three Tube stations within its range and good shopping and entertainment opportunities along Haverstock Hill and Finchley Road. In the middle of the area is the self-styled "Belsize Village" around England's Lane, with pretty little shops and houses. The housing market here is dominated by converted flats in nice examples of red brick and yellow brick Victorian terraces, and you'll find more places to buy than rent as it is the sort of place people aspire to settle in permanently. Further west still is **Swiss Cottage**, which takes its curious name from a Swiss chalet style tavern that was built in 1826, along the path of the Finchley Road. Swiss Cottage is still dominated by the Finchley Road (A41), which is a major route in and out of town. On Finchley you'll find plenty of high street shops, a giant Sainbury's and two multi-screen cinemas. There is also a motley mix of council blocks, faded Victorian grandeur in the shape of large houses converted into flats, and new developments such as the Quadrangles.

In the northern half of the borough are the leafy neighbourhoods that ring Hampstead Heath and offer some of north London's most appealing properties. Their position on a ridge of hills rising above the rest of the city provides lovely views and the airy atmosphere of hilltop villages. Hampstead Heath is an extensive and varied park and is a major asset to all the areas that surround it. **Hampstead** itself is south of the Heath and is a classy and settled neighbourhood. The poet John Keats lived and worked here, and his house on Keats Grove is now open to the public during the summer months. Hampstead retains a highbrow literary image with many of England's best known novelists having lived here; so much so that there is a literary sub-genre known as "the Hampstead novel." Its housing stock consists largely of lovingly maintained terraces on quiet roads closed off from the main thoroughfares. Hampstead brings to mind the quintessential London village, although there's a bit too much traffic and bustle for it to seem truly rural. Prices match its reputation for exclusivity and reach their apex on The Bishops Avenue, London's original "millionaires' row." Many wealthy newcomers from overseas look for homes here. Hampstead High Street and Heath Street have plenty of clothes shops, delicatessens, cafes and housewares stores, as well as a Northern line Tube station. **Gospel Oak** is part of the same Hampstead community. **West Hampstead** stretches over the Finchley Road and the narrow but very busy West End Lane to reach the border with Brent. West Hampstead was previously thought to be a cheaper alternative to the rest of Hampstead, and has traditionally housed a higher population of young people and students, but prices are rapidly catching up. Young professionals settling here are attracted by the convenient train route to the City as well as a Jubilee line Tube station. The stations are all on West End Lane, which is where you will find the area's local stores, bars, and cafes.

On the eastern side of the Heath is **Highgate**, and on the main Highgate High Street, which meanders up a hill northeast of the heath, you'll find specialty grocers, estate agents, a bookshop, and a few bistros and wine bars. The lovely Waterlow Park, sloping off the south side of the high street, offers magnificent views over the centre of town, and leads to Highgate Cemetery. This lovingly maintained cemetery spanning the 19th and 20th centuries holds the graves of Karl Marx, George Eliot (buried under her real name Mary-Ann Evans), Michael Faraday, and Radclyffe Hall, among many others. This area too is known for its literati. Property here, as you'd expect, is expensive and generally of a very high standard. There are highly prized Georgian cottages located in the pretty conservation area around Pond Square, on the eastern side of the Highgate High Street, and to the west Georgian townhouses surround a green called The Grove. There are also plenty of late Victorian terraces and semidetached villas, often with several bedrooms and large gardens. Property in the two apartment blocks, Highpoint I and II, built in the 1930s by respected architect Berthold Lubetkin, are also much sought after. As is the case with Hampstead, Highgate is heavily owner-occupied, and any rented property will be at the priciest end of the market.

Spinning back to where we started, out in the far south of the borough at Camden Town Tube and heading south this time down Camden High Street, lies the Mornington Crescent Tube. Here the high street forks, with one road, Eversholt Street, leading off to Euston station, and the other, Hampstead Road, to Tottenham Court Road. The unexpected thing about the borough of Camden is that it reaches all the way south into Bloomsbury. Going down Eversholt Street you pass Somers Town, a collection of council estates, to reach the Euston Road with its three major mainline railway stations: King's Cross, Euston, and St. Pancras. The latter is fronted by the Midland Hotel, a spectacular late Victorian gothic masterpiece designed by George Gilbert-Scott. Next to it lies the British Library, famous for being several years late in its completion and several millions of pounds over budget. Eventually St. Pancras station will become a terminus on the new fast Channel Tunnel Rail Link to the continent. With such plans in the pipeline, the local **King's Cross** area which was previously a wasteland of disused 19th century industrial heritage with a red light district reputation, is now ripe for reinvention. Gentrification is already cleaning up the edges with speculative residential developments and warehouse conversions like Ice Wharf next to the Regent's Canal.

Cross the Euston Road and you've arrived in **Bloomsbury**. This elegant patch is built on the square and crescent street formation so beloved of late

18th and early 19th century planners. It is an area stuffed full of academic institutions and student residences. The neo-Greek of the British Museum, the imposing thirties rectitude of Senate House library, and the proliferation of blue plaques emphasise Bloomsbury's starring role in the intellectual and artistic life of London. To live and be clever here is the dream of any literary admirers of Virginia Woolf or any of her Bloomsbury set cohorts. Most of the houses on the genteel squares are now given over to offices and classrooms connected with the University of London, but some are still residential, and there are mansion blocks of flats too. As you would expect, prices are high and opportunities to rent or purchase rare. Further south lies **Holborn**, which borders the City and where there are many offices. The eponymous main street is surrounded by the picturesque Inns of Court that have been the centre of London's legal profession since the Middle Ages.

Web site: www.camden.gov.uk

Postcodes: WC1, NW1, NW3, NW5, N6, N19

Council Office: Town Hall, Judd Street, WC1H, 020 7278 4444

Main Post Offices: 19 High Holborn, WC1; 181 High Holborn, WC1; 33 Marchmont Street, WC1; 9 Russell Square, WC1; 84 Theobald's Road; 6 Chester Court, NW1; 13 Euston Road, NW1; 220 Eversholt Street, NW1; 10 Parkway, NW1; 79 Hampstead High Street, NW3; 173 Haverstock Hill, NW3; 212 Kentish Town Road, NW5; Customer Helpline, 0345 223344

Police Stations: 70 Theobalds Road, WC1X, 020 7404 1212; 76 Kings Cross Road, WC1, 020 7704 1212; 12a Holmes Road, NW5, 020 7388 1212; 407 Archway Road, N6, 020 8340 8055; 26 Rosslyn Hill, NW3, 020 7431 1212

Accident and Emergency Departments: Royal Free Hospital, Pond Street, NW3, 020 7794 0500; Whittington Hospital, Highgate Hill, N19, 020 7272 3070

Public Libraries: Belsize, Antrim Road, NW3, 020 7413 6518; Camden Town, Crowndale Centre, Eversholt Street, NW1, 020 7911 1563; Chalk Farm, Sharpleshall Street, NW1, 020 7413 6526; Heath, Keats Grove, NW3, 020 7413 6520; Highgate, Chester Road, N19, 020 7860 5752; Kentish Town, 262-266 Kentish Town Road, NW5, 020 7485 1121; Swiss Cottage, 88 Avenue Road, NW3, 020 7413 6527

Cultural Resources: Camden Arts Centre, Arkwright Road, off Finchley Road, NW3, 020 7435 2643; The Freud Museum, 20 Maresfield Gardens, NW3, 020 7435 2002; The Jewish Museum, 129-131 Albert Street, NW1, 020 7284 1997; London Canal Museum, 12-13 New Wharf Road, N1, 020 7713 0836; Etcetera Theatre, Oxford Arms, 265 Camden High Street, NW1, 020 7482 4857; Hampstead Theatre, 98 Avenue Road, NW3, 020 7722 9301; New End Theatre, 27 New End,

NW3, 020 7794 0022; ABC Hampstead, Pond Street, NW3, 020 7794 6603; Odeon Camden Town, 14 Parkway, NW1, 020 8315 4229; Odeon Swiss Cottage, 96 Finchley Road, NW3, 020 7586 3057; Screen on the Hill, 203 Haverstock Hill, NW3, 020 7435 3366

Leisure Centre: Mornington Sports Centre, 142-150 Arlington Road, NW1, 020 7267 3600

TRANSPORT

Time to City: 10 to 20 minutes; **Time to West End**: 10 to 20 minutes

Tube: **Circle, Metropolitan, Hammersmith & City lines**: King's Cross, Euston Square; **Northern line**: Euston, King's Cross, Camden Town, Mornington Crescent, Kentish Town, Chalk Farm, Belsize Park, Hampstead, Highgate; **Piccadilly line**: King's Cross, Russell Square, Holborn; **Victoria line**: Euston, King's Cross

Rail: **Silverlink**: Camden Road, Kentish Town West, Gospel Oak, Finchley Road & Frognal, Hampstead Heath; **Thameslink**: King's Cross, Kentish Town, West Hampstead Thameslink; **WAGN**: King's Cross

---

ISLINGTON

Boundaries and contiguous boroughs: **North**: Haringey; **East**: Hackney; **South**: The City; **West**: Camden

CLERKENWELL
ANGEL
BARNSBURY
CANONBURY
HIGHBURY
HOLLOWAY/TUFNELL PARK

Angel Tube has the longest escalator in the city, and it is the gateway to the centre of one of the most happening places in London. Loved and loathed in equal measure, Islington, with its mixture of the glamorous and the squalid, the old and the new, in many ways captures the essence of London. Today it is difficult to imagine Islington as a semi-rural region famous for its spas and dairy farms as it was back in the 18th century. Islington's historical journey is a fascinating one. It was a favoured haunt of Henry VIII who hunted in the woods around what was then a village; the first posthouse north, out of London, along the path of the New River (engineered in 1613 to supply water to the thirsty city); and host to Mary Queen of Scots and Sir Walter Raleigh. Today Islington offers some of the most exciting and salubrious areas in which to live and therefore some of the most sought after. It is one of the smallest London boroughs, covering six, densely populated, square miles. The quality of its architecture is witnessed by the fact that it includes over 4,000 listed buildings. Nineteenth century building expansion and the construction of the Regent's Canal were the catalysts that precipitated Islington's 20th century transformation into an inner-city borough. In the media-inspired popular imagination Islington is often thought of, with a mixture of envy and derision, as the home of champagne socialists and dinner party cliques. This is partly because the area has a long standing association with left-leaning politics with claims to fame, from Thomas Paine to Leon Trotsky to the Prime Minister Tony Blair who made the borough his home until his victory at the polls. In fact this attitude does not reflect the genuinely varied and multicultural communities that make Islington home. Although council housing makes up over half the borough's residential property, and the gentrification of the 1970s created a swath of prime real estate in all but the most run-down corners of the borough, there are always properties on the market to buy or rent, if you are prepared to pay "Islington prices."

Coming out of the northern side of the City is **Clerkenwell**, which is just inside Islington's boundary. The crossing into Islington is marked by the dominance of office space gradually giving way to more residential usage. The dilapidated splendour of Finsbury Town Hall on Rosebery Avenue points to the former status of Clerkentwell as a free standing, blue-collar community before being incorporated into the borough. Likewise the council estates around Old Street, which borders the City, and Exmouth Market, still speak of a working class presence amidst the ever-increasing number of luxury developments and expensive bars. Over the last decade or so Clerkenwell has become a fashionable mid-town location. Alongside its existing leafy squares and terraces, it had many disused warehouses and workshops—perfect spaces for conversion into lofts and apartments. These were marketed to young professionals, many of whom are able to walk to the City from here. Nearly all the available derelict industrial buildings have been converted or have been earmarked for development as either homes or offices. Many new restaurants supplement the existing delis and cafes, some of which date from an influx of Italians immigrants in the early part of the century. The offices of *The Guardian* newspaper, plus the many national charities based here fill the local bars and eateries with a lively mix of media, City, and voluntary sector workers. Sadlers Wells Theatre and the appearance of trendy cafes on St. John Street, which lies at the end of Rosebery Avenue and leads off to Angel Tube if you proceed east, are indicators of the high-quality cultural amenities to be found in Islington.

The area around the Tube station at **Angel** is maniacally busy most of the time, as it is a centre for both a residential and a working population. There are a few high street stores clustered around the junction with

Liverpool Road, Marks & Spencer, Sainsbury's and Woolworth's among them, as well as the cheap and cheerful Chapel Market which sells fruit and vegetables, plus clothes and household items. Recent residential developments are loft apartments in the Clerkenwell mould.

Following Islington High Street along to Islington Green, you can see the hive of activity that is the Business Design Centre, which hosts a wide range of exhibitions and trade fairs. Orbiting around this point are an array of food and drink options from tapas bars, Alsatian restaurants, and pricey bistros, to endless theme pubs and pizza parlours. Camden Passage, on the east side, houses an antique market; the streets behind it, leading off towards the canal and the City, are some of the most peaceful and attractive in the borough. Islington High Street forks at the Green, where you will notice a statue of Sir Hugh Myddelton who devised the New River. To the east is the Essex Road (A104) and to the west is Upper Street (A1); these perpetually busy thoroughfares are historical routes in and out of London. Essex Road is becoming swiftly gentrified with designer houseware and gift shops, and more lofts appearing, but there is perhaps more rented accommodation in its surrounding streets than elsewhere in central Islington.

Upper Street, and the squares and streets that lie behind it, are synonymous with the highbrow public image of Islington. You can still find upmarket antique shops, arty gift shops and quality restaurants nestled in between the council offices and fringe theatres of Upper Street. But in recent years there has been a mushrooming of uninspiring restaurants and featureless pubs as the area has become a "going-out" destination. If you get the chance, take a walk around the lovely Georgian and Victorian streets behind the bustle of the main road. Particularly appealing is the complex of terraces and squares of **Barnsbury** which reach on past Liverpool Road to Caledonian Road in the west of the borough. On the east side of Upper Street, past the Town Hall is **Canonbury**, where there are more lovely examples of domestic 18th and 19th century architecture including Canonbury Square, which has been home to such literary luminaries as George Orwell and Evelyn Waugh. With the dreamy and attractive ambience lent by the grassy squares, and the pleasing proportions of the houses, it is easy to understand why these are such desirable neighbourhoods. Many local residents here are successful in the fields of law, politics or the media. Families dominate in Barnsbury and Canonbury, whereas singles and couples are more likely to be found in the flats and apartments of Clerkenwell and Angel.

At Highbury Corner, marked by the Highbury and Islington Tube station, there is another major intersection where Upper Street meets the St. Paul's Road, which goes off east towards the popular Stoke Newington neighbourhood. The A1 continues as the rumbling Holloway Road taking you north to the Nags Head and Archway, a concrete jungle of converging roads and high-rises. Islington's only full-scale park, Highbury Fields, located opposite the Tube station, has more attractive quiet property in its environs. **Highbury**, as this area is known, carries on to the border with Hackney in one direction, and to Arsenal Football Stadium, a remarkable art deco structure and local landmark, in the other. Highbury Park has delis and local restaurants but the immediate vicinity of the football ground gets crowded and noisy on match days (every other Saturday), which is something to be aware of if you are considering living here. Victorian terraces make up the bulk of the housing here, with the larger ones invariably converted into flats. Highbury Park becomes the much grimier and noisier Blackstock Road, which leads to Finsbury Park station where there are rail links to the City and two Tube lines. From the station Stroud Green Road leads further north to Crouch Hill, which marks the border with the borough of Haringey. There are some huge Victorian houses here too, most divided into flats, and also early 20th century mansion blocks of flats.

The other focal point in the north of the borough is the Nags Head shopping area, which stretches along the central portion of the Holloway Road. Here there are several supermarkets and decent-sized branches of many high street chains. **Holloway**, an area which boasts two prisons, is the rougher, bargain basement end of Islington with many of its Victorian terraces a bit dilapidated and some large council estates dotted about. But it is still a well-placed neighbourhood, with Tube and bus links making travel to the West End or the City very doable. The terraced streets bounded by Holloway Road to the east, Brecknock Road to the west, Camden Road to the south, and Junction Road to the north are known as **Tufnell Park**, which is also the name of the Northern line Tube station which serves residents here. Flat conversions in the ordinary but perfectly reasonable Victorian houses here are popular with renters and buyers.

Web site: www.islington.gov.uk
Postcodes: N1, N4, N5, N7, N19
Council Office: Town Hall, Upper Street, N1, 020 7527 2000
Main Post Offices: 238 Essex Road, N1; 116 Upper Street, N1; 5 Highbury Corner N5; 482 Holloway Road, N7; 14 Junction Road, N19; Customer Helpline: 0345 223344
Police Stations: 2 Tolpuddle Street, N1; 211 Blackstock Road, N5; 284 Hornsey Road, N7; 470 Caledonian Road, N7
Accident and Emergency Department: Whittington Hospital, Highgate Hill, N19, 020 7272 3070
Public Libraries: Central Library, 2 Fieldway Crescent N5; Wenlock Library, Murray Grove, N1; West Library, Bridgeman Road, N1; Lewis Carroll Children's Library, 180 Copenhagen Road, N1; South Library, 115-117 Essex Road, N1; Arthur Simpson Library, Hanley Road, N4; John Barnes Library, 275 Camden Road, N7; North Library, Manor

Gardens, N7; Archway Library, Highgate Hill N19; 020 7527 6900 (ask for required branch);

Cultural Resources: Discover Islington Visitor Centre, 44 Duncan Street, N1, 020 7278 8787, email: VIC@islvic.demon.co.uk; Almedia Theatre, Almeida Street, N1, 020 7359 4404; Crafts Council, 44a Pentonville Road, N1, 020 7278 7700; Kings Head Theatre Club 115 Upper Street, N1, 020 7226 1916; Little Angel Theatre, 14 Dagmar Passage off Cross Street, N1, 020 7226 1787; Hen and Chickens Pub Theatre, 109 St. Paul's Road, Highbury Corner, N1, 020 7704 2001; Tower Theatre, Canonbury Place, N1, 020 7226 3633; Sadlers Wells Theatre, Rosebery Avenue, EC1, 020 7863 8000; Old Red Lion Theatre Club, St. John's Street, EC1, 020 7837 7816; Pleasance Theatre, 41 North Road, N7, 020 7609 1800; Screen on the Green Cinema, 83 Upper Street N1, 020 7226 3520; Holloway Odeon, 417 Holloway Road, N7, 020 8315 4212

Leisure Centres: Caledonian Road Swimming Pool, 229 Caledonian Road, N1, 020 7278 1890; Highbury Pool, Highbury Crescent, N5, 020 7704 2312; Sobell Leisure Centre, Hornsey Road, N7, 020 7609 2166; Archway Leisure Centre, 1 MacDonald Road, N19, 020 7281 4105; Ironmonger Row Baths, Ironmonger Row, EC1, 020 7253 4011

TRANSPORT
Time to City: 15 to 30 minutes; **Time to West End**: 10 to 25 minutes

Tube: **Northern line**: Old Street, Angel, Tufnell Park, Archway; **Piccadilly line**: Caledonian Road, Holloway Road, Arsenal, Finsbury Park; **Victoria line**: Highbury and Islington, Finsbury Park

Rail: **Silverlink**: Canonbury, Highbury and Islington, Caledonian Road and Barnsbury; **WAGN**: Old Street, Essex Road, Highbury and Islington, Drayton Park, Finsbury Park

---

HACKNEY

Boundaries and contiguous boroughs: **North**: Haringey; **East**: River Lea/Waltham Forest; **South**: Tower Hamlets/The City; **West**: Islington

HOXTON/SHOREDITCH
DALSTON
STOKE NEWINGTON/STAMFORD HILL
HACKNEY CENTRAL
LONDON FIELDS

Hackney started out as a leafy village spread out along roads running north out of the City, but its incorporation into the old East End in the 19th century was the beginning of a decline in its desirability, and it is now one of the poorest areas in the country. Its name means "dry land amid marshes" and the Hackney Marshes still mark the eastern boundary of the borough. There are, oddly, no Tube stations in the whole of the borough despite its relative centrality, and such an absence has not helped the borough's fortunes. Plans for new extensions and lines into Hackney have been regularly mooted since the 1950s, but have yet to materialise. The long-term future of the borough probably rests on whether improvements to its transport situation ever come to fruition. In the meantime its residents must rely on buses and overland train services which are actually surprisingly comprehensive. From the Hackney Downs railway station you can get to Liverpool Street in the heart of the City in under ten minutes.

Hackney's economic activity was once centred on the furniture trade and light industry, but today the area suffers from a collapsed infrastructure and dwindling opportunities. Many of the poorest immigrants and asylum seekers wind up here in run-down council estates or in shoddy conversions. Years of political infighting and the constant whiff of corruption coming from the local town hall haven't helped its image. The same goes for the appalling reputation of the borough's schools. But on the more positive side, recent years have seen a boom in arts activity, and publicity for the borough now confidently claims the largest community of artists in Europe. What's more, the big guns of central government have been brought in to sort out the education situation, and the borough also offers welcome surprises in the quality and amount of green space; Hackney Downs, London Fields, Clissold Park, and Victoria Park are all nice examples of urban open spaces. There are some unusual attractions too, such as Sutton House, the only red brick Tudor house in London, and the Geffrye Museum, which charts the changing face of English domestic interiors. Hackney also has a fascinating multi-cultural history that extends into the present. The parts of the borough nearest the City and Islington have undergone some gentrification but it still remains cheaper to live on these northeastern city fringes than the northern frontier of Islington. Because of the slightly dicey reputation of Hackney as a whole, it's possible to find property bargains even in the nicest parts of the borough, although prices are rising fast. Those who have adopted Hackney as their home point to its indomitable community spirit, its chaotic charms, the excitement of living in such a quintessentially urban area, and reasonable property rates as reasons for their choice.

The south end of Hackney borders on the City, Tower Hamlets and Islington. **Hoxton** and **Shoreditch**, the areas centring on Hoxton Square and Old Street, have recently experienced a large influx of artists and small design enterprises. In an effort to keep the area a productive one, many new flats here are sold on a double usage basis to artists as live/work loft apartments. As often happens, the poorer up-and-coming artists who were the first to make their mark here are now being priced out as the neighbourhood becomes more desirable. There is a new arts centre including an arthouse cinema, The Lux, a number of small art galleries, plus a smattering of smart bars and restaurants amid old industrial buildings and council estates. There is not much yet in the way of everyday shops but the stores around Liverpool Street Station, including a Marks & Spencer Food Hall, and the markets of Spitalfields are all within walking distance.

The main road leading north of the City beyond Shoreditch is the Kingsland Road (A10), running along the path of what was one of the main Roman roads out of London. The Kingsland Road takes you through **Dalston**, a vibrant, ethnically mixed area with large Turkish, Kurdish, Afro-Caribbean, and white working class communities. Regeneration money has flooded into this area producing the gleaming Dalston Cross Shopping Centre complete with a big Sainsbury's, and there are promises of a multi-screen cinema to come. While Dalston remains a poor neighbourhood with a bit of a rough reputation, it is otherwise notable for Ridley Road street market, one of London's oldest, and its 24-hour bagel bakery (until very recently London's only one!). Next stop on this route, which is lined with Turkish groceries, hot-bread shops and mini-cab firms, is **Stoke Newington**. It is here that most of Hackney's gentrification has been concentrated. Stoke Newington Church Street, which dives off the west side of the A10, has a relaxed atmosphere, interesting shops, a jazz club, cafes and a terrific variety of restaurants. An annual summer festival is hosted by the amiable Church Street community. The Abney Park Cemetery, which extends away from the northern side of the road, is a lovely walk complete with crumbling headstones looming out of the undergrowth. At the bottom of Church Street, Clissold Park is always humming with young families and assorted others knocking footballs about, feeding the goats or finding refreshment at the park's popular cafe situated in a dilapidated manor house. Hovering over the park in the distance are the turrets of the Castle, the grand facade that once hid a Victorian pumping station, and now holds an indoor climbing wall. Local sports enthusiasts are pleased too by the development of the reservoir north of the park as a watersports centre. The terraced streets around the immediate area of Church Street and stretching over to Newington Green are of the familiar Victorian design, and middle class buyers are taking over. There are plenty of converted flats as well. The resident profile here tends to be young and socially aware, with many working in healthcare, education or local government. There are a high number of young families in Stoke Newington, a mix of cultures, and the area is also popular with gays and lesbians. However, the further you get from Church Street, and especially if you stray to the east side of the A10, the more unpredictable the standard of accommodation becomes. Be aware that the popularity of the N16 postcode (which designates Stoke Newington) has led to a cramped and overpriced rental sector. The stretch of the A10 that is Stoke Newington High Street has a reasonable selection of shops and there are two Safeway supermarkets further along where Stoke Newington borders with the borough of Haringey in the north. **Stamford Hill**, the neighbourhood that straddles the two boroughs, is synonymous with its large Hasidic Jewish community.

In the east of the borough is **Hackney Central**. Mare Street, the grimy and busy main street, houses a Marks & Spencer but offers an otherwise mediocre selection of shops, the town hall (a regular feature on the television news every time a new scandal about the council hits the headlines), and Hackney Central train station. The pride of Mare Street is the Hackney Empire, a music hall dating from the 19th century and now a buzzing theatre, comedy and variety club, which sadly is in a constant battle to raise enough funds to secure its future. There are a few nicer enclaves among the council estates and the tall Victorian houses ruthlessly divided up into flats. The north and west sides of Clapton Square, just north of Mare Street, for instance, have amazing pilastered, five-storey houses dating from the Georgian period, which are complete with fanlights, huge bay windows and cast-iron balconies. This is a conservation area so the streets and the centre of the square are neat and picturesque, offering an Arcadian interlude amongst the surrounding noise. West of Mare Street you'll find elegant, flat-fronted Victorian terraces in the streets leading to the open space of **London Fields**. Buyers in this neck of the woods tend to be middle class, encouraged by the council's efforts to improve the nearby council estates. A certain Tony Blair lived here once. On the southeastern edge of the borough Victoria Park marks the border with Tower Hamlets. The streets approaching the park are quiet and leafy and property here tends to get bigger, as do prices.

Web site: www.hackney.gov.uk
Postcodes: E5, E8, E9, N1, N16
Council Office: Town Hall, Mare Street, E8, 020 8356 5000
Main Post Offices: 101 Hoxton Street, N1; 138 Stoke Newington High Street, N16; Mount Pleasant Lane, E5; 481 Cambridge Heath Road, E2; 290 Seven Sisters Road, N4; 118 Kingsland High Street, E8; 176 Shoreditch High Street, E1; 250 Stamford Hill, N16; Customer Helpline 0345 223344
Police Stations: 4-6 Sheperdess Walk, N1, 020 7253 1212; 2 Lower Clapton Road, E5, 020 8986 1212; 33 Stoke Newington High Street, N16, 020 7739 1212; minicom 020 7932 3834
Accident and Emergency Department: Homerton Hospital, Homerton Row, E9, 020 8510 5555
Public Libraries: Clapton, Northwold Road, E5; CLR James, Dalston Lane, E8; Homerton, Homerton High Street, E9; Mare Street, E8; Shoreditch,

Hoxton Street, N1; Stamford Hill, Portland Avenue, N16; Stoke Newington Church Street, N16, 020 8356 5000 (ask for required branch).

Cultural Resources: Rio Cinema, 107 Kingsland High Street, E8, 020 7254 6677; The Lux Centre, 2-4 Hoxton Square, N1, 020 7684 0201; Hackney Empire, 291 Mare Street, E8, 020 8985 2424; Hoxton Hall, 130 Hoxton Street, N1, 020 7739 5431; Comedy Cafe, 66 Rivington Street, EC2, 020 7739 5706; Chats Palace, 42-44 Brooksby Walk, E9, 020 8533 0227; Circus Space, Coronet Street, N1, 020 7613 4141; Vortex Jazz Bar, 139-141 Stoke Newington Church Street, N16, 020 7254 6516; The Blue Note, 35 Coronet Street, N1, 020 7729 8445; Angela Flowers Gallery, 282 Richmond Road, E8 & Flowers East Gallery, 199-205 Richmond Road, E8, both 020 8985 3333; numerous small galleries, see press for details.

Leisure Centres: Britannia Leisure Centre, 40 Hyde Road, N1, 020 7729 4485; Haggerston Pool, Whiston Road, E2, 020 7739 7166; Kings Hall Leisure Centre, 39 Lower Clapton Road, E5, 020 8985 2158

TRANSPORT
Time to City: 10 to 20 minutes; **Time to West End**: 20 to 45 minutes

Rail: **Silverlink**: Dalston Kingsland, Hackney Central, Homerton, Hackney Wick; **WAGN**: Cambridge Heath, London Fields, Hackney Downs, Clapton, Stoke Newington, Rectory Road, Stamford Hill

TOWER HAMLETS

Boundaries and contiguous boroughs: **North**: Hackney; **East**: Newham; **South**: The Thames; **West**: Hackney/The City

WHITECHAPEL/SPITALFIELDS
BETHNAL GREEN
STEPNEY/BOW
DOCKLANDS/ISLE OF DOGS
LIMEHOUSE/SHADWELL/WAPPING

Tower Hamlets is a borough of startling and sometimes brutal contrasts. In a sweep along the northeastern edge of the Thames, it encompasses the epoch-defining Docklands development and the major tourist attraction of the Tower of London as well as some of the most impoverished areas of London. The borough of Tower Hamlets was created in 1965 out of the old metropolitan boroughs making up the infamous East End, and no area of London is so steeped in urban mythology. The infrastructure of these areas was heavily hit, as was the population, during the air raids of the Second

World War, and although many of the residential areas destroyed were undoubtedly slums, the high-rise estates that replaced them frequently offered little improvement. This damage combined with the decline of the traditional dockland industries meant the region was left to decay in the decades that followed. It was not until the 1980s that the borough experienced a change in fortunes with regeneration attempting to capitalise on its terrific commercial potential. Today, Tower Hamlets is a heady mix of old working class cockney communities, immigrant settlements and newly gentrified areas occupied by the upwardly mobile. If you work or study in the City or its outpost in Docklands, this is a convenient base, though its high-octane life will not suit everyone.

The areas of Tower Hamlets bordering the City, Spitalfields and **Whitechapel**, are famous for dark and dramatic associations both with Jack the Ripper, whose crimes loomed so large in the Victorian imagination, and the criminal underworld of the 1960s inhabited by the Kray Twins. The hectic and rather unlovely Whitechapel High Street (A11) takes you the length of the East End and into Newham—its name changing along the way to Whitechapel Road, Mile End Road, and Bow Road. Things to watch out for include the impressively marble-fronted Whitechapel Art Gallery, the old-world charm of the Whitechapel Bell Foundry (which has numbered among its commissions the Liberty Bell and Big Ben), and the East London mosque which serves the neighbourhood's substantial Muslim community.

The **Spitalfields** area to the north of Whitechapel, dominated by Hawksmoor's imposing Christ Church, underwent a certain amount of gentrification during the 1980s with the rediscovery of some beautiful and untouched early Georgian townhouses in the atmospheric narrow streets between Brick Lane and Commercial Street. Residents, like English artists Gilbert and George, were followed here by others in the arts and media sectors. With an ever-increasing number of galleries opening the area has become a focal point for London's burgeoning art and fashion scenes. Another central feature of this area is its long street markets. On Petticoat Lane you'll find cheap clothes are the main commodity. Brick Lane is the place to go to find an eclectic range of stalls, from fruit and vegetables to bikes and electrical goods of dubious origin to obscure odds and ends. The wholesale fruit and vegetable market for which Spitalfields was once best known has relocated. Now occupying its shell is a market specialising in organic produce and where you can find stalls selling trendy retro clothes and second hand books. A jazz venue, restaurants, and fashionable furniture shops line the edges. Old warehouses and industrial buildings nearby are being hastily transformed into "stunning loft apartments" to cash in on the hipness of this fringe area, and prices have begun to spiral upwards. The Spitalfields area has a long and rich tradition of providing a haven for refugees starting with Flemish weavers and Scandinavians in the 16th century and followed by French Huguenots who came over in the 17th century, all of whom helped establish the area's position in the rag trade. There are still vast numbers of small clothing manufacturers and wholesalers on Commercial Street and on nearby Commercial Road (A13), many of which are now run by those of Asian descent. At the end of the last century Jewish escapees from the Russian pogroms made their homes here creating a large Jewish community, which has dwindled in the last thirty years or so. Today it is the Bangladeshi community that thrives in this part of town along with the art school crowd—Brick Lane being renowned for its selection of curry houses and now dubbed "Banglatown." On Fournier Street there is a building which charts all these changes. Built as a Huguenot chapel in the 18th century, it was later to become a synagogue and is now a mosque. Notwithstanding its inclusive and varied history the area saw a certain amount of racial tension in the 1970s and '80s, and council estates still tend to divide along racial lines.

Bethnal Green, located to the northwest of Brick Lane and bounded by Hackney Road in the north and the railway line in the south, is the archetypal East End neighbourhood of run-down estates, boxing clubs and rough pubs. There have been some new developments in old factory buildings, and new schools added as of late, especially near the Tube, but gentrification is still only making tentative inroads here. South of the railway line is **Stepney** and **Bow**, where you will find more terraced properties and more rental accommodation at a medium price. This is due in part to the proximity of Queen Mary and Westfield College, a part of the University of London, whose main building, the People's Palace, can be spotted from the Mile End Road. The area around Victoria Park—a sea of tranquillity in this heavily built-up borough—has some very pleasant streets. The most appealing examples of Georgian and Victorian squares and terraces are preserved as part of the Bow Conservation Area beyond the north of the Bow Road. Tredagar Square is listed and its tall stuccoed houses with Ionic columns and period architraves fetch upwards of half a million pounds. The Roman Road offers another example of a street market complete with quipping cockneys and dirt-cheap goods, and there's a Safeway here too. Down towards the river, south of the Bow Road, are sweeps of tower blocks, only occasionally interspersed with old terraces or new, more luxurious low-rise housing developments aimed at young professionals. The Blackwall Tunnel Northern Approach Road (A102), part of a major north-south route and regular scene of some of London's worst traffic snarl-ups, marks the eastern boundary of both Bow and the borough.

The curious name of the **Isle of Dogs** (it's not an island), is derived, depending on what story you believe, either from the 16th century practice of kennelling the royal dogs here out of the earshot of the palace at Greenwich, or is simply a derisory nickname which stuck. With the decline of the local docks and industries after the Second World War, the Isle became a deprived and wretched place. The Thatcherite era inspired the development of **Docklands** in the early 1980s as an enterprise zone, and the area came under the auspices of a specially created regeneration body, the London Docklands Development Council. This council was criticised for offering little to the beleaguered local communities, as development brought apartments and facilities for an incoming class of upwardly mobile city slickers, rather than jobs and homes for local people. Most of the national newspapers moved their production to this new zone in the early '80s where ultra-modern business premises, unprecedented in this country and radically different from the dusty alleyways and severe Victoriana of the City, were built, along with more residential developments. Canary Wharf tower, the capital's biggest skyscraper by far, which you can see winking at you from points all over town, quickly became an icon representing London's determination to modernise. Add to this the Docklands Light Railway, a new transit system linking these new points on the map, and the proximity of London City Airport, offering a super-convenient route to the continent, and you have a very attractive business environment. The residential areas in particular still have an unreal toytown feel to them but there is no doubt they offer good amenities like off-street parking and on-site gyms, not to mention spectacular views of the river. It's noticeable too that children don't enter much into the equation, and the area is still a bit light on workaday shops, though there are new malls at Canary Wharf and Tobacco Dock. Cinemas and restaurants are springing up too. The recession of the early 1990s meant the Brave New World of Docklands did not turn out quite as planned, with acres of empty office space and various financial problems bringing accusations of over-arching ambitions. However, the development has survived, the offices are occupied and construction continues. The Jubilee line extension has given Docklands a fast link to Westminster and the rest of the Tube network. Over 25,000 people now come to work in Docklands every day, and with major financial institutions such as HSBC and Citibank moving in, this figure is expected to rise to the 100,000 mark by 2005.

The warehouse conversions and new apartment blocks continue all the way west through **Limehouse** and **Shadwell** to **Wapping**, and there are some poignant contrasts between rich and poor, luxury developments and council estates, in all these regions. The Regent's Canal, an arc running east, north and west of London, with links to the canal network in the rest of the country, begins its journey at Limehouse Basin. As Wapping is within walking distance of the City, it was the first of these East End areas to "go up," and Cher is among those celebrities who have chosen a warehouse conversion in Wapping for their London base. On and around Leman Street there are Indian restaurants and a few bars. There are few facilities for children in all these areas, and property is dominated by one and two bedroom flats and penthouses—pretty much split equally between renters (rents are medium to high), and owner-occupiers. At the western boundary of the borough is the renovated St. Katherine's Dock, complete with pleasure craft, luxury flats, and a high-rise hotel. The major tourist attractions lie at the boundary of the borough: the Tower of London, Tower Bridge and HMS Belfast, a naval museum housed in Europe's largest preserved warship.

Web site: www.towerhamlets.gov.uk
Postcodes: E1, E2, E3, E14
Council Office: Town Hall, Mulberry Place, 5 Clove Crescent, London, E14, 020 7364 5000
Main Post Offices: 75 Whitechapel Road, E1; 206 Whitechapel Road, E1; 502 Commercial Road, E1; 223 Bethnal Green Road, E2; 481 Cambridge Heath Road, E2; 138 Roman Road, E2; 2 Stroudley Walk, E3; Cabot Place, E14; Customer Helpline 0345 223344
Police Stations: East Arbour Street, E1, 020 7790 1212; 25 Brick Lane E1; 74 Leman Street, E1, 020 7790 1212; 98 Wapping High Street, E1, 020 7481 1212; 111 Bow Road, E3, 020 8980 1212; 29 West India Dock Road, E14, 020 7515 1212; 12 Victoria Park Gate Square, E2, 020 7983 1212; 160 Manchester Road, E14, 020 7515 1212; 2 Market Way, E14, 020 7515 1212
Accident and Emergency Department: Royal London Hospital, Whitechapel Road, E1, 020 7377 7000
Libraries: Bancroft, Bancroft Road, E1, 020 8980 4366; Stepney, Lindley Street, E1, 020 7790 5616; Whitechapel, 77 Whitechapel High Street, E1, 020 7247 5272; Bethnal Green, Cambridge Heath Road, E2, 020 8980 3902; Limehouse, 638 Commercial Road, E14, 020 7987 3183
Cultural Resources: Tower Hamlets Tourist Information Centre, 18 Lamb Street, E1, 020 7375 2549; Canary Wharf Tourist Information Centre, Canary Wharf Station, DLR Ticket Office, E14, 020 7512 9800; The Spitz, Old Spitalfields Market, Commercial Street, E1, 020 7392 9032; Spitalfields Market Opera, 4-5 Lamb Street, E1, 020 7247 2558; Tower of London, Tower Hill, E1, 020 7709 0765; HMS Belfast, E1, 020 7940 6300; Whitechapel Art Gallery, Whitechapel High Street, E1, 020 7522 7888; Bethnal Green Museum of Childhood, Cambridge Heath Road, E2, 020 8980 2415; Ragged School Museum, Copperfield Road, E3, 020 8980 6405; numerous small galleries, see press for details.
Leisure Centres: Market Sports, 1 Lamb Street, 020 7377 1300; Tiller Leisure Centre, Tiller Road, E14, 020 7987 0500; York Hall Leisure Centre, Old Ford Road, E2, 020 8980 2243; Mile End Climbing Wall, Cordova Road, E3, 020 8980 0289; Langdon Park Centre, 7 Byron Street, E14, 020 7987 3575

TRANSPORT
Time to City: 5 to 25 minutes; **Time to West End**: 10 to 45 minutes
Tube: **Central line**: Bethnal Green, Mile End; **District**, **Hammersmith & City lines**: Aldgate East, Whitechapel, Mile End, Stepney Green, Bow Road; **East London line**: Shoreditch, Whitechapel, Shadwell, Wapping; **Jubilee line extension**: Canary Wharf
Docklands Light Railway: Bow Church, Devons Road, All Saints, Poplar, West India Quay, Canary Wharf, Heron Quays, South Quay, Crossharbour and London Arena, Mudchute, Island Gardens, Westferry, Limehouse, Shadwell, Blackwall, East India
Rail: **WAGN**: Bethnal Green, Cambridge Heath

SOUTHWARK

Boundaries and contiguous boroughs: **North**: Thames; **East**: Lewisham; **South**: Croydon/Bromley; **West**: Lambeth

THE BOROUGH/BANKSIDE
BERMONDSEY/ROTHERHITHE/SURREY QUAYS
WALWORTH/OLD KENT ROAD/ELEPHANT AND CASTLE
CAMBERWELL
PECKHAM/NUNHEAD
EAST DULWICH/HERNE HILL
DULWICH VILLAGE

Southwark was the first major settlement on the south side of the river and dates from Roman times when the first bridge was built over the Thames. London Bridge, as it became known, was rebuilt periodically and remained the only permanent structure crossing the Thames until 1750. For this reason Southwark remained in a prominent position—its name derives from "south works" referring to Anglo-Saxon defences which were constructed here to safeguard the City. The area was London's first borough, known, naturally, as "The Borough." It was here, just outside the jurisdiction of the City, that inns and brothels were established, leading to its description as "a wild disorderly haunt of rakes, drunkards and whores." This reputation was earned in spite of the fact that Southwark was also an important site for royalty and the Church. The so-called "Lost Palace" of Edward II overlooked the river at Rotherhithe, and a powerful coterie of bishops met at Winchester Palace, which stood close to where Southwark Cathedral is situated today—itself one of the oldest religious sites in London. By Elizabethan times though, the area was primarily London's entertainment zone. Revellers went to watch Shakespeare's plays at the Rose and the

Globe theatres, where they were performed alongside bear baiting and cockfighting. Today you can view the amazing reconstruction of the Globe Theatre overlooking the Thames at London Bridge, the result of a labour of love by the late American director Sam Wanamaker. Further east on the riverbank at Rotherhithe is the spot from which the Pilgrim Fathers set sail on their historic journey to America in 1620, marked by the Mayflower pub. Today Southwark's boundaries extend southward through the urban heartlands of Camberwell and Peckham, and as far as the greenery and ancient woodland of Dulwich Village and Sydenham Hill.

The north of the borough faces the City of London across the river. Once the site of wharves, warehouses and intense commercial activity, earning it the nickname "London's Larder," this riverside section is undergoing rejuvenation similar to that of Docklands, with new commercial and residential developments up and going up. **The Borough** or **Bankside**, as this part of Southwark is becoming known, is being marketed as London's "left bank." It includes the stunning and wildly popular new Tate Modern, which is housed in the hulking shell of the old Bankside power station, and smart new shopping precincts, such as Butlers Wharf and Hay's Galleria with their wine bars and luxury goods shops. These shops are juxtaposed with the olde-worlde Dickensian cobbled streets that surround the historic Southwark Cathedral and Borough market, and make for an exciting mix of the old and the new. (It was here on Borough High Street, in a debtors' prison, that Dickens used to visit his father as a child, an experience which left an indelible mark on his life and writing.) The media, financial, and retail sectors are filling in the gaps left by the closing of the docks, including Canadian Imperial Bank, IPC Magazines, Express Newspapers, and the Australian and New Zealand banks. There are also plenty of tourist attractions concentrated here, including the London Dungeon, the Design Museum, and a string of Conran restaurants. A lovely new footbridge arches across the Thames, linking the Tate to St. Paul's Cathedral, and offering great views without bothersome traffic. The extension of the Jubilee line with stations at Southwark, Bermondsey, and Canada Water provides a valuable link with the West End and Docklands. Encouragingly, the regeneration of the Bankside neighbourhood has been praised for its blend of commercial, cultural, and community interests, and for the inclusion of cheaper housing amidst the Docklands-style luxury developments and the surviving cache of up-market Georgian houses and terraces near Guys Hospital. It is hoped that such mixed housing will reduce some of the tension between established residents and newcomers, which has been such an unhappy feature of Docklands development. Another tremendous gain for this part of town will be the City Hall, which is being built here to house the newly-created London wide authority. The design, by Norman Foster, is a giant glass bubble overlooking the Thames, and promises to be one of the most modern and striking city halls anywhere in the world.

Moving along the waterfront eastward past Tower Bridge into the northerly part of **Bermondsey** and into **Rotherhithe**, things become less diverse with every available space snapped up for apartment blocks and warehouse conversions, and at the expense of the local community. The result of this quick-fire development is that the south side of the river now mirrors the Docklands side of the river, complete with its homogenous, young stockbroker/banker profile. The southern part of Bermondsey has an old village centre at Bermondsey Street, where there is a famous antique market though few other amenities or shops as yet. Away from the riverfront there is a mix of council and housing association homes, some loft conversions of old schools and industrial buildings, and a sprinkling of modest Victorian houses and flats. **Surrey Quays**, a part of Rotherhithe, offers a departure from the area norm, with a selection of new family houses with gardens. Surrey Quays shopping centre has a supermarket and one of the few collections of practical shops around here.

The central part of Southwark, covering what is loosely termed as **Walworth** or the **Old Kent Road** or "the Elephant," is still a relatively run-down stretch with busy, grimy roads converging on the **Elephant and Castle** junction. Here you'll find the universally loathed pink shopping mall, which is even more uninspiring inside with its bargain basement shops, surrounded by acres of unattractive concrete buildings and council housing. Some of the estates are now being gentrified, and the once reviled Alexander Fleming office development, a gigantic concrete form designed by uncompromising modernist Hungarian architect Ernst Goldfinger, has been successfully turned into private apartments. On the whole however, Elephant and Castle has yet to become a place where people are especially keen to live and rental accommodation is thus still cheap. The Old Kent Road (A2), running northeast, is famous as one of the few south London locations to feature on the Monopoly board, and is, culturally at least, part of the East End. In the area beyond Elephant and Castle junction which is serviced by a Tube station at the end of the Northern and Bakerloo lines, you'll be reliant on rail services which take you into Victoria or London Bridge, or on bus services. From the Elephant, the Walworth Road (A215) leads down to **Camberwell,** the central west section of the borough, which has a comprehensive if rather scruffy shopping area at Camberwell Green and a couple of gentrified pubs. Camberwell is an oft-scoured locale by those looking for affordable London housing with period charm, which exists here in the form of Georgian and Victorian properties, often hidden behind the roaring roads and the grim council buildings. Also, there is a fair amount of low to medium priced rented accommodation in converted houses which caters to a large student population attending the Camberwell Art School and nurses working at the King's College and

Maudsley Hospitals. Neighbouring **Peckham** is solidly working class with a large Afro-Caribbean community. There is a massive new shopping mall at Peckham Rye, as well as plenty of Caribbean-influenced grocery stores, barbers, and record shops on Rye Lane. Burgess Park is a welcome open space in this heavily built-up patch. The **Nunhead** area, tucked away east of Peckham Rye Common, is more popular with middle class buyers seeking out solid Victorian terraces. West of the Common are **East Dulwich** and **Herne Hill**. These are spacious suburban regions, laid out by the Victorians as "railway suburbs" to house City workers. Today they are still popular as modest but respectable places to live.

The idea of "London villages" is often talked up by estate agents in misleading ways, but **Dulwich Village,** at the southerly tip of Southwark, is genuinely a world apart from the urban scrum. This is in part because much of the land is owned by a trust which has been wary of letting in the developers. The area boasts attractively laid out, spacious (and expensive) houses from every period, from Georgian to the present day. The only surviving tollgate in London, the mill pond, the golf course and Dulwich Park, where you can hire recumbent two-seater bicycles, all contribute to the untroubled gentility of Dulwich, which, if too expensive for most to live in, is at least a great place to visit for a taste of English countryside. Along leafy College Road are the architectural set pieces of the Dulwich Picture Gallery, the 19th century's first purpose-built public gallery, designed by Sir John Soane, and Dulwich College.

Web site: www.southwark.gov.uk
Postcodes: SE1, SE5, SE15, SE16, SE17, SE21, SE22
Council Office: Town Hall, Peckham Road, SE5, 020 7525 5000
Main Post Offices: 239 Borough High Street, SE1; 91 Newington Butts, SE1; 25 Denmark Hill, SE5; 19a Borough High Street, SE15; 121 Peckham High Street, SE15, 199 Rye Lane, SE15; 158 Jamaica Road, SE16; 234 Walworth Road, SE16; 76 Lordship Lane, SE22; Customer Helpline: 0345 223344
Police Stations: 209 Tooley Street, SE1, 020 7403 1212; 323 Borough High Street, SE1, 020 7378 1212; 22a Camberwell Church Street, SE5, 020 7703 1212; 177 Peckham High Street, SE15, 020 7732 1212; 99 Lower Road, SE16, 020 7231 1212; 12/28 Manor Place, SE17, 020 7701 1212; 173 Lordship Lane, SE22, 020 8299 3911
Accident and Emergency Departments: Guy's Hospital, St. Thomas Street, SE1, 020 7955 5000; Kings College Hospital, Denmark Hill, SE5, 020 7737 4000; St. Thomas's Hospital, Lambeth Palace Road, SE1, 020 7928 9292
Public Libraries: Blue Anchor, Market Place, Southwark Park Road, SE16, 020 7231 0475; Brandon, Maddox Way, SE17, 020 7735 3430;

Camberwell, 17-19 Camberwell Church Street, SE5, 020 7703 3763; Dulwich District, 368 Lordship Lane, SE22, 020 8693 5171; East Street/Old Kent Road, 168 Old Kent Road, SE1, 020 7703 0395; Grove Vale, 25 Grove Vale, SE22, 020 8693 5734; John Harvard, 211 Borough High Street, SE1, 020 7407 0807; Kingswood, Seeley Drive, SE21, 020 8670 4803; Newington, 155-157 Walworth Road, SE17, 020 7703 3324; North Peckham, 600-608 Old Kent Road, SE15, 020 7639 1255; Nunhead, Gordon Road, SE15, 020 7639 0264; Peckham, 167 Peckham Hill Street, SE15, 020 7639 1624; Rotherhithe, Albion Street, SE16, 020 7237 2010

Cultural Resources: Southwark Tourist Information Centre, Hay's Galleria, Tooley Street, SE1, 020 7403 8299; Coronet Cinema, New Kent Road, Elephant & Castle, SE1, 020 7703 4968; Premier Cinema, Moncrieff Street, SE15, 020 7732 1010; Tom Blau Photographic Gallery, 21 Queen Elizabeth Street, SE1, 020 7378 1300; Dulwich Picture Gallery, College Road, SE21, 020 8693 8000; South London Gallery, 65 Peckham Road, SE5, 020 7703 6120; Bramah Tea and Coffee Museum, Clove Building, Maquire Street, SE1, 020 7378 0222; Shakespeare Globe Museum, New Globe Walk, SE1, 020 7902 1500; see **Cultural Resources** chapter for major museums.

Leisure Centres: Camberwell, Camberwell Church Street, SE5, 020 7703 3024; Dulwich, 45 East Dulwich Road, SE22, 020 8693 1833; Elephant & Castle, 22 Elephant & Castle, SE1, 020 7582 5505; Orchard Sports Centre, William Booth Road, SE20, 020 8778 3500; Peckham, McKerrell Road, SE15, 020 7732 3516; Seven Islands, Lower Road, SE16, 020 7237 3296; Southwark Park Sports Complex, Hawkstone Road, SE16, 020 7231 9442; Surrey Docks Watersports Centre, Greenland Dock, Rope Street, SE16, 020 7237 4009

TRANSPORT

Time to City: 5 to 30 minutes; **Time to West End**: 10 to 40 minutes

Tube: **Bakerloo line**: Elephant and Castle; **East London line**: Rotherhithe, Surrey Quays; **Jubilee line**: London Bridge, Southwark, Bermondsey, Canada Water; **Northern line**: Elephant and Castle, Borough, London Bridge

Docklands Light Railway: Surrey Quays

Rail: **Connex South Central**: London Bridge, South Bermondsey, Queen's Road Peckham, Peckham Rye, East Dulwich, North Dulwich; **Connex South Eastern**: London Bridge, Elephant and Castle, Denmark Hill, Peckham Rye, Nunhead; **Thameslink**: Elephant and Castle, London Bridge

LAMBETH

Boundaries and contiguous boroughs: **North**: Thames; **East**: Southwark; **South**: Croydon; **West**: Wandsworth

SOUTH BANK
VAUXHALL/KENNINGTON
STOCKWELL
BRIXTON/TULSE HILL
CLAPHAM
STREATHAM

There are four bridges over the Thames that lead into the Borough of Lambeth: Waterloo, Westminster, Lambeth, and Vauxhall. Large buildings that run along the riverbank and include the London Weekend Television's Studios and the South Bank Centre occupy the spaces between the first three bridges. Also along the bank, County Hall, a grand, early 20th century Portland stone building, sits just in sight of the Houses of Parliament on the opposing bank. County Hall was once home to the Greater London Council (GLC), London's last city-wide authority and a symbol of London opposition to the Thatcher government. Against much resistance, the GLC was abolished in 1986, and after a lot of wrangling the building was turned into the London Aquarium. Lambeth Palace, the official residence of the Archbishop of Canterbury, is nearby too. Cutting a swathe alongside the river and extending down to meet Croydon, Lambeth is a borough with a great deal going on beyond these most visible signs of public, official, and tourist activity. Travelling south you'll find pleasant contrasts in Lambeth, from the wine bars of Clapham, the lively markets and rough edges of Brixton, to the quiet, almost suburban, reaches of Tulse Hill and Streatham.

At the top end of Lambeth the Thames dips steeply southward, and this part of the borough is dominated by the South Bank Arts Complex (see **Cultural Resources**) and Waterloo station. Waterloo, long a major rail and Tube intersection, recently has been made busier still by the opening of the Channel Tunnel rail link. The elegant Eurostar trains now leave from the Waterloo station bound for Paris and Brussels. Waterloo Bridge sweeps over to the Strand, which runs through the middle of the busy West End, creating a perpetual stream of traffic. In the early 1990s, the **South Bank** area was much vaunted as an up and coming bit of the inner-city in which to live, resulting in the building of new apartment blocks and the smartening up of council estates. There are some expensive restaurants and new bars around the station but due mainly to the high volume of through-traffic it doesn't feel much like a neighbourhood.

Vauxhall, the area immediately south of Waterloo, was the cradle of industry in London in the mid-17th century. Pottery and glassworks came first, followed by the boat-builders, distilleries, and vinegar and glue works, which sprang up during the Industrial Revolution. Now the only vestige remaining of the great 19th century industries is the Royal Doulton Factory, a fine, Italian-style building that once housed a pottery works and is now a business centre. As with many other ex-industrial riverside areas, apartment blocks and warehouse conversions have been developed in the area. Around Vauxhall Tube there is a noisy conflagration of busy main roads bringing traffic across the river and radiating out north and south to Lambeth (Albert Embankment, South Lambeth Road), Kennington (Kennington Lane), and Wandsworth (Wandsworth Road). In the 17th, 18th and 19th centuries the Vauxhall Pleasure Gardens occupied a site next to Kennington Lane, providing music, dancing, and other sorts of ribald entertainment. The London Balloon, now moored on the small remaining bit of parkland called Spring Gardens, is all that survives of this fairground spirit. Venture further down into **Kennington** and you'll find pretty Georgian and Victorian squares such as Cleaver Square, Walcot Square, St. Mary's Gardens, and West Square, interspersed with tower blocks and low-rise estates. The Oval cricket ground is here as is the Imperial War Museum. Kennington Park provides the area with some welcome breathing space. Along some of the main routes, Kennington Park Road (A3) and Kennington Road (A23) are some more splendid Georgian houses, but the amount of traffic can be off-putting. Kennington lies just across and down river of Westminster and down the road from Waterloo and so the nicest family homes often attract members of Parliament and other notables. The Duchy of Cornwall Estate (belonging to the Prince of Wales) has owned a parcel of land west of Kennington Road for centuries and the homes built by the Estate are now on the open market or are rented out by a housing association. Area residents tend to be a mix of professionals seeking cheaper period properties and council tenants. Along South Lambeth Road there are several lively tapas bars, an indication of the area's resident Portuguese community, and nearby Clapham, with its wine bars and more expensive restaurants, is well within reach. There is a Sainsbury's off Wandsworth Road, a Tesco superstore is planned for Kennington Lane, and there are enough local stores for the day to day basics.

Moving south the borough broadens out into **Stockwell** where you'll find a wide variety of housing, including some surviving terraces, semis, and detached houses dating back to when the area was first developed in the early 19th century. There are pockets of flats and houses from just about every era since, including a lot of council housing. Perhaps because it is a bit of a mish-mosh the area has yet to succumb fully to gentrification. Bugbears such as tower blocks and roaring thoroughfares, make Stockwell's full potential as an upscale and desirable environ unconvincing to some. The group of streets to the east of the Stockwell Road is known collectively as "Stockwell Park" and this, with its large Regency family homes, is the poshest part of the neighbourhood.

The east-west running Coldharbour Lane leading into Acre Lane, and the north-south A23 Brixton Road, which becomes Brixton Hill before heading off to Clapham, are the two major arteries which bisect Lambeth and they cross at **Brixton**, the heart of the borough. In the early 1980s Brixton was the scene of riots, caused by the frustrations of local unemployment and police harassment of the black community. Since that time government money has been channeled into the area through a revitalization project called the "City Challenge." The culmination of this regeneration effort has been the creation of over 600 new businesses and a significant number of jobs. Gradually, what was once a notorious inner-city ghetto has been rehabilitated, due in large part to the strength and commitment of the local community. However, a riot in 1995 demonstrated that all the problems have not been entirely solved and gives Brixton an edgy reputation, though this arguably attracts as many people as it turns off. The clubs and street life of Brixton are for those who embrace noise, bustle, and a heady mix of youth cultures—heaven for some, hell for others. Amenities in the area include the Brixton Academy on Stockwell Road, a large music venue which attracts a steady stream of big-name bands, and going south, Brixton Road is lined with small branches of high street stores and sports shops where the local youth buy their trainers. In amongst the railway arches of Electric Avenue, so named because in the 1880s it was the first street in London to be lit by electricity, is Brixton Market where there are spectacular mounds of tropical fruit, vegetables, and fish on offer. Continue south and you'll come upon a junction marked by a triangle of green; on your right, at the beginning of Brixton Hill, is the Fridge, a cavernous and popular club which hosts all kinds of dance nights, and on your left, past the turn-off to Coldharbour Lane, is the renovated Ritzy Cinema, an excellent independent multi-screen. Brixton Hill leads south towards Streatham, and it is in this direction that the best quality housing can be found. The roads here are wide and the houses are large architect-designed Victorian affairs with big gardens. Effra Road also runs south from the junction and offers well-kept terraces. Effra Road becomes **Tulse Hill,** which overlooks Brockwell Park with its delightful Lido, an outdoor swimming pool. Housing prices here are reasonable, by London standards, with young professionals and first-time buyers attracted by Brixton's relative affordability, and the fast Tube link into Central London via the Victoria line. There is also a good slice of mid-price rented accommodation in shared houses and flats.

Families may be a bit intimidated by Brixton's reputation and the perceived poor standards of local schools. Those with children are more likely to head for **Clapham** in the west of the borough, where there are several good primary schools in the vicinity of Clapham Common. The Common itself is an excellent resource for kids, joggers, dog-walkers and kite flyers alike. North of the Common and south of Wandsworth Road is the oldest part of the neighbourhood, with houses of every date from the early 18th century onwards, though the bulk are Victorians. The streets south of Clapham Common are popular too with Abbeville Road running through the middle of the area and acting as a mini-high street, complete with cafes and gift shops. Located here are some elegant period properties including large four- or five-bedroom late Victorian terraces and maisonettes, attracting professionals and City workers, often with children. Filling in the gaps between these two most desirable bits of Clapham are council housing, the odd new development and a few scruffier terraced streets where there are a higher number of conversions and rented flats. Clapham High Street has a big Sainsbury's, plenty of bars and restaurants, and a Tube station at each of its ends. As with Brixton, the presence of the Tube is a big plus as many other parts of south London are ill-served by public transport. Clapham is one of those areas to which residents become quite devoted and to which others aspire to live, but where you will still find a multi-cultural populace spanning the income divides.

In the southern half of the borough, below the South Circular Road (A205), lies **Streatham**, a large mostly Victorian and Edwardian-built area. The busy Streatham High Road (A23) is a major route running north into the capital. This is the area's main street, but the heavy traffic and closed-down shops lend it a rather besieged feel. Streatham's many large terraced houses have given rise to plenty of conversions which provide relatively cheap property to rent or buy, but there are still many family houses too. Apart from a low-key red light district between Streatham High Road and Tooting Bec Common, the area is generally quiet and its relative anonymity has kept prices reasonable. The northeastern Streatham Park corner is popular as it is particularly green and spacious and it sneaks into Wandsworth's boundary. Commuters rely on the rail services to Victoria from the three overland stations in the area.

Web sites: www.lambeth.gov.uk; www.brixton.co.uk
Postcodes: SE1, SE11, SW2, SW4, SW8, SW9, SW12, SW16
Council Office: Town Hall, Brixton Hill, SW2, 020 7926 1000
Main Post Offices: 125-131 Westminster Bridge Road, SE1; 410 Kennington Road, SE11; 161 Clapham High Street, SW4; 833 Wandsworth Road, SW8; 347 Wandsworth Road, SW8; 225 Clapham Road, SW9; 250 Ferndale Road, SW9; 92a Balham High Road, SW12; 1348 London Road, SW16; 136 Streatham High Road, SW16; 330 Streatham High Road, SW16; Customer Helpline: 0345 223344
Police Stations: 367 Brixton Road, SW9; 49 Kennington Road, SE1; 51

Union Grove, SW8; 101 Streatham High Road, SW16; 66 Central Hill, SE19; 47 Cavendish Road, SW12; Switching Centre: 020 7326 1212, ask for the station you require; Help desk, 101 Streatham High Road, SW16 to deal with non-urgent calls only, 020 8649 2929.

Accident and Emergency Departments: Guy's Hospital, St. Thomas Street, SE1, 020 7955 5000; Kings College Hospital, Denmark Hill, SE5, 020 7737 4000; St. Thomas's Hospital, Lambeth Palace Road, SE1, 020 7928 9292

Public Libraries: North Lambeth, 114-118 Lower Marsh, SE1, 020 7926 8690; Durning, 167 Kennington Lane, SE11, 020 7926 8682; South Lambeth, 180 South Lambeth Road, SW8, 020 7926 0705; Clapham, 1 Northside, Clapham Common, SW4, 020 7926 0717; Clapham Park, Poynders Road, SW4, 020 7926 0108; Streatham, 63 Streatham High Road, SW16, 020 7926 6768; Streatham Vale, 162 Eardley Road, SW16, 020 7926 6591; Carnegie, 188 Herne Hill Road, SE24, 020 7926 6050; Brixton, Brixton Oval, SW2, 020 7926 1056; Minet, 52 Knatchbull Road, SE5, 020 7926 6073

Cultural Resources: The 198 Gallery, 198 Railton Road, Herne Hill, SE24, 020 7976 8309; Sabbokai Gallery 101 Acre Lane, SW2, 020 7737 7063; Brixton Artists Collective, 35 Brixton Station Road, SW9, 020 7733 6957; Clapham Picture House, 76 Venn Street, SW4, 020 7498 3323; MGM, Streatham High Road, SW16, 020 8970 6033; Ritzy Cinema, Brixton Oval, Coldharbour Lane, SW2, 020 7737 2121; Odeon, Streatham High Road, SW16, 020 769 2221; South Bank Centre (National Film Theatre; Royal National Theatre; Royal Festival Hall; Queen Elizabeth Hall and Purcell Room; Hayward Gallery), South Bank, SE1, 020 7928 3002; The Old Vic, Waterloo Road., SE1; Oval House Arts Centre, 52-54 Kennington Oval, SE11, 020 7582 0080; White Bear Theatre, Kennington Park Road, SE11, 020 7793 9193

Leisure Centres: Queen Mother Sports Centre, 223 Vauxhall Bridge Road, SW1, 020 7630 5522; Brixton Recreation Centre, Brixton Station Road, SW9, 020 7926 9780; Brockwell Lido, Brockwell Park, SW2, 020 7274 3088

TRANSPORT

Time to City: 20 to 40 minutes; **Time to West End**: 10 to 40 minutes

Tube: **Bakerloo line**: Lambeth North; **Northern line**: Kennington, Oval, Stockwell, Clapham North, Clapham Common, Clapham South; **Victoria line**: Stockwell, Brixton, Vauxhall

Rail: **South West Trains**: Waterloo, Vauxhall; **Thameslink**: Streatham, Tulse Hill, Herne Hill, Loughborough Junction; **Connex South Central**: Streatham, Streatham Hill, Streatham Common, Tulse Hill, Clapham High Street; **Connex South Eastern**: Herne Hill, Brixton

WANDSWORTH

Boundaries and contiguous areas: **North**: Thames; **East**: Lambeth; **South**: Merton; **West**: Wimbledon Common/Richmond-upon-Thames

BATTERSEA
WANDSWORTH
SOUTHFIELDS/EARLSFIELD
BALHAM/TOOTING
PUTNEY/ROEHAMPTON

The River Wandle, which runs through the centre of this borough to the Thames, made Wandsworth an early industrial heartland. Mills and bleachers used the river water as early as the 13th century, and brewers, fur-makers, and arms manufacturers came and went over the centuries. Huguenots, who arrived in the 18th century and made iron, copperware, and hats, brought Wandsworth fame throughout Europe for the quality of its headgear. In the 18th century successful businessmen began to build grand houses near the open space which is now Wandsworth Common. (It became commonland when the poor of the area formed a society to prevent the wealthy from enclosing it for their private use.) The coming of the railways and the industrial revolution were the catalysts for much 19th century development. Today, as industry has declined, the borough of Wandsworth is often thought of, with Westminster, as an enclave of wealthy conservative voters holding out against the town hall socialism of its inner-city neighbours. The local council prides itself on its low council tax, which is something to set against the high cost of property here. The "right to buy" policy of the 1980s was enthusiastically promoted by the council with the result that Wandsworth is unusual in the high proportion of council built property which is now bought, sold or rented on the open market. Sure the borough has its grubbier corners, but in general it is an area of wide streets, proud residents, and generous green space.

Battersea, in the north of the borough, is famous chiefly for two things: its power station and its home for stray dogs. Battersea Power Station looms over the banks of the Thames and is a superb example of industrial architecture. It was built in two sections, the first completed in 1935 and the extension finished in 1955. After a relatively short working life, it has lain idle since 1983 whilst developers, locals, and the council squabble endlessly over what is to become of it. Proposals for various schemes have fallen in and out of favour over the years, but the most likely outcome is some sort of leisure and entertainment complex. Tucked below the stretches of industrial estate and a jumble of railway lines, the residential bits of Battersea have been desirable since the 1980s. This side of the Thames, between Albert and Wandsworth bridges and beyond, is now festooned with acres of spanking new residential quarters—penthouses and loft conversions of old schools, facing their counterparts across the river. The residential pockets are interspersed with remaining industrial sites and the Westland Heliport (beware of the noise). A typically ambitious residential development is the Montevetro, designed by British architect Richard Rogers. This massive glass structure has 103 luxury flats with prices rarely below half a million pounds. You'll find vestiges of the old village of Battersea located in a couple of 18th century buildings at the top of Battersea High Street. Around Battersea Park are good quality mansion blocks of flats. Ex-council flats and houses in the area also have no trouble selling or renting. Queenstown Road, running along the eastern side of the park, offers a nice selection of trendy restaurants and shops. You'll find that Victorian flat-fronted townhouses and conversions are the norm. There is also the unusual Shaftesbury Estate built in the 1870s by the Artisans, Labourers, and General Dwellings Company as cheap accommodation for the working classes. Today these delightful little cottages with gothic details are now a popular buy with middle-income first timers. Lavender Hill, which is lined with restaurants, bars and estate agents, takes you east to the boundary with Lambeth. The southwestern part of Battersea is marked by Clapham Junction station, nationally notorious as a particularly busy railway intersection servicing the commuters of south London and beyond. Close to the station at Clapham Junction there is a department store, Arding and Hobbs, and a giant Asda Superstore. Walk a few blocks beyond this hive of activity and you quickly will be rewarded with some lovely streets of Victorian houses bordering on the western side of Clapham Common. Running south from the junction is St. John's Road/Northcote Road which offers more good quality shopping facilities with top end high street names, and delis, butchers, wine bars, and antique shops taking over as you move south. The streets leading off the main drag are pleasant terraced streets of family homes. Battersea Rise veers off to the east bringing into view the plains of Clapham Common. The area sandwiched between Wandsworth Common and Clapham Common is thick with Victorian and Edwardian family homes and a smaller number of conversions. Known by estate agents as "Nappy Valley," this patch has one of the highest concentrations of young families in the city. There are several popular schools, both state and fee-paying, and traffic is hellish during the school run.

Further to the west, **Wandsworth** proper is the area stretching diagonally southeast from Wandsworth Park by the Thames to Wandsworth Common. Wandsworth's town centre is located in the middle of the busy tangle of roads at Wandsworth High Street (A3). Here lies the Arndale shopping mall plus other high street shops, and there is a sports centre along Garratt Lane (A217). The residential heart of the area is to the east. Four highly desirable streets off Baskerville Road, with their spacious double-fronted houses with gardens and sometimes pools, attract well-off families, despite their proximity to both Wandsworth Prison and the noisy Trinity Road. Prices are high by south London standards, and developers continue to fill available space with more large houses aimed at a similar market. Wandsworth Common station provides a rail link to Waterloo. Running along the southern end of the Common, trendy Bellevue Parade has posh shops, estate agents, a Marco Pierre White restaurant as well as the wine bars which have become a feature of the whole area.

Southwest of Wandsworth town centre things get more sleepy and suburban in the streets of **Southfields**, which is separated from its neighbour Earlsfield by the north-south running River Wandle and a strip of playing fields. Southfields is laid out south of the West Hill section of the A3 and extends down to reach the borough boundary with Merton. The housing is a happy mix of Edwardian and later 1930s suburban developments of semidetached and detached houses. Property on 1960s and 1970s council estates is increasingly coming onto the open market. Near Southfields Tube, which is on the District line, is an even grid of Edwardian planned streets with a mix of maisonettes, converted flats and whole houses. Replington Road has basic shopping facilities but most residents travel out to do major shopping. The area attracts young families looking to settle in a respectable neighbourhood with modestly-priced accommodation and who are prepared to forgo "going-out" opportunities in favour of proximity to Wimbledon Common (see **Parks and Open Spaces**). The large car owning demographic and the main thoroughfares of the A3, Merton Road (A218), Wimbledon Park Road, and Garratt Lane (A217), combine to create ongoing traffic and parking problems in the area. Southfields Tube is actually the most convenient for the All-England Tennis Club so the Wimbledon Park Road gets clogged up with pedestrians during Wimbledon fortnight. Around the River Wandle is a strip of land which houses light industry and playing fields, but west of Garratt Lane the area becomes more residential again. **Earlsfield** is the less favoured and less well-defined of the two neighbourhoods, and so prices are lower and there are more renters. It is distinguished by a fine 1920s and '30s council-built estate with cottage-style, three bedroom properties with large gardens—now mostly in private ownership. The rest is a motley collection of turn of the century terraces, Edwardian maisonettes, a few 1930s semis, and modern council and privately built houses and flats.

Until relatively recently, south London's **Balham** and **Tooting** were considered to be cheaper and much less fashionable than Wandsworth and nearby Clapham. However, the property boom of the 1980s reinvented them as cheerful and convenient neighbourhoods complete with Tube stations and rail links, and a reliable standard of property (due in part to a council policy of restricting conversions). Balham High Road (A24) has a reasonable selection of shops, takeaways, and a couple of up-market bars, and Sainsbury's and Safeway supermarkets are close by. Balham's property is mostly Victorian-built terraces and a few mansion blocks of flats. The nearer to Clapham Common you get, the more the prices become comparable to the rest of Clapham. The A24 then slopes southwards into Tooting. Off the eastern side of this main road, on the edge of Tooting, is the Heaver estate, much of which is a conservation area where you'll find the best period houses in the vicinity—vast three-storey redbrick terraced houses with plenty of detail to delight architecture buffs. Those that have been converted into flats command high prices, those left intact will fetch upwards of half a million. Tooting has the benefit of a large open space, Tooting Common, and also has Tooting Bec Lido, an outdoor swimming pool. It has the archetypal south London mix of Victoriana, Edwardian terraces, and streets of between-the-wars housing. There is a large Asian community here, which influences the shops and restaurants along the bustling Tooting High Road/Upper Tooting Road stretch of the A24. The most popular streets are around Tooting Bec Tube or close to the common. New developments are still rare but the 600 new flats and houses built at the end of the 1990s on an old hospital site at Tooting Bec is surely the first of many. The further south you travel towards the boundary with Merton, the further away from amenities you get and the lower the house prices.

The borough of Wandsworth also encompasses **Putney** in the west, a long established up-market area, the south London equivalent of Chelsea. Here the young and upwardly mobile hunt for flats, while older and already successful business people buy houses. The rental market is geared toward the short-term luxury let. The north-south running Putney Hill (A219) neatly divides the area in two, with the western half being more plush, offering vast detached houses with enormous gardens. Impressive Victorian mansion blocks of flats line the riverfront, and there are some good modern blocks of flats on Putney Hill itself. On the eastern side housing is rarely on such a grand scale, mostly mid- and late-Victorian terraces and Edwardian houses built for the middle classes, but due to Putney's desirability, they fetch high prices, often as converted flats. Council built property is the cheaper option and there is good supply of this in **Roehampton** on the southwestern borough boundary. Putney Heath gives residents access to vast green vistas of the Richmond Park/Wimbledon Common continuum. It is a very conservative community with an active Putney Society, which polices new developments. A constant headache for residents is the ever escalating traffic and parking problems of the area near the South Circular Road (A205). East Putney and Putney Bridge Tube stations are on the District line but many residents here rely on their cars. Putney High Street, which leads to Putney Bridge, has a good range of shops, coffee bars and pubs. Here you will also find the Putney Exchange shopping mall, complete with a Waitrose supermarket and branches of the classier high street clothes stores.

Web site: www.wandsworth.gov.uk

Postcodes: SW11, SW12, SW15, SW17, SW18

Council Office: Town Hall, Wandsworth High Street, SW18, 020 8871 6000

Main Post Offices: 583 Battersea Park Road, SW11; 202 Lavender Hill, SW11; 92a Balham High Road, SW12; 214 Upper Richmond Road, SW15; 2 Gatton Road, SW17; 63 Trinity Road, SW17; 1 Arndale Walk, SW18; Customer Helpline, 0345 223344

Police Stations: 112 Battersea Bridge Road, SW15, 020 7350 1122; 176 Lavender Hill, SW11, 020 7228 1212; 146 High Street, Wandsworth, 020 8870 9011; 215 Upper Richmond Road, SW15, 020 8785 1212; 117 Danebury Avenue, SW15, 020 8788 1103; Mitcham Road, SW17, 020 8672 9922

Accident and Emergency Departments: St. George's Hospital, Blackshaw Road, SW17, 020 8672 1255; Kingston Hospital, Galsworthy Road, KT2, 020 8546 7711

Public Libraries: West Hill Library, West Hill, SW18, 020 8871 6386; Putney, Disraeli Road, SW15, 020 8871 7090; Battersea, Lavender Hill, SW11, 020 8871 7466; Balham, Ramsden Road, SW12, 020 8871 7195

Cultural Resources: Battersea Arts Centre, 176 Lavender Hill, SW11, 020 7223 2223; Jongleurs Comedy Club, 49 Lavender Gardens, SW11, 020 7564 2500; Putney ABC, Putney High Street, SW15, 020 8788 3003

Leisure Centres: Balham Leisure Centre, Elmfield Road, SW17, 020 8772 9577; Latchmere Leisure Centre, Burns Road, SW11, 020 7207 8004; Putney Leisure Centre, Dryburgh Road, SW15, 020 8785 0388; Tooting Bec Lido, Tooting Bec Road, SW17 (no phone number); Wandle Recreational Centre, Mapleton Road, SW18, 020 8871 1149

TRANSPORT

Time to City: 20 to 45 minutes; **Time to West End**: 20 to 45 minutes

Tube: District line: Putney Bridge, East Putney, Southfields; **Northern line**: Clapham South, Balham, Tooting Bec, Tooting Broadway

Rail: Connex South Central: Battersea Park, Clapham Junction, Wandsworth Common, Balham; **South West Trains**: Queenstown Road, Clapham Junction, Wandsworth Town, Putney, Earlsfield; **Thameslink**: Tooting, Haydons Road

HAMMERSMITH AND FULHAM

Boundaries and contiguous boroughs: **North**: Brent; **East**: Kensington & Chelsea; **South**: Thames; **West**: Hounslow/Ealing

FULHAM
BARON'S COURT/WEST KENSINGTON
HAMMERSMITH/RAVENSCOURT PARK/BRACKENBURY/BROOK GREEN
SHEPHERD'S BUSH

The two vicinities of Hammersmith and Fulham form two quite distinct neighbourhoods within this west London borough. Fulham occupies a teardrop shaped area bounded by the Thames, and Hammersmith inhabits the higher end of the borough where the river runs northwards. Sport is the borough's main claim to fame—the sprinter Linford Christie grew up and trained in the north of the borough, and three professional football clubs have their grounds here.

Before major development got under way in the last two decades of the 19th century, **Fulham** was renowned for its market gardens, and then for most of the 20th century, the area's terraced streets were occupied by a stable community of skilled workers. However, in the last twenty years middle class buyers have swarmed in, attracted by Fulham's proximity to Kensington and Chelsea. The survival of working class culture in the area can be found in the local pubs and eateries close to the Chelsea Football Club, located in Fulham at Stamford Bridge. They are in marked contrast to the ongoing development of the stadium itself, which includes a luxury hotel and restaurants. Also in contrast to the smart set of Chelsea proper is the public housing of the Clem Atlee estate. You'll find the riverside here to be a strange mix of industrial sites—which may have a bright future as warehouse conversions—and a scattering of new luxury developments. Central to these and adding to the area's prestige, despite its location downwind of a council refuse dump, is the recently constructed Chelsea Harbour, a fancy marina with residential and office developments. As with many up-market riverside developments, Chelsea Harbour seems antiseptic and eerily deserted, and you may find yourself wondering if children are banned. There is a large Sainsbury's on the waterfront but otherwise few shops. The whole lot is overlooked from behind by the massive disused gas cylinders of Sands End (which are soon to be developed.)

Further north of the river the grid of terraced streets around Fulham Palace Road offers plenty of modest housing. The area is home to middle- to high-income families, there are few conversions and not much in the way of rentals. Fulham is quite popular with foreign residents, and there's also a sprinkling of celebrities brought in by the area's schools and the countrified atmosphere. For shopping needs Fulham has a large Safeway and a small shopping centre, a street market at North End Road, and a coterie of antique shops around New King's Road. A bit of heritage can be uncovered at Fulham Palace, with a museum and grounds open to the public. The Palace is in Bishops Park, which covers a stretch of riverside westwards from Putney Bridge.

North of Lillie Road, which bisects the borough, is the **Baron's Court/West Kensington** region. The area offers a high number of conversions of late Victorian houses making it rich hunting grounds for well placed flats in the rented sector, though they don't come cheap. Property ranges from impressive red brick Victorian houses and solid mansion blocks around the conservation area of Queen's Club Gardens, to solid 19th and 20th century terraces (mostly converted into small flats) to council estates. The area has convenient public transport on the District and Piccadilly lines.

The A4 Talgarth Road/Great West Road links with the M4 motorway to Heathrow and beyond. North of it is the glossy Broadway Mall at Hammersmith Tube station. The new mall was built in the early 1990s, precipitating the area's recent rise in prominence. Formerly an outlying industrial hamlet of Fulham, **Hammersmith**, until recently, retained a certain feeling of noise and grime around the Tube, due to an ill-conceived system of roads and underpasses. The recent bright redevelopment of the station area, melding office space (the European headquarters of Coca-Cola is here), and shops has helped immensely. The web of roads swirling around the Tube at least ensures excellent road links both into the centre of London and westward. Hammersmith Tube is also well placed for those going to Heathrow and the West End. King Street, leading west from the station, and with the Kings Mall situated on it, has an excellent range of high street stores. The Lyric Theatre, often staging productions that go on to play the West End, adds a bit of gravitas to King Street, hiding a Victorian auditorium behind its unprepossessing modern frontage. The Hammersmith Apollo, the big concert hall here, brings in evening crowds to the many pubs near the Tube. The streets beyond the main roads offer a wide variety of living quarters, from the grand to the bland. West, along King Street (which runs roughly parallel to the Thames) towards Ravenscourt Park, the area becomes distinctly posh. The grand St. Peter's Square on the south side has vast four-storey, colonial-style semidetached villas, and the surrounding streets three-storey, cottagey Georgian terraces. This is a pleasant conservation area where it is something of a surprise to still hear the dull roar of traffic ploughing along the Great West Road. On the northern side of King Street the streets around **Ravenscourt Park** are also a conservation area, with highly prized houses. Ravenscourt Park itself, once the grounds of an 18th century manor, is now a neatly landscaped and cheery park providing the local community with the familiar attractions of children's playgrounds and duckponds.

In the eastern end of Hammersmith, **Brook Green** and **Brackenbury** have some quiet streets with a mix of cottagey Victorian terraces and larger properties. Brackenbury is the less pretentious neighbourhood with a blend of middle-class owner occupiers and young renters in conversions. Brook Green is more exclusive with families looking to settle into sturdy Victorian houses with large gardens.

The Great West Road, also running parallel to the Thames, cuts most of Hammersmith off from the river. However, if you manage to negotiate crossing the road successfully you'll find a sliver of riverside to explore. The Riverside Studios, an arts complex with cinema, theatre, gallery, and cafe is a great local resource. There are the obligatory new residential complexes by the river, plus some older mansion blocks and houses in the area near the handsome Hammersmith Bridge. As always, apartments with river views fetch the highest prices and are in the greatest demand. There is a charming stretch of riverside walk from the bridge along the Mall where you'll find some grand old merchants' homes, including Kelmscott House, which was one of the homes of 19th century designer and artist William Morris.

Shepherd's Bush Road runs due north of Hammersmith to Shepherd's Bush Green junction where it meets with a number of other large roads— the Uxbridge Road leading straight west into Ealing and beyond, Wood Lane which runs north to Brent, plus Holland Park Avenue and Holland Road going east into different parts of Kensington. **Shepherd's Bush** is famous for the BBC TV Centre in Wood Lane; with 8,000 workers it's the borough's biggest employer. Nearby White City stadium held the 1908 Olympic games before it was used for dog racing and was then sold off to (you guessed it) the BBC. The borough, as a whole, is also home to the offices of Disney, EMI and Polygram; in general entertainment and service industries are replacing the old manufacturing ones. Some ugly concrete buildings and its position as a main intersection compromise the appeal of Shepherd's Bush, but the area is gaining in popularity. Those on a modest income are starting to see the benefits of the neighbourhood's proximity to the BBC and a Zone 2 Tube station on the Central line. There is an excellent fringe theatre too, the Bush, located above the pub on the southern corner of the green. It was from an inn on this site in 1657 that a group of Royalists planned to assassinate Oliver Cromwell. Close by is the Shepherd's Bush Empire, originally a music hall dating from 1903, it now hosts rock concerts. Shepherd's Bush Market has an Afro-Caribbean slant with exotic vegetables and brightly-coloured fabrics commonplace. An upsurge in young Australian and South African newcomers renting here has led to the opening of large Aussie-themed pubs. Residential property is mostly made up of closely packed plain Victorian terraces with prices climbing fast for those in the best condition. The rental sector, which has always been quite big here, is still lively despite the area becoming more popular with buyers.

Further north, past the Westway, is Hammersmith Hospital, Wormwood Scrubs Prison, and Wormwood Scrubs itself. At 200 acres it is one of the largest surviving pieces of common land in London and is a functional rather than aesthetic space, with football and rugby pitches. In the northwestern end is Tent City, a campsite where visitors to London can pitch their tents.

Web Site: www.lbhf.gov.uk

Postcodes: SW6, W6, W12, W14

Council Office: Town Hall, King Street, W6, 020 8748 3020

Main Post Offices: 815 Fulham Road, SW6; Hammersmith Broadway, W6; 88 North End Road, W14; 66-69 Shepherd's Bush Green, W12; Customer Helpline, 0345 223344

Police Stations: 226 Shepherd's Bush Road, W6, 020 8563 1212; Heckfield Place, SW6, 020 7385 1212; 252 Uxbridge Road, W12, 020 8740 1212

Accident and Emergency Departments: Charing Cross Hospital, Fulham Palace Road, W6, 020 8383 0000; Chelsea and Westminster Hospital, 369 Fulham Road, SW10, 020 8746 8080; Hammersmith Hospital, DuCane Road, W12, 020 8383 1000

Public Libraries: Hammersmith, Shepherd's Bush Road, W6, 020 8576 5050; Askew Road, 87/91 Askew Road, W12, 020 8576 5064; Shepherd's Bush, 7 Uxbridge Road, W12, 020 8576 5060; Barons Court, North End Crescent, W14, 020 8576 5258; Fulham, 598 Fulham Road, SW6, 020 8576 5252; Sands End, The Community Centre, 59-61 Broughton Road, SW6, 020 8576 5257

Cultural Resources: Bush Theatre, Shepherd's Bush Green, 020 8743 3388; Lyric Theatre, King Street, W1, 020 8741 2255; Riverside Studios, Crisp Road, off Queen Caroline Street, W6, 020 8237 1111

Leisure Centres: Broadway Squash & Fitness Centre, Chalk Hill Road, W6, 020 8460 4797; Fulham Pools, Lillie Road, SW6, 020 7385 7642; Lillie Road Fitness Centre, Lillie Road, SW6, 020 7381 2183; Janet Adegoke Leisure Centre, Bloemfontein Road, W12, 020 8743 3401

TRANSPORT

Time to City: 25 to 35 minutes; **Time to West End**: 15 to 25 minutes

Tube: **Central line**: White City, Shepherd's Bush; **District line**: Hammersmith, Barons Court, Ravenscourt Park, West Kensington, West Brompton, Fulham Broadway, Parsons Green, Putney Bridge; **Hammersmith & City line**: Hammersmith, Goldhawk Road, Shepherd's Bush; **Piccadilly line**: Hammersmith, Barons Court

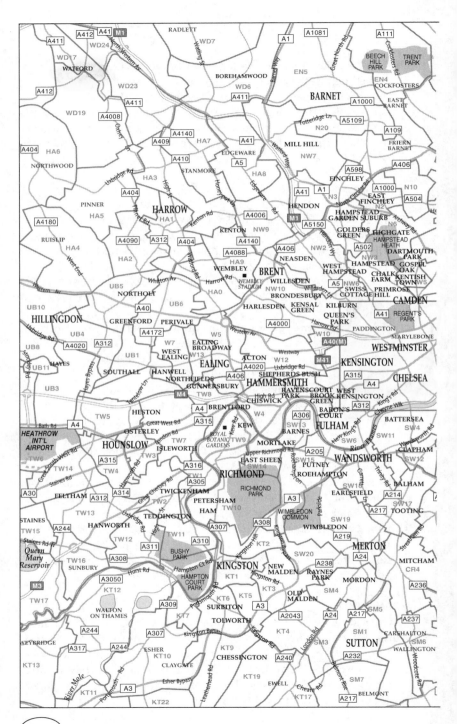

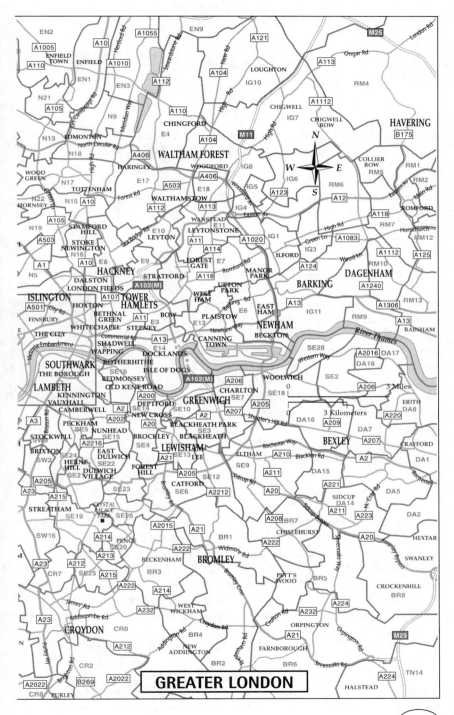

GREATER LONDON

OUTER LONDON

HARINGEY

Boundaries and contiguous boroughs: **North**: Enfield; **East**: Waltham Forest; **South**: Hackney/Islington/Camden; **West**: Barnet

CROUCH END/HORNSEY
MUSWELL HILL/ALEXANDRA PARK
HARRINGAY GREEN LANES
WOOD GREEN
TOTTENHAM

Haringey is a north London borough encompassing a mixed bag of neighbourhoods with contrasting reputations. Much of the borough is poor and struggling—youth unemployment in the northern and eastern parts of the borough is staggeringly high. Prospects are much brighter on the western side of the borough. With the gentrification of Islington and the ever-soaring popularity of Hampstead and Highgate leading to a shortage of reasonably-priced properties in north London, Crouch End and Muswell Hill have become more in vogue among middle-class Londoners. For residents of these neighbourhoods the area's lack of transport links over the years has proven to be an asset. Being off the beaten track encouraged little development and allowed for much of the area's architecture to remain intact.

Residents of **Crouch End** who rely on public transport to get them in and out of town must use Finsbury Park Tube and local buses. Finsbury Park station, whilst warren-like and dank, boasts two Tube lines plus a rail link to the City. Buses to and from the station are frequent, with a route along the Stroud Green Road and up the steep Crouch Hill where you cross the border from Islington into Haringey. (Traffic here can make the journey take longer than it should.) Off the main road, the tree-lined streets with late Victorian terraces are pleasantly quiet, mixing family homes with conversions, many of which are occupied by young professionals. Nestled in a hollow at the bottom of the hill, Crouch End Broadway has a homely but useful selection of shops: butchers, fishmongers, bakers, small supermarkets, gift shops and bookstore. There is an enticing range of restaurants and coffee bars too. The Broadway converges on the distinctive Clock Tower built in 1895 to commemorate H.R. Williams—chairman of the Local Board and the man with foresight enough to save nearby Highgate Wood from development. Topsfield Parade, two rows of shops which sit back to back, are particularly appealing architectural examples dating from the late Victorian period when much of this area was developed. The same builder also worked on Muswell Hill Broadway. Crouch End borders on Highgate to the west and the largest, most expensive properties are on the Highgate border (a part of Highgate is technically in Haringey but it is covered here under Camden). Crouch End is a popular neighbourhood in its own right and is tenaciously guarded by its residents, called "Crouch-Enders," who tend to oppose any development which may threaten the character of the place (McDonalds is among those who have failed to get their plans past the local community.) It remains a fairly mixed community but gentrification and escalating house prices give it an increasingly middle-class profile. It is popular with singles, and couples in their late twenties and thirties looking for one or two bedroom conversions. Unconverted family homes are becoming rarer and prohibitively expensive. Legions of neighbourhood toddlers make use of Priory Park and the outdoor swimming pool in Park Road. Crouch End merges with **Hornsey** to the east along Tottenham Lane where prices begin to drop a notch.

The west of Haringey is a series of hills, and the neighbourhood of **Muswell Hill** perches at the top of one. The area was developed steadily in the early 20th century with streets of red brick houses providing an air of architectural harmony. Large Edwardian semis and detached houses can offer panoramic views across London. Prices are quite high but have yet to reach the dizzying heights of Hampstead or Highgate. The area has, until quite recently, had a sleepy rarefied quality, despite the traffic heavy convergence of roads at the Muswell Hill Broadway roundabout. In the last few years an increasing numbers of eateries, cafes, and barn-sized pubs have opened. The streets radiating off from the roundabout are host to various restaurants and an eclectic mix of delicatessens, houseware shops and high street stores including a WH Smith and a Sainsbury's supermarket. There's also an Odeon cinema. The residential roads of Muswell Hill fan out to the nearby grand Alexandra Palace and Park, where the BBC made its first broadcast in 1936. The enchanting ancient Highgate Wood, on Muswell Hill Road augments the overall impression of mossy greenness. The area is popular with young and middle-aged media professionals with healthy bank accounts, and also those with children as the local schools have good reputations. With the market demand for houses with period features, modern houses and flats can be picked up relatively cheaply, and prices generally get lower as you head north toward the border with Enfield or south toward Wood Green. Muswell Hill is bounded by the North Circular Road (A406) but, if you don't have access to a car or bike, buses are the order of the day since the nearest Tube can be quite a hike. **Alexandra Park** railway station offers a stop on a commuter line into the City at Moorgate.

The east of the borough finds the **Harringay Green Lanes** area. Green Lanes (A105) is a major thoroughfare, running from Stoke Newington in Hackney to Wood Green, but traffic snarl-ups are commonplace as it is not quite up to coping with the daily volume of traffic. The stretch of road from the bottom of Finsbury Park to Wood Green has many Greek and Turkish Cypriot groceries and the ever present scent of freshly baked bread (it is also one of the few parts of the capital where you'll find stores open 24 hours). The roads marching off to the west of Green Lanes are known as "the ladder" due to their regularity. The streets leading off both sides of the main drag offer many cheap and mid-priced rented flats and studios, mostly in converted late Victorian terraces, making the area popular with students and those on a modest income.

Wood Green is best known locally as a shopping destination. Its recently renovated shopping mall, Shopping City, coupled with the busy Wood Green High Road (a continuation of the A105), create an insanely busy atmosphere most of the time. The Wood Green area itself has a fairly mixed reputation. However, with the opening of an arts centre and two huge new multiplex cinemas there has been a concerted effort to regenerate the area. Wood Green's terraces are run-of-the-mill Victorian, but they scrub up quite well and the area is on the way up. As you proceed north into Bounds Green, life becomes distinctly calmer and more suburban. **Tottenham**, in the north of the borough, despite some grand buildings on the High Road hinting at a more illustrious past, is the site of most of the borough's poverty. But South Tottenham has some nice pockets of terraces that attract first time buyers, and there is plenty of cheaply priced rented accommodation here and around Seven Sisters Tube station.

Web site: www.haringey.gov.uk
Postcodes: N8, N10, N15, N17, N22
Council Office: Civic Centre, High Road, N22, 020 8489 0000
Accident and Emergency Department: Whittington Hospital, Highgate Hill N19, 020 7272 3070
Central Library: Central Library, High Road, N22, 020 8888 1292; Hornsey, Haringey Park, N8, 020 8348 3351
Cultural Resources: The Chocolate Factory, Clarendon Road, N22; Muswell Hill Odeon, Fortis Green Road, N10, 020 8315 4217; Bruce Castle, Lordship Lane, N17, 020 8808 8772
Leisure Centres: New River Sports Centre, White Hart Lane, N22, 020 8881 1926; Tottenham Green Leisure Centre, 1 Philip Lane, N15, 020 8365 0322 (minicom, 020 8801 0515); Park Road Pools, Park Road, N8, 020 8341 3567; Alexandra Palace Ice Rink, Alexandra Palace Park, N22, 020 8365 2121

TRANSPORT
Time to City: 15 to 25 minutes; **Time to West End**: 15 to 25 minutes
Tube: **Piccadilly line**: Finsbury Park, Turnpike Lane, Wood Green,

Bounds Green; **Victoria line**: Finsbury Park, Seven Sisters, Tottenham Hale

Rail: **Silverlink**: South Tottenham, Harringay Green Lanes, Crouch Hill; **WAGN**: Finsbury Park, Stamford Hill, Seven Sisters, Bruce Grove, White Hart Lane, Tottenham Hale, Harringay, Hornsey, Alexandra Palace, Bowes Park, Palmers Green

BARNET

Boundaries and contiguous boroughs: **North**: Green Belt **East**: Enfield/Haringey **South**: Camden **West**: Brent/Harrow

FINCHLEY
EAST FINCHLEY
HAMPSTEAD GARDEN SUBURB
GOLDERS GREEN
HENDON/MILL HILL

The borough of Barnet offers some of outer north London's most solidly respectable and well-established neighbourhoods. The names of Barnet's subdivisions are likely to be most familiar as exits from the North Circular Road (A406). The area of **Finchley** is split into two sections by the North Circular, with the northern side of the road, which encompasses Central, North and West Finchley, being more homogenous and suburban. There are many commuters living here who can reach either the City or the West End within three-quarters of an hour or so via the numerous Northern line Tube stations in the area. Family houses predominate and there is a high level of car ownership creating the usual parking problems. Any conversions in the area crowd around Finchley Central Tube. There are plenty of shopping facilities; the quaintly named Tally-Ho Corner, at the junction of the High Road and Ballards Lane, has a Sainsbury's supermarket, and there are more shops on Ballards Lane. The giant Brent Cross shopping centre is nearby as well. The Finchley Lido on the High Road has excellent leisure facilities including a swimming pool, bowling alley, and multiplex. The many major roads in the area are off-set by two golf courses and various recreation grounds and small woodlands. In the most westerly part of Finchley the even more exclusive Woodside Park and Church End sub-neighbourhoods have the largest houses and luxury flats.

    East Finchley is the area below the North Circular Road. The neighbourhood strings along the Great North Road (A1000) from East Finchley Tube station up to the junction with the North Circular. On the main street there are shops, cafes, delicatessens, a cinema, and the British headquarters of McDonalds. Sought after modern blocks of flats, big Victorian terraced houses, and semis from between the wars all appear in the leafy streets that border Muswell Hill to the east. First-time buyers often pursue flats in Victorian conversions and maisonettes. Although still quiet and respectable, East Finchley is less suburban and a bit more affordable than the rest of Finchley. However, the relatively small proportion of rentals here and throughout the borough tends to be aimed at professionals. In the corner bounded by North End Road, the A1 and the North Circular Road, there are some roomy 1920s and '30s semidetached houses with garages along quiet and pleasantly green streets. Finchley is home to a large Jewish community and is also a favoured destination for affluent settlers, many from Japan and Greece.

Crossing Lyttleton Road (A1), which forms the southern boundary of East Finchley, takes you into **Hampstead Garden Suburb**. "The Suburb," as it is known, was the idea of a philanthropist named Mrs. Henrietta Barnett who wished to create a pleasant residential area in which "all classes would live together under right conditions of beauty and space." The garden city movement originated in the late 19th century as a town planning ideal and was first attempted in 1903 at Letchworth in the English county of Bedfordshire. The Hampstead Garden Suburb is remarkable in a city such as London where development traditionally had been opportunistic and lacking an overall scheme. Begun in 1907, Hampstead Garden Suburb was planned and laid out on land north of Hampstead Heath (and included an extension of Hampstead Heath) and had the input of various notable architects of the day, including Sir Edwin Lutyens. The result, including major additions after the First World War, is an enclave of spacious, tree lined streets and cul-de-sacs with strictly demarcated property. Small flats were designed for artisans, medium sized villas for the petit bourgeois and large houses with views were earmarked for the wealthy retired. In keeping with the idea of creating a community there is also a library, an adult education centre, schools, churches, and a synagogue. However, Mrs. Barnett's noble ideal of providing people from all points on the social scale with the opportunity to live happily and productively side by side has fallen by the wayside as the high standard of even the smallest properties has pushed prices way beyond the reach of those for whom they were originally intended. The aesthetically pleasing and harmonious red brick streets are still managed by the Hampstead Garden Suburb Trust, which has pushed with success for many of its houses to be listed. Still the Suburb has a rather strange atmosphere as there are only a couple of small shops, and no restaurants or bars, making it an unlikely choice for younger people. There is a high car to person ratio reflecting the affluent profile of its residents, although Golders Green Tube station is not unreasonably far away and the area has its own nippy little bus route. It is a popular choice with wealthy Jewish, American, and South

African residents, often with young families (for teenagers the lack of things to do might be oppressive) seeking a green and pleasant haven within easy reach of the rest of London. Be aware, prices in Barnet are above average, and homes here are at a premium.

Golders Green is best known for its large, well-established Jewish community. A large number of London's first Jewish immigrants lived in the East End, but during the second half of the 20th century many of their descendents moved out to these north London suburbs. At the main intersection of Golders Green Road and Finchley Road (A598) there is the Tube station and also a National Express coach station, where long-distance coaches travelling up and down the country begin and end their journeys. The architecture at the busy crossroads is reminiscent of Muswell Hill and Crouch End (see Haringey), with its tall terraces of red-brick Victorian shop fronts. At the junction, and along Golders Green Road, you'll find a selection of high street stores and cafes as well as discount designer clothes stores and other locally owned shops. Because the housing stock includes a good many Edwardian villas which make great family houses, but not many conversions and rented properties, residents here tend to be middle-aged and long time homeowners.

The M1 motorway cuts through the western side of the borough. **Hendon** and **Mill Hill** fill in the spaces between the major traffic arteries that bunch around this corner. Both neighbourhoods, although they have Tube stations on the outer reaches of the Northern line and are thus attractive to some commuters, suffer from a lack of a centre. Hendon is known chiefly as the home of a Royal Air Force museum and a police training school. The Burroughs is the main street at Hendon; here the old Victorian Town Hall houses Barnet's council offices and the Church Farm House, the borough's local history museum. Middlesex University has a campus here, though the immediate vicinity, with its luxury flats and houses, is a bit out of the reach of most students' means. In less appealing west Hendon beyond the M1 motorway, prices are a bit cheaper and there is the added bonus of the nearby Welsh Harp reservoir, home to a watersports centre. The massive Brent Cross shopping mall is at the junction of Hendon Way (A41) and the North Circular (A406). Boasting an IKEA, a John Lewis department store, and large branches of high street chains, it brings in a steady stream of traffic from outside. Things continue to become more suburban and staid as you progress further north into Mill Hill, which straddles the M1 motorway and extends north to meet green belt land.

Web site: www.barnet.gov.uk
Postcodes: N2, N3, N20, NW4, NW7, NW9, NW11, EN5, HA8
Council Office: The Town Hall, The Burroughs, Hendon, NW4, 020 8359 2000

Accident and Emergency Departments: North Middlesex, Sterling Way, N18, 020 8887 2000; Royal Free, Pond Street, NW3, 020 7794 0500

Central Libraries: East Finchley, 226 High Road, N2, 020 8883 2664; Golders Green 156 Golders Green, NW11, 020 8359 2060; Hampstead Garden Suburb, 15 Market Place, NW11, 020 8455 1235

Cultural Resources: London Museum of Jewish Life, Sternberg Centre, East End Road; Royal Air Force Museum, Grahame Park Way, NW9, 020 8205 2266; The Bull Theatre, Gallery & Studio, 68 High Street, EN5, 020 8449 0048; Garden Suburb Theatre, The Institute, Central Square, NW11, 020 8455 6669; All Saints Arts Centre, Oakleigh Road North, N20, 020 8445 8388; Phoenix Cinema, 52 High Road, N2, 020 8444 6789; ABC Golders Green, 612 Finchley Road, NW11, 020 8455 1724; Odeon, Finchley Road, NW3, 020 7586 3057; Odeon Barnet, Great North Road, EN5, 020 8441 2574; Warner Village Cinema, Great North Leisure Park, Chaplin Square, N12, 020 8446 9933

Leisure Centres: Ashmole Leisure Centre, Burleigh Gardens, N14, 020 8368 4984; Copthall Sports Centre, Great North Way, NW4, 020 8457 9900; Queen Elizabeth Centre, Meadway, EN5, 020 8441 2933

TRANSPORT

Time to City: 20 to 30 minutes; **Time to West End**: 20 to 30 minutes

Tube: **Northern line**: Golders Green, Brent Cross, Hendon Central, Colindale, Burnt Oak, Edgware, East Finchley, Finchley Central, West Finchley, Woodside Park, Totteridge & Whetstone, High Barnet, Mill Hill East

Rail: **Thameslink**: Cricklewood, Hendon, Mill Hill Broadway

BRENT

Boundaries and contiguous boroughs: **North**: Harrow/Barnet; **East**: Barnet/Camden; **South**: Westminster/Kensington and Chelsea/Hammersmith and Fulham/Ealing; **West**: Ealing/Harrow

KILBURN/BRONDESBURY
QUEEN'S PARK
KENSAL GREEN
WILLESDEN/HARLESDEN
NEASDEN/WEMBLEY

The London Borough of Brent is named after the river that runs through it. Brent prides itself on being the most racially and culturally mixed of all the local authorities in England. Black and Asian communities make up nearly half the population. That Brent is twinned with South Dublin is a testament to the remarkable statistic that nearly a tenth of its residents are Irish by birth. With such a mix of ethnic backgrounds, cultural events in the borough include a huge Irish Festival and a Hindu Navrati Festival. In general terms the southern half of the borough, incorporating Willesden and Harlesden, has higher rates of unemployment and social deprivation than the more affluent and green northern half of Brent. The North Circular Road (A406), which crosses the borough, and the Kilburn High Road/Cricklewood Broadway (A5), which forms its eastern boundary, provide major road links with the centre of town and surrounding areas. In addition there are several Tube stops and rail stations.

The neighbourhood of **Kilburn** lies west of the Kilburn High Road (A5), which marks the borough boundary with Camden, and north of Maida Vale in Westminster. Traditionally a more modest prospect than its Westminster and Hampstead neighbours, Kilburn has a fair bit of concrete and urban sprawl. However, ranks of respectable terraces which were mainly built in the latter Victorian period make up the spaces in between, and their presence is somewhat responsible for the area's up-and-coming status. The rail stations of the North London Line which give it a link to the north and east of London, plus numerous Tube stations on both the Bakerloo and Jubilee lines into the West End, make it a particularly fortuitous area from which to commute. Most of these stations are in Zone 2, which helps as well, and the new fast link to Heathrow from nearby Paddington station is an extra boon. Though becoming less apparent with the influx of non-Irish newcomers, Kilburn traditionally has been home to a large Irish population, and includes the Irish Centre on the High Road. The Kilburn High Road is endearingly scruffy with lots of inexpensive household goods and clothes for sale, tatty pubs, and a market, alongside small branches of Sainsbury's, Safeway, and Marks & Spencer. For cafes, bars and more sophisticated shops, you'll have to go back east to the Finchley Road. But there is a popular and exciting local theatre, The Tricycle, on the High Road, which has the added boon of an arthouse cinema. The standard of housing tends to improve as you travel north along the High Road into **Brondesbury** and towards Gladstone Park. In the conservation area bounded by the High Road (A5), Willesden Lane (A4003) and Walm Lane/Chicele Road (A407), the houses evolve into large Edwardian villas with spacious gardens. There is a thriving market in mid-priced rented flats and shared houses in Kilburn, while buyers focus on good-sized terraced houses.

The large houses of **Queen's Park**, west of Willesden Lane Cemetery, were also built in the Edwardian period after the opening of the 30-acre park of the same name in 1887. (Queen's Park is also the name of the estate of Victorian artisan's cottages laid out south of here in West Kilburn, which is in the boundary of Westminster). The wide streets of Queen's Park, between Salusbury Road and around the park itself, hold generously-proportioned houses with gardens. These residences are fast becoming popular with media executives and their families, many of whom have found themselves priced out of the market in nearby areas such as super-trendy Notting Hill—though it won't be long before prices here have caught up. Between Chamberlayne and Harrow Road (A404) the smaller terraces of **Kensal Green** are cheaper and less desirable but are beginning to feel the knock-on effects of Queen's Park's popularity. There is a nearby Sainsbury's superstore at the top end of Ladbroke Grove. The central-south portion of the borough is made up of **Willesden** and **Harlesden**, which are less favoured as they have some grim council estates and fewer amenities.

Much of the western and northern reaches of Brent are commuter-belt crisscrossed by numerous roads. **Neasden** is famous for its spectacular white marble Hindu temple and there is a large Asian community in this part of the borough. The huge Brent Cross shopping centre, just over the border in Barnet, brings traffic by the shed load to this portion of the North Circular (A406), which should be avoided during the Christmas rush! The Welsh Harp reservoir and Fryent Country Park make the northern end of the borough quite green. Over to the western fringe of the borough, **Wembley** Stadium, where cup finals and international football matches are played, and Wembley Arena, a huge indoor venue that attracts the biggest name performers, are responsible for the occasional traffic nightmare. Wembley is also the site of a large industrial estate, leaving the residential part of it feeling a bit hemmed in.

Web site: www.brent.gov.uk
Postcodes: NW2, NW6, NW9, NW10, HA0, HA1, HA3
Council Office: Brent Town Hall, Forty Lane, Wembley, HA9; 0208 8937 1234
Accident and Emergency Departments: Central Middlesex Hospital, Acton Lane, NW10, 020 8965 5733; Northwick Park Hospital, Watford Road, HA1, 020 8864 3232
Central Libraries: Kilburn, Salusbury Road, NW6, 020 8937 3530; Town Hall, Brent Town Hall, Forty Lane, HA9, 020 8937 3550
Cultural Resources: Tricycle Theatre & Cinema, High Road, Kilburn, NW6, 020 7372 6611; Carib Theatre, 73 Lancelot Road, HA0, 020 8795 0576
Leisure Centres: Charteris Sports Centre, 24-30 Charteris Road, NW6, 020 7625 9842; Willesden Sports Centre, Donnington Road, NW10, 020 8459 6605; Vale Farm Sports Centre, Watford Road, HA0, 020 8908 6545

TRANSPORT
Time to City: 15 to 40 minutes; **Time to West End**: 15 to 35 minutes

Tube: **Bakerloo line**: Kilburn Park, Queen's Park, Kensal Green, Willesden Junction, Harlesden, Stonebridge Park, Wembley Central, North Wembley, South Kenton, Kenton; **Jubilee line**: Kilburn, Willesden Green, Dollis Hill, Neasden, Wembley Park; **Metropolitan line**: Wembley Park, Preston Road, Northwick Park

Rail: **Chiltern Railways**: Wembley Stadium; **Silverlink**: Brondesbury, Brondesbury Park, Kensal Rise, Kilburn High Road, Queen's Park, Kensal Green, Willesden Junction, Harlesden, Stonebridge Park, Wembley Central, North Wembley, South Kenton, Kenton

EALING

Boundaries and contiguous areas: **North**: Harrow/Brent; **East**: Hammersmith and Fulham; **South**: Hounslow; **West**: Hillingdon

ACTON
EALING BROADWAY
NORTHFIELDS/WEST EALING
HANWELL
SOUTHALL
NORTHOLT/GREENFORD/PERIVALE

Ealing is one of the more culturally mixed of the outer-western boroughs of London. Built up in the late 19th century and the first decade of the 20th century, Ealing is a large and sprawling suburban region incorporating many green spaces (18 at last count). With its large houses and rural pretensions, the borough was marketed to the middle classes as the "queen of the suburbs" by its original developers. Its name was made famous though, by its association with the Ealing Studios, which in the 1940s and 1950s produced some of the best loved British feature film comedies of all time, starring the likes of Peter Sellers and Alec Guinness.

In common with some of the other outer London boroughs, Ealing sometimes feels like a small satellite town rather than a part of the capital, something that can be advantageous for its citizens. For those who work in the west London area or who are prepared for a long commute into the City, Ealing offers a good local infrastructure, plentiful shopping opportunities, and an overall high standard of living. It has a good range of public transport links including Ealing Broadway, which is at the end of the Central and District lines, and a very quick rail link to Paddington. The rest of the borough is peppered with stops on the Piccadilly and District lines and rail stations. Journey times by Tube and rail are reasonable into the West End but can be quite long if you're headed for east London; it takes the best part of an hour to get to the City from most parts of Ealing. As for roads, the Western Avenue (A40) skirts the northern boundary of the borough, meeting with the North Circular Road (A406) at the perpetually busy, and fiendishly difficult to navigate, Hangar Lane gyratory.

The Uxbridge Road runs east-west through the middle of the borough travelling through all of Ealing's major sub-divisions. At the westerly end is **Acton**, where you'll find a standard mix of council housing and modest terraces. It has a bustling high street with a Safeway supermarket, Woolworth's, and plenty of other run-of-the-mill shops, as well as a couple of popular local restaurants. Acton also boasts one of the highest density Tube and rail stations in London. The area has been boosted by the popularity of nearby Chiswick (see Hounslow), and Acton's image of being a bit dull is now changing as those priced out of more expensive parts of west London move in. The dinky two-bedroom Victorian cottages and maisonettes in the series of streets known as Poets' Corner, north of Churchfield Road, are some of the most sought after in and around these parts by upwardly mobile young families.

The borough's centre is at **Ealing Broadway**, west of Acton. There are two malls here—the large and comprehensive Ealing Broadway Centre and another one directly across the road. In the surrounding residential areas impressive large properties and newer private developments predominate. Although housing is expensive here, it isn't wildly overpriced. Particularly notable are the streets around open spaces: Walpole Park, Ealing Common, and Pitshanger Park. Pitshanger Lane has a genteel meandering quality with small specialty shops that contrast nicely with the big chain stores to be found in the nearby malls. The central Ealing area is popular with older media executives (Ealing is handy enough for the BBC in Shepherd's Bush) and other professionals, especially those with families, who are attracted by spacious properties with big gardens, excellent leisure amenities, and reasonable state schools. Polish and other immigrant communities are here as well, and are represented by churches and ethnic delicatessens. Ealing Broadway is home to many foreign residents, both permanent and temporary, with swarms of continental students attending language schools here in the summer. The rented sector is fairly lively, though again there is little available for bargain hunters. Due to the impracticality of travelling out of the borough for nightlife, the Broadway offers its own range of restaurants, pubs and clubs, which get pretty lively on Friday and Saturday nights.

The Uxbridge Road carries on west past the solid, terrace-lined streets of **Northfields** and **West Ealing**, where there are yet more chain-stores and a supermarket. Northfields' quiet rows of terraced streets recently have been noticed by estate agents, and as a previously under-exploited source of good quality and compact family homes they are quickly becoming hot properties. Northfields Avenue curls northeast back round towards Acton, and has a motley collection of old and new retail outlets, including hardware, antique and computer shops next to restaurants and estate agents.

Next stop along the Uxbridge Road is **Hanwell**; this neighbourhood is comprised of the roads and estates around the central north-running road of Church Avenue/Greenford Avenue. Hanwell Village, the small area immediately around Hanwell Station and the golf course, has the grandest and most expensive semidetached and detached houses in the area. The rest of the housing includes plenty of late Victorian terraces of all sizes, 1930s mock-Tudor houses on attractive tree lined streets, as well as some large council estates. A local landmark is Brunel's dramatic railway viaduct, a triumph of 19th century engineering, which runs through the pretty Brent Valley Park (referred to by locals as the bunny park).

Southall is farthest west along the Uxbridge Road and is without a London postcode. Historically a quite unremarkable industrial part of the borough (its biggest factory produced margarine), it is now the most striking of Ealing's neighbourhoods. Southall's large Asian community dates from the 1950s when a local firm began recruiting employees from the Indian sub-continent, making it one of the first established Asian communities in Britain. Many aspects of Asia's cultures are expressed here—in the curry houses, sweet centres, fabric and jewellery shops, in the local grocers, and in the mosques, temples, and community centres. Since 1698 Southall Market has been the site of London's original horse auctions, which are still a weekly event, but there is also now a more useful Saturday market that deals in cheap clothes and household goods. The Tube does not service Southall, and residents tend to be firmly rooted, often working locally. The housing stock encompasses some very spacious semis, a lot of average Victorian terracing, and some pretty rough council estates. There is generally little movement in the market due to the substantial number of long-term residents.

Greenford and **Northolt**, in the northwest of the borough and edging out of the London postal area, are generally pleasant and quiet, if rather nondescript areas, with little to distinguish them except the high standard of accessible parkland. Supermarkets are plentiful and conveniently located, and there is another clutch of everyday shops in Greenford. Nearby **Perivale** has fewer residential areas as it is dominated by a huge industrial estate and various golf courses.

Web site: www.ealing.gov.uk
Postcodes: W3, W5, W6, W7, W13, UB1, UB6
Council Office: Town Hall, Uxbridge Road, W5, 020 8579 2424
Accident and Emergency Department: Ealing Hospital, 020 8967 5000
Central Library: 103 Ealing Broadway Centre, W5, 020 8567 3670

Cultural Resources: Questors Theatre, Mattock Lane, W5, 020 8567 0011; Virgin Cinema, Uxbridge Road, W5, 020 8567 1333; Warner Bros. Cinema, Royale Leisure Park, Park Royal, 020 8896 0066; Pitshanger Manor Gallery, Mattock Lane, W5

Leisure Centres: Acton Baths, Salisbury Street, W3, 020 8992 8877; Dormers Wells Leisure Centre, Dormers Wells Lane, Southall, 020 8571 7207; Gurnell Leisure Centre, Ruislip Road East, W13, 020 8998 3241; Northolt Swimarama, Eastcote Lane North, Northolt, 020 8422 1176; Walford Sports Centre, Bengarth Road, Northolt, 020 8841 0953

TRANSPORT

Time to City: 35 to 50 minutes; **Time to West End**: 20 to 35 minutes

Tube: **Central line**: East Acton, North Acton, West Acton, Ealing Broadway, Hanger Lane, Perivale, Northolt, South Ruislip, Ruislip Gardens, Greenford; **District line**: Acton Town, Ealing Common, Ealing Broadway; **Piccadilly line**: Acton Town, Ealing Common, North Ealing, South Ealing, Park Royal, Northfields, Boston Manor

Rail: **Silverlink**: South Acton, Acton Central; **Thames Trains**: Acton Main Line, Ealing Broadway, West Ealing, Hanwell, Southall, Drayton Green, Castlebar Park, South Greenford, Greenford

---

HOUNSLOW

Boundaries and contiguous boroughs: **North**: Ealing; **East**: Hammersmith and Fulham; **South**: Thames/Richmond-Upon-Thames; **West**: Green Belt/Hillingdon

CHISWICK/GROVE PARK/BEDFORD PARK
GUNNERSBURY
BRENTFORD
ISLEWORTH
HOUNSLOW/OSTERLEY/HESTON/FELTHAM/HANWORTH

The London Borough of Hounslow marks the move from the urban mix of Hammersmith to the wealthy suburban reaches of west London as Hammersmith's King Street (A315) becomes Chiswick High Street. **Chiswick** is an appealing old London village turned suburb, situated around the grounds of Chiswick House, an 18th century manor house in Palladian style, designed by Victorian architect Lord Burlington. The Great West Road (A4), which leads onto the M4 motorway, neatly splits the area in two, providing some sharp contrasts between its Georgian heartland and the 20th century encroachments of flyovers and thundering traffic. William Hogarth, the 18th century artist and chronicler of London life who lived in Chiswick and whose house is now open to the public, has the dubious honour of having one of London's busiest roundabouts named after him. On the south side of the A4 is Chiswick House (now a museum), and Chiswick Mall. The Mall runs close to the river—too close for some as there is a risk of flooding—and its most expensive houses are three-storey Georgian terraces with river views. During low tide it is possible to walk out to the Chiswick Eyot Island. A large patch of allotments also huddle by the river (allotments are an endearing British phenomenon where a strip of land is divided into plots to be rented out by willing gardeners). Further west the **Grove Park** region of Chiswick is bounded by the Great West Road (A4) and has high quality suburban houses spanning from the Edwardian era to the 1930s. On the north side of the A4 are the chain cafe-bars, restaurants, and high street stores. Turnham Green Terrace has delicatessens and cafes. The area is sold as villagey and picturesque, but the ever-present metropolitan roar ensures you don't lose sight of the fact that you are still in London. Towards Stamford Brook Tube are smaller Victorian cottage-style terraces as well as larger properties with a mix of those that are intact and those that have been converted.

Bedford Park, a self-contained conservation area, is part of Chiswick. Building began on this garden suburb in 1879 and there are contributions from notable architects of the time. Bedford Park's earliest residents were satirised at the time as pretentious arty types. Now its wide tree lined roads are eminently respectable. The detached Art and Crafts red-brick houses often with five or more bedrooms, most of which are now listed, are among the most sought after family homes in the capital, with prices fetching as much as one million pounds.

The 18th-century Strand-On-The-Green in **Gunnersbury** is another lovely riverside stretch, and is only a step across the bridge to Kew. Gunnersbury Park has a boating lake and miniature golf and is a great local asset. The narrow corridor of the borough of Hounslow widens out westwards into **Brentford** and Isleworth. These areas do not have London postcodes and are part of the county of Middlesex. Brentford has a historic position on the western Roman route out of London, and a battle was fought here in 1642 during the English Civil War. Brentford became heavily industrialised in the 19th and 20th centuries, and its older stock of housing was largely replaced during the post-war years by social housing. The M4 motorway is a dominating presence. The neighbourhood of Old Brentford around a central square called "The Butts" is what remains of the earlier settlements. Brentford extends along the riverbanks of both the Thames and the Brent rivers, and a marina is located where the two intersect with each other and also with the mouth of the Grand Union Canal. Around the marina is the Brentford Dock, a residential development dating from 1970s, which has a good supply of all sizes of flats and houses. Other residential developments are likely to spring up around these waterways over the next few years. As Brentford has yet to make much of an impact in the property market, it may be worth investigating for housing bargains. **Isleworth** has an illustrious history as the site of a manor house and of the still standing Syon House, which now has the London Butterfly House and the Heritage Motor Museum on its large grounds (see **Parks and Open Spaces**). The riverside location of Isleworth made it a popular choice for the well-off during the 18th century. It was with the opening of Isleworth station in the mid 19th century that many of the gentry's estates were sold and more modest residential development, as well as local industry, took off. A large number of council houses were built in the latter half of the 20th century, contrasting with the area's churches and grand buildings, reminders of Isleworth's illustrious past. Some of these early buildings have contributions from architects such as Christopher Wren and Robert Adam, and the quintessential English landscape gardener Capability Brown.

   Hounslow is a large sprawling area of west London, and covers many old villages turned suburbs including **Osterley**, **Heston**, **Feltham** and **Hanworth**. Aircraft noise from nearby Heathrow is a constant issue for residents, though the proximity of the airport makes for good road and Tube connections. The high street running through the town centre is a major thoroughfare (A30), which runs along the route of the Roman road out of London to Silchester. Indeed Hounslow long relied on its position as a stopover for its trade and industry, and was the haunt of highwaymen in the 18th century. It was the arrival of the railways followed by the Tube that changed the face of the locality from country wealth to increased population/urbanisation. Hence Victorian residential development in the northern and central parts of Hounslow was supplemented with some large tracts of 1930s houses which date from the opening of the Piccadilly line. The large Treaty shopping centre caters to the local community's shopping needs.

Web site: www.hounslow.gov.uk
Postcodes: W4, TW3, TW7, TW8, TW13
Council Office: The Civic Centre, Lampton Road, TW3, 020 8583 2000
Accident and Emergency Department: Ealing Hospital, Uxbridge Road, Southall, Middlesex, UB1, 020 8967 5000
Central Library: Hounslow Library Centre, 24 Treaty Centre, TW3, 020 8570 0622
Cultural Resources: Hounslow Tourist Information Centre, The Treaty Centre, High Street, TW3, 020 8572 8297; Chiswick House & Gardens, Burlington Lane, W4, 020 8995 0508; Hogarth's House, Great West Road, W4, 020 8994 6757
Leisure Centre: Brentford Fountain Leisure Centre, 658 Chiswick High Road, Middlesex, TW8, 020 8994 9596

TRANSPORT
Time to City: 30 to 50 minutes; **Time to West End**: 25 to 45 minutes
Tube: **District line**: Turnham Green, Chiswick Park, Gunnersbury;
   Piccadilly line: Turnham Green, Osterley, Hounslow East, Hounslow
   Central, Hounslow West
Rail: **Silverlink**: Gunnersbury; **South West Trains**: Chiswick, Brentford,
   Syon Lane, Isleworth, Hounslow

RICHMOND UPON THAMES

Boundaries and contiguous boroughs: **North**: Thames/Hounslow;
East: Wandsworth; **South**: Kingston upon Thames/Thames; **West**: Green
Belt/Hounslow

BARNES
MORTLAKE
EAST SHEEN
KEW
RICHMOND
HAM/PETERSHAM
TWICKENHAM
TEDDINGTON

When looking at a map of Richmond upon Thames, the first thing you'll
notice is that a massive chunk of the borough is green. The second thing
you'll become aware of is that the borough is unique in being the only one
to straddle both sides of the river. In fact it even has a territory in the *middle*
of the Thames, the delightfully named Eel Pie Island. At Richmond, the river
narrows, winding its way southward, and gradually presents a more rural
and picturesque prospect. Richmond is a borough, mostly outside the
London postal district, which boasts both small charms and big tourist
attractions. From the Royal Botanical Gardens at Kew in the north of the
borough, to the historic Hampton Court Palace in the south—previously a
country retreat of royals, from the Tudors onward until Queen Victoria
opened it to the public—there is never a shortage of things to do. In addition to the river meandering through the borough, there are large and
inviting open spaces. The most notable is the 2,470-acre Richmond Park in
the east of the borough, which is the largest urban park in the country.
Enclosed in the time of Charles I as a hunting ground, you can spot herds
of red and fallow deer roaming freely today—of course hunting them is no
longer encouraged! The acres upon acres of green space make for abundant sport and leisure opportunities. All the neighbourhoods that make up

Richmond have long and distinguished histories as manors, with some striking examples of Queen Anne and Georgian architecture surviving and lending the borough a special air. The chief downside to all this is the cost of living. Richmond residents tend to be wealthy and established, having chosen the area for its prestige and amenities. The borough also has several well known and high performing independent schools in its environs. Rental property usually takes the form of luxury houses or flats aimed at overseas visitors or dignitaries, and you'd be unlikely to find much for less than £900 per month.

Over the past couple of years **Barnes**, located in the far east of the borough, has overtaken areas such as St. John's Wood (see Westminster) in the popularity stakes, reflecting the soaring prestige of riverside locations. Its position on the Heathrow flight path no longer seems to put people off. Its houses are quintessential, large, turn-of-the-century villas or pretty little Victorian cottages. Famous residents have included Gustav Holst and, when he wasn't cleaning up the streets of Westminster, novelist Henry Fielding. It's a popular area for those with money, and those who settle here are apt never to leave, making for a rather slow-moving market. It has little nightlife other than a clutch of olde-worlde pubs and cafe-bars and so some find Barnes a bit stuffy. The high street converges on Barnes Pond, which comes complete with well-fed ducks and geese in residence. The shops on Church Street and Barnes High Street number a handful of pricey independents including a butcher and a baker, and a couple of appealing restaurants. Additional shopping requires a hike over the bridge to Hammersmith or venturing into East Sheen.

House prices decrease as you get into **Mortlake** and nearer the industrial area around the brewery on the riverbank. Further south, **East Sheen** is a more modest and typically suburban area. Most people in these areas own cars, with public transport providing a link to the City through the crowded commuter trains which run to Waterloo.

Following the river round on this south side brings you to **Kew**, which is best known for its fabulous botanical gardens (see **Parks and Open Spaces**), attracting many visitors to the village centre around Kew Gardens Tube station. Local shops tend towards the expensive and impractical but a recently opened retail park nearby has brought new, more down-to-earth shopping possibilities for residents. The M4 motorway, here situated just north of the Thames, grants quick access to Heathrow. Be aware, noise from Heathrow is bothersome to Kew residents who, even now, brace themselves against the prospect of a fifth terminal added to the airport. Housing prices seem unaffected by the sound issue, with large but fairly standard Victorian terraces here costing upwards of half a million pounds. The Kew Road (A307), leading south off Kew Bridge, brings you down into **Richmond** town centre, with both Kew and Richmond having Tube stations on the District line. There are great shopping facilities here with major branches of high street clothing stores, including a Dickins and Jones department store, housewares shops, specialty grocers, and a variety of restaurants and pubs. The area is replete with historical and royal associations. Henry VII built a royal palace here naming it after his favourite Yorkshire earldom of Richmond. Richmond Green is a grand manifestation of the past, once the scene of medieval jousting tournaments it is now a square of perfectly manicured green overlooked by period Georgian and Victorian houses. Built in the 1770s, picturesque Richmond Bridge is the one of the Thames' oldest surviving crossing places. An idyllic stretch of river between Twickenham and Richmond bridges is home to several lively pubs and cafe-bars whose patrons spill out onto the grass and riverbank on long summer evenings. Richmond Park, where the deer are the residents of note (see **Parks and Open Spaces**), occupies a big patch of the rest of the borough's area south of the river, leaving only the old manors of **Ham** and **Petersham**. Ham has a common that joins up with Richmond Park on its eastern side, and there are some notable 18th century houses nearby in the old village centre. Ham House, with an amazing position on the Thames, is another historical gem. Originating in the 17th century Stuart period, it was passed down the centuries through the same aristocratic family, the Dysarts, who were lords of the manor. It is now owned by the National Trust, which has restored its splendid interior and formal gardens, and opened it to the public. Petersham acquired its period houses in the 17th century too, and has a matching, though not quite as magnificent, manor house.

North of the river the principal neighbourhoods are **Twickenham** and **Teddington**. Twickenham is home to English rugby, and has some fine period houses and preserved stretches of riverfront as well. The area's main shopping facilities are at High Street and Broad Street. Hampton Court dominates the area, and on either side of Hampton Court Road (A308) are parks. Bushy Park to the south was the tranquil base from which General Eisenhower planned the D-Day operation in 1944. A picturesque little footbridge crosses the Thames at Teddington Lock where there is another old village centre. Boat trips are a popular pursuit for visitors to the borough, with craft shuttling between Hampton Court, Kingston, Richmond and Westminster offering glimpses of all the many facets of west London.

Web site: www.richmond.gov.uk

Postcodes: SW12, TW1, TW2, TW9, TW10, TW11, TW12

Council Office: Civic Centre, 44 York Street, Twickenham, TW1, 020 8891 1411,

Accident and Emergency Departments: Teddington Memorial Hospital, Hampton Road, TW11, 020 8977 2212; Queen Mary's Hospital, Roehampton Lane, SW15, 020 8789 6611

Central Library: Richmond, Little Green, TW9, 020 8940 0981
Cultural Resources: Tourist Information Centre, Old Town Hall, Whittaker Avenue, TW9, 020 8940 9125; Landmark Arts Centre, St. Albans, Teddington, TW11, 020 8977 7558; Orleans House Gallery, Riverside, Twickenham, TW1, 020 8892 0221; Richmond Theatre, Richmond Green, TW9, 020 8940 0088; Orange Tree Theatre, Clarence Street, 020 8940 3633; Odeon Cinema, Hill Street, 01426 915474; Odeon Studio, Red Lion Street, 01426 915474; Richmond Film Studio, 3 Water Lane, 020 8332 0030; Royal Botanic Gardens, Kew, 020 8940 1171; Hampton Court Palace, 020 8781 9500; Twickenham Experience & Museum of Rugby, Rugby Football Union, Rugby Road, Twickenham, TW1, 020 8892 8877

TRANSPORT
Time to City: 40 to 60 minutes; **Time to West End**: 35 to 50 minutes
Tube: District line: Kew Gardens, Richmond
Rail: South West Trains: Kew Bridge, Barnes, Barnes Bridge, Mortlake, North Sheen, Richmond, St. Margarets, Twickenham, Strawberry Hill, Teddington, Hampton Wick, Whitton Fulwell, Hampton, Hampton Court, Thames Ditton; **Silverlink**: Kew Gardens, Richmond

KINGSTON UPON THAMES

Boundaries and contiguous boroughs: **North**: Richmond upon Thames; **East**: Merton/Sutton; **South**: Green Belt; **West**: Green Belt/Thames

ROYAL PARK/KINGSTON TOWN CENTRE
SURBITON
TOLWORTH
NEW MALDEN
OLD MALDEN
CHESSINGTON/MAIDEN RUSHETT

The river forms part of the northwestern boundary of the widest part of the Royal Borough of Kingston upon Thames, which is shaped a little like a map of Africa. It is one of those boroughs with a dual identity, a London borough with a Surrey address, and the further south in Kingston you go, the less identifiable as a part of London it becomes. There is a proud history of royal connections for which the borough has earned the "royal" prefix. It is believed to have been the place where seven Anglo-Saxon kings were crowned, and Queen Elizabeth I often came here to hunt. Kingston has a very similar composition to neighbouring Richmond with plenty of open spaces, village greens, independent schools and excellent shopping facilities.

The **Royal Park** area of the borough borders the expanse of Richmond Park. Further south on the eastern side of the river **Kingston Town Centre** is famed for its concentration of shops as well as the maddening one way traffic system that encircles it. Happily the whole shopping area is pedestrianised. In between the new malls, The Bentall Centre and Eden Walk, are little streets and alleyways that often date back to medieval times. There is also some interesting sculpture scattered about, notably David Mach's group of leaning telephone boxes on London Road. Market Place, at the junction of Church and Thames streets, is the town's heart with the interesting looking Market House providing a focal point. Kingston Town's residential areas are quite established with commuting professionals and their families being the norm. The highly rated local schools attract those with children, which has pushed up the price of family sized homes. It's no surprise, given the extent of Kingston's shopping facilities, that retail is a major source of local jobs. The presence of Kingston University means there is a lively student population, giving the area a bit more of a mix of ages and races than next door Richmond. Richmond Park, Bushey Park, and Home Park are all within walking distance of the town centre, and, while there is no Tube station, there is a useful rail link to Waterloo and road access to central London via the A3, M3 or M25. One of the area's few drawbacks is the aircraft noise which plagues these stretches of west London. Property prices in Kingston are high but not unreasonably so given the standard of living. There are plenty of large Victorian family houses, as well as some newer, trendier riverside developments such as Charter Quay, which tend to attract younger buyers.

Elsewhere in the borough things are quieter and more uniform. **Surbiton,** as its name suggests, is an orderly Victorian creation of suburbia, as is **Tolworth**, which offers good quality, if uninspiring, 19th century houses and a large commuting population. **New Malden** and **Old Malden** are villagey and quite remote from London. **Chessington** is home to the popular theme park, the World of Adventures, and a zoo, and looks directly onto green belt countryside. In the southerly tip of the borough is the village of **Maiden Rushett**, where the pace of life suits those who need to be near the city but wish to live somewhere more reminiscent of a traditional English country village.

Web site: www.kingston.gov.uk
Postcodes: KT1, KT2, KT3, KT4, KT5, KT6
Council Office: Guildhall, High Street, Kingston upon Thames, 020 8546 2121
Accident and Emergency Department: Kingston Hospital, Galsworthy Road, KT2, 020 8546 7711

Central Library: Kingston, Fairfield Road, KT1, 020 8547 6400
Cultural Resources: Tourist Information Centre, The Market House, KT1,
020 8547 5592; Kingston Museum, Wheatfield Way, KT1, 020 8547
6738; Cannon Cinema, Clarence Street, KT1, 020 8546 0404; Options
Nightclub & Cinema, 154 Clarence Street, KT1, 020 8547 2848;
Chessington World of Adventures, Leatherhead Road, Chessington,
01372 729 560
Leisure Centres: Kingfisher Leisure Centre, Fairfield Road, KT1, 020 8546
1042; Albany Park Canoe & Sailing Centre, Albany Park Road, 020 8549
3066; Chessington Sports Centre, Garrison Lane, Surrey, 020 8974
2277; Tolworth Recreation Centre, Fullers Way North, 020 8391 0684;
Malden Centre, Blagdon Road, New Malden, 020 8949 3330

TRANSPORT
Time to City: 35 to 50 minutes; **Time to West End**: 35 to 50 minutes
Rail: South West Trains: Kingston, Norbiton, Berrylands, Surbiton, New
Malden, Malden Manor, Tolworth, Chessington North, Chessington South

---

MERTON

Boundaries and contiguous boroughs: **North**: Wandsworth; **East**:
Lambeth/Croydon; **South**: Sutton; **West**: Kingston upon Thames/Richmond
upon Thames

WIMBLEDON/WIMBLEDON VILLAGE
RAYNES PARK
MERTON PARK
MITCHAM
MORDEN
COLLIERS WOOD

Merton, a leafy and suburban borough in the southwest of London, is
home to more than 60 parks and recreation grounds, not to mention the
river Wandle it shares with Wandsworth. Horatio Nelson, English hero of
the 1815 Battle of Waterloo, lived here for a time with his lover Emma
Hamilton who dubbed it "Paradise Merton." Parts of the borough are still
very desirable but large-scale 20th century development has made it more
socially mixed than its historical image might suggest. Merton is quite well
placed for transport into London, with plenty of rail stations and journey
times of around 15 minutes to Waterloo. Both Heathrow and Gatwick airports are easily accessible by road.

   Wimbledon, home of the genteel All-England Lawn Tennis Association, delivers the luxurious, suburban ambience you would expect. Apart from those two weeks in July when queues of tennis fans, ticket touts, autograph hunters, and souvenir merchants wind their way along Wimbledon Park Road, it is usually a quiet place. Wimbledon Common offers an enormous park with a golf course, an iron-age hill fort, a renovated Windmill, woodland, open space, and plenty of wildlife. The hilly area around the Common is fast becoming a playground of the rich, with the grandest houses fetching upwards of a million pounds. There are luxury flats converted from 18th century mansions as well as some new developments. The area further south, known as **Wimbledon Village**, is the most fashionable part of the area. The high street, which runs down through the old village, offers restaurants and many expensive little shops. New developments emulate the small mews cottage style of older Victorian artisan houses and are aimed at the high-income bracket. The houses around Wimbledon Park come as both semidetached and detached, and are considered reliable, if less glamorous, family houses. Wimbledon Broadway is at the bottom of Wimbledon Hill. It is the town centre of the borough and as such is a less bucolic prospect, with a busy main shopping area including a supermarket and a shopping mall, Centre Court. The area was built-up in the mid-Victorian era, with the arrival of the railways, and consequently is made up of familiar tracts of commuter belt terraces and semis within easy reach of Wimbledon station, which has an overland link to Waterloo and a stop on the District Line. Cheaper housing consisting of Edwardian houses and maisonettes can be found further south in the **Raynes Park** area, which has the railway line running through it.

To the southwest of Wimbledon is **Merton Park**, an innovative estate that pre-dates the garden suburb movement. The houses here were built over a period of some 60 years beginning in the 1870s. Different trends in house building are reflected in the variety of styles, from little cottages to large Arts and Crafts homes to the villas of the Edwardian era.

The rest of the borough was historically in the county of Surrey and is without a London postcode. **Mitcham** is in the southeast of the borough. Its fertile loam soils established farming as a significant player in the local economy from Neolithic times all the way through to the mid-20th century when its market gardens finally closed. During the Middle Ages Mitcham was popular as a country seat for the nobility. You'll find a rich seam of picturesque inns, manor houses and commonland next to the tracts of solid residential suburbia which have been built up steadily since the 1880s, with the arrival of the trams, which were later replaced by trains. (Trams, incidentally, are making a comeback to the area with the new Tramlink network linking Wimbledon with Croydon.) Further south **Morden** was a settlement that grew up along the Roman road Stane Street, between London and Chichester, and became an early Surrey parish. The last stop on the Northern line terminus, built here in 1926, put an end to its life as a village, establishing it as a London's suburb. **Colliers Wood,** on the border with Wandsworth, has its High Street on Stane Street. The area first sprang up as a farming community on the banks of the river Wandle, then developed as estates of the nobility before becoming a home for a growing working class population in the 19th century. Both Morden and Colliers Wood are favoured by City commuters as they have Tube stops, with journey times of about half an hour into the City or West End.

Web site: www.merton.gov.uk

Postcodes: SW19, SW20, SM4, SM5, CR4

Council Office: Merton Civic Centre, London Road, Morden, Surrey SM4, 020 8543 2222

Accident and Emergency Departments: St. Georges Hospital, Blackshaw Road, SW17, 020 8672 1255; St. Helier Hospital, Wrythe Lane, Carshalton, SM5, 020 8644 4343

Central Library: Wimbledon, Wimbledon Hill Road, SW19, 020 8946 7979/7432

Cultural Resources: Odeon, Broadway, SW19, 020 8542 2277; Polka Children's Theatre, 240 Broadway, SW19, 020 8542 4250; Wimbledon Theatre, Broadway, SW19, 020 8946 5211; Merton Heritage Centre, The Canons, Madeira Road, CR4, 020 8640 9387; Wimbledon Lawn Tennis Museum, All England Club, Church Road, SW19, 020 8946 6131; Wimbledon Windmill Museum, Windmill Road, SW19, 020 8788 7655

Leisure Centres: Canons Leisure Centre, Madeira Road, CR4, 020 8545 8544; Morden Park Pool, Morden Park, 020 8640 6727; Wimbledon Recreation Centre, Latimer Road, SW19, 020 8542 1330

TRANSPORT

Time to City: 45 to 60 minutes; **Time to West End**: 35 to 50 minutes

Tube: District line: Wimbledon Park, Wimbledon; **Northern line**: Colliers Wood, South Wimbledon, Morden

Rail: South West Trains: Wimbledon, Raynes Park, New Malden, Berrylanads, Motspur Park; **Thameslink**: Wimbledon, Wimbledon Chase, South Merton, Morden South, St. Helier

LEWISHAM

Boundaries and contiguous boroughs: **North**: Thames; **East**: Greenwich; **South**: Bromley; **West**: Southwark

DEPTFORD/NEW CROSS
BLACKHEATH
LEE
LEWISHAM
BROCKLEY
FOREST HILL
CATFORD

Lewisham is a large south London borough that fans out to encompass a bewildering number of interlinked neighbourhoods. As a whole, the borough has suffered from poor transport links; its only Tube connection was the East London Line which ends at New Cross. Happily, the situation has changed for the better with extensions to the Docklands Light Railway and the Jubilee line both skirting the top half of the borough. For the southern half, beyond Lewisham Town Centre, public transport options remain limited to rail lines and buses.

The areas of **Deptford** and **New Cross** are notable for Goldsmiths College, part of the University of London, which has an Art Department of enormous influence (movers and shakers of the infamous BritArt movement like Damien Hurst and Gavin Turk studied here). This urban northern end of the borough, which has a high percentage of council housing, is trying to shake off an image of blight and inner-city problems which date back to the 16th century when playwright and Shakespeare contemporary Christopher Marlowe was killed in a bar room brawl in Deptford. The new transport links have helped bring the area closer to Docklands money, but Lewisham is unlucky in that only a short stretch of riverbank falls within its boundaries, so wholesale gentrification here is still a bit of a long shot.

Blackheath, located in the northeastern corner of the borough, is the grandest and proudest part of the borough. Exiting the southern end of Greenwich Park you are confronted by the whizzing traffic of Shooter's Hill Road (A2—the London to Canterbury road) which marks the borough boundary. The dizzyingly flat and wide expanse of the heath itself, populated by kite-flyers and dog-walkers, is surprising and slightly surreal. There is a wealth of history attached to the heath; the Romans built a road across it; Wat Tyler's revolting peasants assembled here in 1381; and various kings have shown off here to the cowering masses. The Paragon, proudly overlooking the heath, is an impressive and rare example of a crescent of semidetached Georgian houses, grandly connected by single-storey strings of colonnades. Blackheath Village is a well preserved parish with some lovely Georgian architecture as well as good quality Victorian terraces and 20th century housing developments. There is a railway station on a commuter line that takes you into London Bridge and Charing Cross in less than 15 minutes. The shops on Tranquil Vale are a pretty little mix of cafes, antique shops, bookshops, and some small branches of high street stores. The period houses are hotly pursued as prices generally are a bit lower than areas with similar village atmospheres such as Highgate or Chiswick, due to the general lower prestige of south London. The local community, however, is firmly convinced of Blackheath's superiority and would prefer to keep the area a secret, especially from tourists.

The southern half of the borough is mostly suburban, keeping a low profile. There is a cheerful amount of green space, some of which is part of the south London wide Green Chain Walk. Tucked north alongside the eastern boundary of the borough is **Lee**, with its Georgian Manor House, now made over into a public library. The cluster of spacious streets south of its grounds and west of Burnt Ash Road were built in the 1870s and are now a conservation area. Some of the large three storey houses, complete with double fronts, mansard roofs and Parisian style ironwork, are quite splendid, and have shot up in value over the last few years as buyers spill over from Blackheath.

The central part of **Lewisham,** south of New Cross and west of Blackheath, has several pleasant hilly streets with a few massive Victorian houses, some of which have been broken up into flats and others are fabulous family homes. There are some great views to be had from Hilly Fields park, and Lewisham High Street has a vast shopping area with a good selection of high street chains. The high street has been partially pedestrianised so a daily market thrives too, and your shopping experience is not blighted by traffic as it is on many of London's high streets. The town centre also boasts a Victorian clock tower and quite a few new pubs and restaurants. The best bit of neighbouring **Brockley** is a conservation area which is pretty, tree lined and has many flats converted from tall Victorian houses, eagerly sought by first time home buyers for their relative affordability and decent size. Flats on the ground floor will often have access to large gardens. Further south **Forest Hill** has more pleasant Victoriana and the telltale signs of gentrification, such as converted flats being turned back into houses. Forest Hill is located 12 minutes from London Bridge and half an hour from Victoria by rail, and residents benefit from being close to the open spaces of Dulwich and Sydenham golf course.

Catford, in the south of the borough below the South Circular Road (A205), is unusual in having a large tract of identically styled roads set out on a grid. These roads were filled in with houses by Victorian developer,

Archibald Corbett. The Corbett estate remains a popular buy with professionals looking for family homes; properties range from large to very large with front and back gardens. Bromley Road supplies the area with shops, but drinkers be warned: Corbett did not allow any pubs to be built on his land and there still aren't many about!

Web site: www.lewisham.gov.uk

Postcodes: SE4, SE6, SE8, SE13, SE14, SE23, SE26

Council Office: Town Hall Chambers, Catford Road, SE6, 020 8695 6000

Accident and Emergency Departments: Lewisham Hospital, Lewisham High Street, SE13, 020 8333 3000; Guys and St. Thomas, St. Thomas Street, SE1, 020 7955 5000

Central Library: Lewisham, 199-201 Lewisham High Street, SE13, 020 8297 9677

Cultural Resources: Lewisham Tourist Information Centre, Lewisham Library, 199-201 Lewisham High Street, SE13, 020 8297 8317; Lewisham Theatre, 020 8690 0002; Blackheath Concert Halls, 23 Lee Road, SE3, 020 8463 0100; The Albany Centre, Douglas Way, SE8, 020 8691 3277; The Bird's Nest Theatre, 32 Deptford Church Street, SE8, 020 8694 2255; Brockley Jack Theatre, 410 Brockley Road, SE4, 020 8291 1206; ABC Catford, 020 8698 3306; Horniman Museum, 100 London Road, SE23, 020 8699 1872

Leisure Centres: Ladywell Leisure Centre, Lewisham High Street, SE13, 020 8690 2123; Crofton Leisure Centre, Manwood Road, SE4, 020 8690 0273; Forest Hill Pools, 020 8699 3096; The Bridge Sports & Leisure Centre, Kangley Bridge Road, SE26, 020 8778 7158; Wavelengths Leisure Pool, Creek Road, 020 8694 1134

TRANSPORT

Time to City: 12 to 40 minutes; **Time to West End**: 15 to 40 minutes

Tube: East London Line: New Cross, New Cross Gate

Docklands Light Railway: Deptford Bridge, Elverson Road, Lewisham

Rail: Connex South Eastern: New Cross, Deptford, St. Johns, Lewisham, Blackheath, Ladywell, Catford, Catford Bridge, Bellingham, Beckenham Hill, Lower Sydenham, Crofton Park; **Connex South Central**: New Cross Gate, Brockley, Honor Oak Park, Forest Hill, Sydenham

GREENWICH

Boundaries and contiguous boroughs: **North**: Thames; **East**: Bexley; **South**: Bromley; **West**: Lewisham

GREENWICH
BLACKHEATH PARK
CHARLTON
WOOLWICH

Greenwich is best known as the location of the Meridian line, longitude zero. Indeed Greenwich capitalised on its significance as the home of Greenwich mean time, marketing itself grandly as the "millennium borough." Billions of pounds were poured into the borough, with the construction of the controversial Millennium Dome on the Greenwich peninsula swallowing the most. In addition to its special place in the space-time continuum, Greenwich has a proud history of royal connections. It's the birthplace of both Henry VIII and Elizabeth I and, while the Tudor royal residence, The Palace of Platentia, was replaced in the late 17th century by Christopher Wren's Royal Naval College, the original Tudor crypt remains. The area is jammed full of tourist attractions—the tea clipper Cutty Sark, the National Maritime Museum, and the Old Royal Observatory (where you can have your photo taken standing with one foot in the western hemisphere and one in the eastern). Central Greenwich is distinguished with some fine period homes, but the rest of the borough is a more varied affair with typical south London suburbia and some dank ex-industrial corners. Greenwich is less multi-cultural than most London boroughs, having a mostly white population. It also has the largest undeveloped area of waterfront in London, though don't expect that to last much longer!

The nicest way to approach Greenwich is via the Thames, and tourist boat services take advantage of this by shuttling up and down from Charing Cross pier. From the river you get a picture-postcard view of the twin towers of the Royal Naval College's western entrance. Designed as a hospital and with contributions from all the major English architects of the early 18th century; Christopher Wren (who takes most of the credit), Nicholas Hawksmoor and John Vanburgh, the building became a training college for officers of the armed forces in 1873. In addition to its tourist attractions, Greenwich has a hugely popular weekend market with a jaunty array of stalls, shops, cafes, and pubs bringing in the crowds. The green slopes of Greenwich Park afford spectacular views of the river, Docklands, the City, and the Dome. On the western side of the park, the residential streets are influenced by the area's grand Georgian roots and contain nice examples of housing from all periods since. The streets, such as Crooms Hill, which overlook the pleasing landscape of the park and the river below, are particularly notable. Further east housing tends to be more modest, dating from the waterfront's time as a working port with small Victorian terraced cottages predominating. These would once have been working class homes but occupants are now likely to be from further up the social scale and working in Docklands or the City. Traffic and parking are ongoing issues in Greenwich and public transport has hitherto been rather inadequate. Rail services take most of the strain carrying commuters over the river to the City, with journey times around 15 minutes into London Bridge. The picture has altered significantly with the extension to the Docklands Light Railway, encompassing Greenwich station and a new terminal at Cutty Sark, and with the stations on the Jubilee line extension.

The Greenwich peninsula, a bump of land jutting out from the shoreline, was, until the late 1990s, nothing more than the Blackwall Tunnel Approach Road (A102) and a disused gasworks. Amid much fanfare and controversy the enormous circular structure of the Millennium Dome was constructed, representing the country's millennium celebrations. During 2000 the 20-acre structure hosted a massive exhibition with a millennial theme. However, inadequate planning, poor financial management, and disappointing visitor numbers combined to ensure it became a political embarrassment and a huge drain on the public purse—the overall cost was upwards of £500 million. It has since been sold off to become a business park amidst ridicule and recrimination. Behind the Dome an additional £250 million was spent to construct the Millennium Village, an ambitious flagship scheme to build 1,400 environmentally friendly houses and flats on reclaimed and decontaminated "brownfield" land. The Swedish architect hired on to undertake the design, Ralph Erskine, described the peninsula as the bleakest place he has ever worked! This project too was dogged with problems but at any rate offers something of an alternative vision to the homogeneity of the luxury riverside developments that dominated the 1980s and '90s. Ecological terracing on the peninsula and plans to make this part of the riverbank friendlier to wildlife and humans alike were also welcome moves.

Below Greenwich Park and Blackheath proper (see Lewisham) is **Blackheath Park** (sometimes called the Cator Estate after its original architect John Cator who first developed the area in the early 19th century). This is an inward looking private estate with carefully proscribed entrances. It has some splendid houses from the Victorian and Edwardian eras and some 1930s mock-Tudors. As these homes are frequently quite luxurious with several bedrooms, large gardens, and even swimming pools, they attract some very wealthy occupants.

East of Rochester Way (A1020—Blackwall Tunnel Approach Road) is **Charlton**. Its waterfront area is heavily industrial but the residential part, further back from the river and south of the Woolwich Road (A206), has some good Victorian terraces. Going along the river's eastern edge are less expensive homes. **Woolwich** is also quite industrial near the river and has a long history as a shipbuilding dockyard. Its name is most commonly associated with the Woolwich Arsenal, a giant munitions complex dating back to the 1600s which still exists today, though on a smaller scale. Arsenal Football Club originated here before migrating to its current north London home at Highbury. There are plenty of old maritime buildings to see on the waterfront and the Woolwich ferry shuttles between here and North Woolwich. In the area bounded by Woolwich Church Street to the north (A206) and Shooters Hill Road (A207) to the south, there are several parks and some more terraced streets with Victorian period houses. Thamesmead is a new-town style development of high and low rise housing located in the far east of the borough on the Plumstead marshes. Once council-owned but now private, it has the indignity of being the most unpopular postcode in London.

A band of green across the southern reaches of the borough encompasses several parks, playing fields and woods. Oxleas Woods is of particular interest, it being an ancient woodland, recently saved from developers by the energetic efforts of anti-roads protesters.

Web site: www.greenwich.gov.uk
Postcodes: SE3, SE7, SE8, SE9, SE10, SE18, SE28
Council Office: Town Hall, Wellington Street, SE18, 020 8854 8888
Accident and Emergency Department: Greenwich District Hospital, Vanburgh Hill, SE10, 020 8858 8141
Central Library: West Greenwich, Greenwich High Road, SE10, 020 8858 4289
Cultural Resources: Greenwich Tourist Information Centre, 46 Greenwich Church Street, SE10, 020 8858 6376; Greenwich Cinema, Greenwich High Road, SE10, 020 8235 3007; Blackheath Concert Halls, Lee Road, SE3, 020 8463 0100; Greenwich Theatre, Crooms Hill, SE10, 020 8858 7755; Citizens Gallery, 151 Powis Street, SE18, 020 8317 8687; Woodlands Art Gallery, Mycenae Road, SE3, 020 8858 4631; Cutty Sark, King William Walk, Greenwich Pier, SE10, 020 8858 3445
Leisure Centres: Waterfront Leisure Centre, Woolwich High Street, SE18, 020 8317 1119; Arches Leisure Centre, Trafalgar Road, SE10, 020 8317 5000; Thamesmere Leisure Centre, Thamesmere Drive, SE28, 020 8311 1119; Plumstead Leisure Centre, Speranza Street, SE18, 020 8855 8289; Eltham Pools, Eltham Hill, SE9, 020 8850 4756

TRANSPORT
Time to City: 15 to 40 minutes; **Time to West End**: 15 to 40 minutes
Tube: Jubilee line: North Greenwich

Docklands Light Railway: Greenwich, Cutty Sark
Rail: **Connex South Eastern**: Greenwich, Maze Hill, Westcombe Park, Charlton, Woolwich Dockyard, Woolwich Arsenal, Plumstead, Kidbrooke, Eltham, Mottingham, New Eltham

---

NEWHAM

Boundaries and contiguous boroughs: **North**: Waltham Forest/Redbridge; **East**: A406 North Circular Road/Barking; **South**: Thames; **West**: River Lea/Tower Hamlets

STRATFORD
WEST HAM
CANNING TOWN
CUSTOM HOUSE/BECKTON
PLAISTOW/UPTON PARK/EAST HAM
FOREST GATE/MANOR PARK

The borough of Newham was formed in 1965 with the merger of East Ham and West Ham, two working class areas built around the huge Royal Docks complex on the Thames. As the docks gradually declined over the latter half of the 20th century, possibilities for gainful employment in the area dwindled as well. The Second World War had already exacted a hefty toll on existing housing stock in the area, and the large tracts of tower blocks which were built to replace the lost homes did little to enhance the picture. Consequently, Newham became a deprived collection of neighbourhoods, and this, it has to be said, is still overwhelmingly the case. That said, however, times are changing and area prosperity is improving with the extension of Docklands development east into the Royal Docks area, and the regeneration of the town centre at Stratford.

Stratford is situated where the Romford Road joins the A11 to form a major route into the City. Since the Channel Tunnel Rail Link was opened in the mid-1990s there have been plans to build a new high-speed line (the existing track to Waterloo does not allow the Eurostar trains to reach their top speed) through Kent to north London at St. Pancras and east London at Stratford. The scheme, with its typical on-again, off-again status, finally looks as if it is going ahead. Although the proposed international passenger station is not due before 2003, Stratford has already become an increasingly important feature on the transport map of London. Stratford station is a part of Docklands Light Railway, and has a quick rail link to Liverpool Street, a Tube stop on the Central line, a stop on the Silverlink North London line, and lastly and perhaps most important of all, it is the end-point of the

Jubilee line extension. The station environment, once hidden behind a particularly inauspicious shopping centre, is being completely made over. There is a new bus station and a dramatic glass dome that houses the Jubilee line ticket hall. Newham Council is vigorously promoting Stratford, and millions of pounds are being ploughed into the area in the shape of a regeneration programme. Its rough edges are gradually being cleaned up, the shopping centre is getting better, and there is a new cinema to complement The Theatre Royal Stratford East, one of the oldest repertory theatres in London. New restaurants and wine bars have introduced nightlife to what once was a barren spot of dodgy pubs and takeaways. Stratford Business Village and other office developments have brought new commerce into the area. There are a few new housing developments, and the surviving late Victorian terraced streets are being looked at with fresh eyes. Newcomers are enticed to the area by inexpensive property, and with the notion that Stratford could be "the next big thing." Whether due to residual snobbery, too many busy roads, too many council estates, or a combination of the three, housing prices here remain low, despite the grand plans. Those who have taken the plunge tend to be youngish professionals, maybe working in local government or the public services, who realise this is one of the few parts of town where they can afford to buy a house and are willing to take a gamble on Stratford's upward climb.

On its route to Stratford the Jubilee line extension stops at **West Ham** and **Canning Town**. These hitherto run-down and rather remote areas in the middle of the borough are hoping for positive knock-on effects from this recent link to Greenwich, Docklands and Westminster. In keeping with Newham's East End credentials there are lively street markets at Green Street and on Barking Road.

Given that the borders of Newham extend to the river, and meet with Docklands in the west, it was only a matter of time before the Newham Docklands was invented in an attempt to bring revitalisation to the wasteland of the Royal Docks. City Airport is the most important landmark at this end of the borough, offering easy access to continental Europe for those business travellers coming from east London and the City. A new Docklands Light Railway station with a planned 2004 opening will boost the airport's accessibility. Other developments around the site of the old docks include quality housing at West Silvertown Urban Village and Thames Barrier Park, the latter overlooking the spectacular Thames Flood Barrier. A Royal Docks University Campus, a London International Exhibition Centre and (another) aquarium are also in the pipeline. Current amenities include a massive Sainsbury's Savacentre (discount supermarket), a dry ski slope, and various watersports centres (see **Sports and Recreation**). **Custom House** and **Beckton,** located just to the north of the riverside area, are seeing a tremendous amount of residential development on the back of all this.

There is no reason to suppose that this region of the borough will not continue to thrive and extend the province of Docklands.

North of Newham Way (A13), another trunk road that bisects Newham on its way to the City, are the residential heartlands of the borough. These areas, **Plaistow, Upton Park,** and **East Ham** on the outer reaches of the District line, are more or less untouched by the catacyclisms shaking up the west of the borough and remain a fairly run down but quiet mixture of closely terraced streets, council housing, and uninspiring shopping areas. Further north, strung out along the Romford Road (A118), are **Forest Gate** and **Manor Park,** where there is a significant Asian community as well as large numbers of students attracted by cheap rental accommodation and the proximity of Queen Mary and Westfield College, and the University of East London.

Web site: www.newham.gov.uk

Postcodes: E6, E7, E12, E13, E15, E16

Council Office: Newham Town Hall, Barking Road, East Ham, E6, 020 8472 1430

Accident and Emergency Department: Newham General, Glen Road, E13, 020 7476 4000

Central Library: Stratford, Water Lane, London E15, 020 8557 8968

Cultural Resources: Stratford Picture House, Gerry Raffles Square, E15, 020 8555 3366; Showcase Cinemas, Jenkins Lane, E6, 020 8477 4520; Boleyn Cinema (Asian films), 7-11 Barking Road, E6, 020 8471 4884; The Rex (music venue), High Street, E15, 020 8215 6000; Theatre Royal Stratford East, Gerry Raffles Square, E15, 020 8534 0310; Three Mills Island, Three Mill Lane, Bromley-by-Bow, E3, 020 8215 0050; North Woolwich Old Station Museum, Pier Road, E16, 020 7474 7244

Leisure Centres: Atherton Leisure Centre, Romford Road, E15, 020 8519 5731; Balaam Leisure Centre, Balaam Street, E13, 020 7476 5274; Newham Leisure Centre, Prince Regent Lane, E13, 020 7511 4477

TRANSPORT

Time to City: 10 to 30 minutes; **Time to West End**: 20 to 40 minutes

Tube: Central line: Stratford; **District, Hammersmith & City lines**: East Ham, Upton Park, Plaistow, West Ham; **Jubilee Line**: Stratford, West Ham, Canning Town

Docklands Light Railway: Stratford, Pudding Mill Lane, Canning Town, Custom House, Prince Regent, Royal Albert, Beckton Park, Cyprus, Gallions Reach, Beckton

Rail: Great Eastern: Stratford, Maryland, Forest Gate, Manor Park; **LTS**: West Ham; **Silverlink**: Stratford, West Ham, Canning Town, Custom House, Silvertown & London City Airport, North Woolwich

WALTHAM FOREST

Boundaries and contiguous boroughs: **North**: Epping Forest/Green Belt; **East**: Redbridge; **South**: Newham/Hackney; **West**: Hackney/Haringey/Enfield

LEYTON
LEYTONSTONE
WALTHAMSTOW
UPPER WALTHAMSTOW/CHINGFORD

Waltham Forest is the point where north London meets east London—inner merges with outer. In the south of the borough the river Lea forms the border with decidedly inner-city Hackney, while to the north it meets the wide expanse of Epping Forest and the county of Essex. The Lea Valley, separating the borough from Haringey on the west side, is a flat marshland developed in the 19th century with reservoirs and filtration plants. It is now a designated and rare urban nature reserve. Suburban but not at all sleepy, Waltham Forest offers quick getaways to the countryside and is popular with those who work in town but prefer to live in slightly quieter and more spacious environs. Walthamstow Central station is at the end of the Victoria Line and is also on an overland line to Liverpool Street. Leyton and Leytonstone Tube stations are on the Central line, and there are numerous rail stations throughout the borough. Residents of the borough are close to major roads as well, with access to the M11 via the new M11 link road, which cuts through Leytonstone, and to the North Circular which skirts the northern end of Walthamstow. Property, both to buy and rent, remains cheap in the central and southern parts of the borough, but prices rise significantly near the open spaces of the Wanstead Flats and Epping Forest.

Until the mid-1800s, the vicinity of Waltham Forest was predominately agricultural and popular as a country retreat. The south of the borough encompassing **Leyton, Leytonstone** and Walthamstow is mostly made up of terraced streets, built quickly in the late 19th century to meet the housing demand created by the encroachment of the railways. This housing stock was intermittently augmented in the 1930s, and by the social housing and high rise blocks of the 1960s and '70s. This south side of the borough houses about two thirds of the area's population. Leyton and Leytonstone are generally quite low-key areas, with large Asian and student populations, and a high level of cheap rental accommodation in converted houses. Buyers are becoming more common as prices remain low for small Victorian and early 1900s terraced houses, which make good starter homes. Upper Leytonstone, west of Whipps Cross Road (A114), holds larger houses of a similar vintage, on leafy and respectable streets.

Around its end-of-the-line Tube station and its street market, which claims to be the longest in Europe, **Walthamstow** is East Endish and urban. Students and those on a lower income are attracted by the abundance of rental accommodation in Victorian conversions and maisonettes, and there is a broad racial mix including Asian and Afro-Caribbean communities. Alongside the delights of the market, which extends the length of the high street, there is the fair sized Selborne Walk Shopping Centre. There isn't a great deal of nightlife or culture about and this is part of the reason the area remains inexpensive. To the east of Hoe Street (A112), Walthamstow's main thoroughfare, is the area's posh bit, "the Village," made up of a sweet collection of conservation-area streets. Potential buyers often are drawn to the appealing Victorian cottages here, though property in the village is certainly expensive when compared to the rest of the borough. The Vestry House Museum traces the area's pedigree, offering a glimpse of local life in the Georgian and Victorian periods. Walthamstow's main thoroughfares, Hoe Street (A112), Lea Bridge Road (A104), and Forest Road (A503) are perpetually busy, and form parts of routes in and out of London. Traffic becomes so clogged on the Lea Bridge Road and Forest Road that Walthamstow can seem like an island. At the entrance to Lloyds Park on Forest Road stands the William Morris Gallery in the house where the pre-Raphaelite designer and pioneer socialist thinker was born. Around Lloyds Park are 1930s maisonettes with slices of gardens for both upstairs and downstairs dwellings.

Chingford and **Upper Walthamstow** were developed mostly in the inter- and post-war years, and the houses tend to be large with several bedrooms and generous gardens reflecting a wealthier demographic. You'll find many previous East-Enders happily calling the area home.

Web site: www.lbwf.gov.uk

Postcodes: E4, E10, E11, E17

Council Office: Town Hall, Forest Road, Walthamstow, E17, 020 8527 5544

Accident and Emergency Department: Whipps Cross Hospital, Whipps Cross Road, E10, 020 8539 5522

Central Library: Walthamstow Central Library, High Street, E17, 020 8527 5544

Cultural Resources: William Morris Gallery, Forest Road, E17, 020 8527 3782; Vestry House Museum, Vestry Road, E17, 020 8509 1917; Walthamstow ABC, 186 Hoe Street, E17, 020 8520 7092; Lee Valley UCI 12 Screens, Picketts Lock, Edmonton, 020 8482 5282

Leisure Centres: Waltham Forest Pool & Track, Chingford Road, E17, 020 8527 5431; Cathall Leisure Centre, Cathall Road, E11, 020 8539 8343;

Leyton Leisure Lagoon, 763 High Road, E10, 020 8558 8858; Kelmscott Leisure Centre, 243 Markhouse Road, E17, 020 8520 7464; Lee Valley Park (including leisure centre, riding centre, pitch & putt, watersports etc.), Myddleton House, Bulls Cross, Enfield EN2, information centre: 01992 717711

TRANSPORT
Time to City: 15 to 25 minutes; **Time to West End**: 25 to 45 minutes
Tube: **Central Line**: Leyton, Leytonstone, Wanstead; **Victoria line**: Blackhorse Road, Walthamstow Central
Rail: **Silverlink**: Blackhorse Road, Walthamstow Queens Road, Leyton Midland Road, Leytonstone High Road, Wanstead Park; **WAGN**: St. James Street, Walthamstow Central, Wood Street, Highams Park, Chingford

SURROUNDING BOROUGHS

There are ten remaining outer London boroughs. They all border on the green belt offering a taste of the countryside. They have dual status as London boroughs and parts of English home counties, and all have their own unique aspects and attractions. If suburban life is what you're looking for, you may want to investigate them further. All these areas tend to be heavily owner-occupied, with a relatively low percentage of privately rented accommodation available. Here we take a quick tour clockwise round from Hillingdon in the northwest to Sutton in the south.

HILLINGDON

Hillingdon is a large borough making a bridge between London and the home counties on the northwest side. Its 42 square miles include the world's busiest airport at Heathrow (aircraft noise is a nuisance in some parts of the borough), a university, and a dry ski slope. **Uxbridge** is the borough's main shopping and commercial centre. The site of a Stone Age hunters' campsite, Uxbridge has a long and varied history as a market town on the road from London to Oxford. During the English Civil War it was the frontier between the warring factions of Parliament and the Royalists. Today the borough accommodates the offices of many international companies. The Ruislip Lido is a great outdoor swimming facility and there are plenty of golf courses, parks, and woodland. Three motorways going to other parts of the country, the M4, M40, and M25, pass through Hillingdon, and there is a rail link to Paddington that takes about 40 minutes.

For more information about Hillingdon, contact the Tourist Information Centre, Central Library, 14 High Street, Uxbridge, UB8, 01895 250706; www.hillingdon.gov.uk.

HARROW

Close to the M1, M40, and M25 motorways and located about ten miles northwest of the centre of London, the borough of Harrow is built on the foundations of settlements that originated in Anglo-Saxon times. In the 16th century a local yeoman founded the now world famous Harrow School. It has produced seven British Prime Ministers and many other notable figures in the histories of public life and literature. Harrow-on-the-Hill and Pinner High streets are both full of period character with 16th and 17th century buildings. There are large shopping malls with parking available at **Harrow** town centre and at **Wealdstone**. Harrow has Tube stations on the Piccadilly, Bakerloo and Jubilee lines as well as suburban rail services into town so it is particularly well served for an outer London borough. Harrow has a well-developed enterprise sector with large employers in the borough including Kodak and GEC Marconi. Harrow's housing, away from the posh enclave of Harrow-on-the-Hill, was mostly built between the wars in the typical suburban pattern with a predominance of semidetached family homes supplementing sporadic Victorian and Edwardian growth spurts. There is a large Asian community concentrated in the central part of the borough. All in all the area is thoroughly suburban, with 60% of the borough's residents travelling outside Harrow to work.

Contact the Harrow Tourist Information Centre, Civic Centre, Station Road, Harrow HA1, 020 8424 1103, www.harrow.gov.uk, for more information.

ENFIELD

The outer northern borough Enfield, www.enfield-online.co.uk, is home to the world's first "hole-in-the-wall" cash dispenser, opened at Barclays Bank on Church Street in 1967 by Reg Varney, a sitcom star of the day. The borough is traversed by the A10, which links the two major trunk roads in the north and south of the borough, the M25 orbital motorway, and the A406 North Circular Road. The western side of the borough offers suburbia by the mile with about half the borough's houses built between 1918 and 1939. There is a canal and the Trent Country Park to the northwest of the borough. There are excellent country sport amenities including golf courses and riding schools. New developments on brownfield sites near the Lock are attracting residents who work in the City as the overland train link goes to Liverpool Street. The Piccadilly line reaches the borough at Palmers Green and Oakwood.

REDBRIDGE

The London Borough of Redbridge, www.redbridge.gov.uk, mostly consists of archetypal 1930s suburbia. Indeed, one of its towns, **Ilford**, has gained notoriety due to its very anonymity. Closely allied to the East End and also part of Essex, areas such as Ilford, **South Woodford**, **Snaresbrook**, and **Hainault** have consistently drawn those moving out of inner east London for a higher standard of living. Stations on the Central line and easy journeys to City Airport and Stansted Airport are sweeteners, and property prices tend to be low by London standards. There are major shopping facilities at the Exchange Centre in Ilford, and at **Barkingside** and South Woodford.

BARKING AND DAGENHAM

Areas around Barking and Dagenham, www.barking-dagenham.gov.uk, have been inhabited since the Stone Age. Along the way William the Conqueror used Barking Abbey as his headquarters, and a vast fishing industry grew up around this stretch of the Thames. In the late 19th century docks were built and the area became heavily industrialised. The Beacontree Estate in Dagenham was one of first large public housing projects in Europe providing some 27,000 homes. Barking and Dagenham are also closely linked to the East End and often considered part of Essex. The District and Hammersmith and City Lines trundle their way out to Barking offering a link to central London destinations. The recent closure of the massive Ford car plant in Dagenham has been a big blow to the area's infrastructure.

HAVERING

The borough of Havering, www.havering.gov.uk, is named after the village of Havering-atte-Bower where a palace stood on a hillside, used by English royals from the Norman Conquest to the 17th century. Today it retains its village atmosphere despite being just a stone's throw from the M25 motorway. In contrast the neighbourhood of **Romford** is a new, populous, and busy area, which like nearby **Harold Hill**, was built up in the 20th century specifically to absorb some of inner London's excess population. The borough is linked to central London via Hornchurch and Upminster stations on the District line and various train stations on routes into Liverpool Street.

BEXLEY

Bexley is located in the far south of London and part of Kent. Many of the component areas, **Erith**, **Crayford**, and **Sidcup**, were agricultural and genteel in character until the 20th century when they became part of suburbia. There are some surviving grand houses and parks. By the 19th century Bexleyheath, the administrative centre of the borough, was an established residential area, providing living quarters for textile workers. The area is traversed by the Rochester Way section of the A2.

Contact the Bexley Tourist Information Centre, Central Library, Townley Road, Bexleyheath, Kent, DA6, 020 8303 9052; www.bexley.gov.uk, for more information.

BROMLEY

Bromley, www.bromley.gov.uk, begins south of Lewisham and Greenwich and, in terms of land area, is London's largest borough. Most of it is solid commuter belt and includes well-known suburban heartlands such as **Chislehurst** and **Penge**. There are ranks of semidetached and detached houses that were built in the 1930s to supplement the earlier terraced streets. The council has made efforts to promote commerce and industry in the borough with the creation of nine business areas, and the town centre is home to the offices of the Bank of America. There is an airfield at Biggin Hill, a concert arena at Crystal Palace Park, and a national sports centre.

CROYDON

The most notable thing about Croydon is its exciting new tram system, linking Croydon town centre with New Addington, Beckenham, and Wimbledon. There are lots of shopping opportunities both in the town centre, which has an enormous Allders department store, and in Drummond Mall and the Whitgift Centre. The Fairfield Arts Centre puts on a wide variety of theatrical and musical performances and has an art gallery, bars and restaurants. The state-of–the-art Clocktower Cultural Centre has similar amenities as well as a cinema and interactive museum. Housing prices remain inexpensive as Croydon has never been considered very fashionable. Industrial and professional office space mixed with tower blocks helps maintain a diverse social mix. The train from the middle of Croydon gets to Victoria in 14 minutes and the borough is also within easy reach of Gatwick Airport.

Contact the Croydon Tourist Information Centre, Katherine Street, Croydon CR9, 020 8253 1009; www.croydon.gov.uk, for more information.

SUTTON

The construction of the London to Brighton road route in 1755 was the impetus for Sutton's original development. Shortly thereafter the borough expanded greatly as one of Victorian era's earliest railway suburbs. It was also known for its thriving lavender and herb-growing industry. Today, in the absence of much local industry, the borough offers houses of all sizes, accommodating a wide range of commuters. The neighbourhoods of Sutton, **Cheam**, **Wallington**, **Carshalton**, **Worcester Park**, **Rosehill**, and **Beddington** all have high streets and local parks and amenities. Rail services take commuters into Victoria or London Bridge.

Go to www.sutton.gov.uk for more information.

LOOKING FOR SOMEWHERE TO LIVE IN LONDON INVOLVES A CRASH course in the layout of the city and in the subtleties and snobberies of the property market. Rents and house prices here are the highest in the country, among the highest in the world, and competition is fierce for places in the most congested middle-income bracket of the market. At the higher end of the scale there is usually plenty to be found, especially to rent. It is an estate agents' cliché that the most important factors in the property game are "location, location, location," and you will soon pick up the extent to which rents and house prices vary according to area—a Georgian house that goes for millions in Chelsea, will be a fraction of that price in Bow. The traditional certainties that north London is better than south, west is miles better than east, are gradually breaking down. The 1990s saw the housing market trend shift to waterfront living, and the rush to fill every available space by the river with luxury residential developments continues, moving ever eastwards. As space by the Thames runs out, developers are turning their attention to London's extensive and neglected canal network which, with its disused wharves and industrial buildings, offers great potential to be transformed into stunning living space. In response to the increased tendency for urban dwellers to live as singles or as couples without children, and the notion that more units equals more money, many new developments are now made up primarily of one- and two-bedroom apartments. This in turn has left family houses at a bit of a premium, and it's not uncommon for period houses converted into flats to be purchased and turned back into single-family homes. The fashion for "loft-living"—the creation of gallery-like spaces with high ceilings and tall windows in ex-industrial buildings—shows no sign of diminishing, and is particularly popular among the young professional classes.

Housing stock can be broken down into four main types:
- **Owner Occupied**: property lived in by those who have bought it.
- **Privately Rented**: property let by a landlord to a tenant or tenants.

The landlord will either be a property company whose business is letting acquired property, or an individual who is making a bit of money on the side. Some landlords let out rooms in the house they themselves occupy.

- **Local Authority** (council housing): local authority owned and managed properties which are let to tenants at a subsidised rent through a system of waiting lists; those in the greatest financial need are given priority. With most local authorities any residents in the borough can put their name down for a council house, but waiting lists are long even for those in the greatest need, and the standard of property is low. Since the early 1980s council tenants have had the right to buy their council houses, meaning some of them are now on the market or available in the privately-rented sector. Ex-local authority property tends to be the cheapest on the market.

- **Housing Association**: property owned by housing associations and let on various criteria of need, usually through referrals made by the local authority. Housing associations have their origins in the philanthropic organisations of the 19th century such as the Peabody Trust, which were created to provide decent homes for the working poor. In recent years housing associations have increasingly taken on the burden of building social housing (housing intended for those who cannot afford to buy or rent at market rates). Their properties are managed in a similar way to local authority housing.

RENTING

Renting from a private landlord is the most feasible and favoured option for those newly arrived in the capital. Although the renting market tends to be more stable than the buying and selling one, since the 1980s rents in London have nonetheless been going up faster than the rate of inflation. Options include renting a whole flat or house from a private landlord or choosing to rent a room in a shared house or flat (referred to as houseshare or flatshare) or renting a room in a landlord-occupied house. You may be lucky and find a place quickly, but as a general rule be prepared for a lot of trekking about before you find somewhere suitable.

FLAT HUNTING

Before embarking on house hunting in earnest, it's best to get some idea of the area of London in which you want to live—proximity to your workplace and ease of access to the amenities you value will be factors. Consult the profiles in this book for help in the evaluation of neighbourhoods, listen to what locals have to say, and most importantly, once you've narrowed down a couple prospective boroughs, visit at different times of the day and on different days of the week. When considering living in the central parts of town you need to weigh the benefits this gives you in terms of ease of access to transport and city facilities against the possible expense. Rents generally will reflect the desirability of a neighbourhood, so you have to ask yourself if you're prepared to pay a premium to live near a park or a high street, or in an area which has become particularly trendy. The outer London boroughs generally offer more space for less rent, but this must be balanced against the costs of commuting if you work or study in the middle of town. If you have children, quality of local schools should also be considered. In contrast to the US, the majority of lets are furnished, and if you prefer to rent somewhere unfurnished, your hunt may take longer. There are a number of methods of looking for rented accommodation. To maximise your chances of success it's best to employ as many as possible. When responding to ads for accommodation, a quick response is advisable, as places can go within hours of publication. When staking a claim remember that the landlord will probably want a deposit and a month's rent in advance, and will most likely expect you to provide a work reference before accepting you as a tenant.

CLASSIFIED ADVERTISEMENTS

- *Loot* is an ads paper which carries a vast amount of agency and privately-rented accommodation usefully broken down by price (agency ads appear in bold type). The paper is published five times a week, and also has a web site, www.loot.com.

- *Time Out*; weekly listings magazine, published on Tuesdays, carries adverts for house and flatshares, and occasionally whole flats and houses to rent.

- *Evening Standard*; London's daily newspaper runs accommodation ads on Tuesdays and Wednesdays. On Wednesdays it publishes a *Homes and Property* supplement which gives useful information about the state of the property market. Check their web site, www.thisislondon.com.

- *The Guardian*; on Thursday a good number of flat/houseshare ads appear in its "Space" supplement.

- *The Pink Paper*; a national, free, lesbian and gay magazine which carries accommodation ads for the London area—mostly for flat/houseshares.

- *Freesheets*; there are an ever increasing number of flimsy free magazines which can be picked up from stands on the streets. Many are aimed at ex-patriot communities: *LAM (Living Abroad Magazine)*, *Southern Cross*, www.southerncross.co.uk, *Footloose*, etc., and carry accommodation ads.

OTHER MEDIA

Look everywhere you can, including: campus noticeboards, local cafes, libraries, community bookshops and newsagents' windows (though this last practice is not as common as it once was). Places in shared houses and flats often go by word of mouth, so inform friends and colleagues that you are looking.

LETTING AGENTS

Many landlords lease their property through letting or estate agents of which there are hundreds in London. Because of the additional fees land-lords pay to the letting agent to find tenants for them, properties rented this way tend to be more expensive. But, if money is no object this is prob-ably the quickest way of finding accommodation. Visit the offices of letting agents in your preferred area, ask what they currently have on their books and phone them regularly to see if anything new has come up. Don't rely on them to contact you! This service should be free; anyone trying to charge you just for looking at lists of accommodation is breaking the law. Companies that belong to the Association of Residential Letting Agents are the most reliable. Sometimes letting agents will charge to register your details or if they successfully find a place for you—which is legal only if they inform you of the cost in advance.

ACCOMODATION SEARCH/RELOCATION SERVICES

There are a number of accommodation agencies aimed at newcomers that will find you somewhere to live for a (hefty) fee. You will see these adver-tised in the freesheets mentioned above or listed in the *Yellow Pages*. Relocation services will also often include in-country orientation, tax and financial advice, etc.

- **Focus Information Service**, 13 Prince of Wales Terrace, London W8, 020 7937 0050, www.focus-info.org; membership to Focus (60£ per year, per couple, 50£ per individual) gives you access to a range of resources and information to help you settle in London, from finding a job, or a doctor to advice about housing or legal issues. Although they won't find accommodation for you, they will help you find someone who can.
- **People and Property Limited**, 18 Coulston Street, London SW3, 020 7225 1313; fax: 020 7225 2765; e-mail: peopleandproperty@btin-ternet.com; offers services similar to those listed above, however, will take clients out to look for housing.

DEPOSITS AND CONTRACTS

With most tenancies you will be required to put down a deposit, in addition to a month's rent in advance. The deposit is usually a sum similar to a month's rent. Deposits are refundable but interest is not payable on them. Once you have signed a contract it is legally binding so be sure to read the small print thoroughly. Consult a Citizens Advice Bureau (see the **Consumer Protection** section of the **Helpful Services** chapter) if you have any worries.

For the renting of a property where the landlord is not resident, the main type of contract you will come across is **Assured Shorthold Tenancy**. In fact all tenancies are automatically on shorthold terms unless the landlord follows the procedure for setting up an **Assured Tenancy**. (Assured tenancies are much less common now, as their terms are more favourable to tenants, giving them greater rights of occupancy.) An assured shorthold tenancy must be for a fixed term of not less than six months. Within the six months there is usually a month's notice period. If they want you to leave after the first six months, the landlord must give you two months notice (and vice versa). Of course mutual agreement between landlord and tenant can override these terms. However the landlord has a guaranteed right to repossess the property through the courts, if you do not leave after having been given notice. The tenancy can be renewed after its initial term is finished.

If a landlord tries unjustly to withhold your deposit at the finish of a tenancy, your legal recourse is through the small claims court. Seek advice from a Citizens Advice Bureau (see **Consumer Protection** in **Helpful Services**), a Law Centre or a lawyer.

For more information on the lengthy terms and conditions of tenancies contact a Citizens Advice Bureau.

CHECKING IT OUT

While most landlords are decent, there are, of course, a few who are not, and with the huge pressure for accommodation in London, they can sometimes get away with providing sub-standard service. In the rush to find somewhere to live, don't lose sight of health and safety issues. It is also wise to try and establish how responsible and willing to undertake repairs a landlord is before agreeing to move in. To help you avoid making a decision you may later regret, here are some specific things to consider when viewing a property:

- Ask yourself how you would escape in the event of a fire—do the windows open properly? Are there smoke detectors?
- Take note of how secure the locks on doors and windows are—this is

especially pertinent if the flat is in the basement or on the ground floor. Pests are another issue which are particularly relevant to lower floor dwellings. Any signs of pest control, mouse traps or rat poison, for instance, should make you think very seriously about whether this is the place for you.

- What is the condition of the appliances? Faulty gas appliances can kill, and landlords are legally required to have these serviced annually
- Is it noisy? Do the windows open onto a busy street? Can you hear noise, such as music or a baby crying, coming from adjacent flats? Flats converted from houses are particularly notorious for poor sound insulation.
- Are there any signs of dampness such as discoloured wallpaper or unseasonable coldness?
- Check the furniture, is it clean and comfortable?
- Is there sufficient storage space for your belongings?
- Is there adequate insulation and heating? London winters have their chilly moments, and gas-fired central heating is by far the most controllable and cost efficient heating source. Anything else—electric storage heaters, individual gas fires, electric bar heaters or fan heaters—is liable to be unreliable, inadequate, and expensive. This will be particularly important if the rental price does not include the cost of heat.
- If the flat is above a shop or business, what sort is it? Mini-cab firms, bars, and late night grocery stores may generate noise into the night.
- If you are considering a room in a shared house, think realistically about whether the facilities will be able to cope with the number of residents. One bathroom and five inhabitants who all get up at 8 a.m. does not a happy situation make!
- Is there a washing machine? If not, is there a launderette nearby?
- How close are you to a grocery store? How far away is the nearest Tube or rail station? What are the local bus routes? How would you get to work or college?
- Finally, don't be afraid to ask questions and be picky! If the landlord has nothing to hide, he/she shouldn't mind going into details.

BUYING

The good news for those considering buying property is that, discounting the initial outlays involved in purchase, mortgage repayments often work out to be cheaper than paying rent. Plus you are making an investment that may benefit you financially in the future. The property market in London, which had been fairly uneventful in the 1970s and early '80s, went mad during the late '80s economic boom with sky-rocketing housing prices. This was followed by a crash in 1991, which saw many homeowners trapped in negative equity. From that low, prices have been climbing steadily and now most have passed their late '80s high. The last few years in particular have again seen some dramatic increases. London's property market is competitive and has a cut-throat reputation. Approach with caution, study the latest trends, and do as much research as you possibly can to give yourself the best chance of making an informed decision. As for prices—in 2000, the average price of a property in London was £163,317. The price for a basic, one-bedroom flat started at around £80,000 in the less prepossessing or far-flung bits of town, and went up from there, depending on amenities. A terraced house containing two or three bedrooms will rarely go for less than £150,000 anywhere.

Unless you have a large amount of capital or your employer has a facility for providing loans to staff, a **mortgage loan** from a bank, building society, specialist mortgage company, or insurance company will be in order for the purchase of a house or flat. There are two types of mortgages: interest-only (generally "endowment policies") and repayment. Repayment mortgages are the most common type of loan. You pay a monthly sum, which covers the interest on your loan, plus an amount that goes toward paying off the debt itself. By the time the mortgage term is up (typical terms are 25 years), the loan will be paid off. Interest-only loans come in a few different sorts, but the idea is that all you pay per month is the interest on the loan whilst at the same time you contribute towards an endowment policy, which should, by the time the mortgage term is up, be worth enough to pay off the loan and leave a lump sum over. Personal pensions or other investments can also be used to repay an interest-only loan. Lenders are often keen to steer you in the direction of endowment mortgages, as they are more lucrative for the lender—so, before making a decision, seek advice, either informally from friends and colleagues who have been through the house-buying process, or from a financial adviser. At any given time there are various "best mortgage deals" and house-buying guides, available in magazine form from newsagents. These too can help you pick your way through all the options currently available. Generally, the maximum amount you will be able to borrow is three times your annual gross salary. Interest rates vary and regular perusal of the financial pages of the papers is the best way of keeping tabs on this area. A deposit of five- to ten-percent of the purchase price is normal, but 100% mortgages are available at less favourable terms. Be prepared for your finances, employment status, and credit record to undergo a thorough examination by the lender.

The initial outlays involved in purchasing property include solicitors' fees, valuation, a survey, and stamp duty. Stamp duty is a tax of one percent of the purchase price if it is between £60,000 and £250,000, three percent if it is over £250,000 but under £500,000, and four percent for anything exceeding that. Taking out mortgage payment protection insurance (MPPI), which insures you against sickness and redundancy, will add another chunk to your monthly outgoing, once the buying process is over.

Property in London is bought either on **freehold** or **leasehold** terms. A freehold is just as it sounds, you own your property free of any conditions or additional payments. In the case of leasehold, someone else owns the freehold. This means that your lease has a time limit and that you will have to pay ground rent. The vast majority of flats, and some houses as well, due to the historical presence of large estate owners in London, are sold on leasehold terms. On top of ground rent, which is usually minimal (a figure of about £100 a year is not unusual), leaseholders usually have to pay a service charge for the maintenance of the shared areas of the building in which they live. This is where you need to take care, as service charges can be high, or can increase suddenly if something structural goes wrong with the building.

The vast majority of property sales happen via **estate agents** so they are the best people to talk to if you have questions about the buying process. The number of estate agents operating in London is huge (property is, after all, the capital's biggest employer) and, once you've found an agent with whom you are comfortable, you'll just need to follow along to view available homes in your target neighbourhood. Other resources include:

- *Hot Property*; (published by *Loot*.) Comes out weekly and contains details of more than 2,000 properties on sale privately. Property details can also be accessed via the internet: www.hot-property.com.
- *Evening Standard*; Wednesday's *Homes and Property* supplement offers invaluable information about the state of the property market and house prices, though it concentrates on the more expensive end of the spectrum. Look here too for commercial advertisements for new residential developments. Visit their web site at www.thisislondon.com.
- **Online Searches** is a burgeoning area with the alluring possibility of viewing properties from the comfort of your own desk. Try these to get an idea of what's on offer:
    - www.findaproperty.com
    - www.homes-on-line.co.uk
    - www.homepages.co.uk
    - www.propertyfinder.co.uk
    - www.propertylive.co.uk
    - www.propertynet.co.uk
    - www.propertyworld.co.uk
    - www.ukpg.co.uk

POUNDS STERLING IS THE CURRENCY OF GREAT BRITAIN. THERE ARE 100 pence (p) to every pound (£). London branches of overseas banks are listed in the *Yellow Pages* and *Thomson Local*.

BANK ACCOUNTS AND SERVICES

After moving to London, opening an account with a British bank will likely be one of your first orders of business. Generally all you need to open a bank account is a UK address and proof of earnings. The last few years have seen a massive expansion of the banking services sector in this country. Banks and building societies used to be a relatively straightforward matter, with most people holding a current (checking) account at one of the main high street banks, a savings account, a mortgage at a building society, and a credit card from one of the credit card companies. Those days are gone. Many building societies have forgone their mutual status and converted into banks. All major banks and building societies offer a comprehensive range of personal financial services. Leading supermarkets Sainsbury's and Safeway have entered the fray offering mortgages, current and deposit accounts too. And then there's banking by phone, and banking by internet. Phew! The only way to work your way through this is to consider what your requirements are and shop around for the best deals. If you're looking for up to-date-tips and comparisons, a couple of good general financial web sites are www.find.co.uk and www.moneynet.co.uk.

CURRENT AND DEPOSIT ACCOUNTS

Banks in Britain are national. Generally high street banks and large building societies offer **current accounts** (referred to as checking accounts by someone from the US). Upon opening such an account you will receive a debit card and a chequebook, and with them the ability to withdraw cash from any cashpoint in the network of which your bank is a part. When choosing which type of current account it's a good idea to make an honest assessment of your financial situation—a current account that pays interest on a credit balance is a good idea, if you never go overdrawn (remember that interest rates on current accounts are low, and large surplus balances will earn you far more money in a savings or investment account). Likewise, if you're apt to sneak into the red, it might be a better idea to find an account with a free "buffer zone" overdraft facility.

Opening a **deposit account** (also known as a savings account) is similar to opening a current account. Deposit accounts vary between those that offer instant access to your savings, and those that require notice before taking out any money. Interest rates improve the larger the initial deposit and the longer the notice period. Interest rates of various accounts can be found on the money pages of newspapers where you can also find out about investments and ISAs, the government's tax-free savings scheme.

All the banks and building societies listed below also have a wide variety of savings accounts, insurance, investment and property services. Nearly all of the high street banks now offer online and telephone banking services as well. Bank branches generally are open 9 a.m. to 5 p.m., Monday-Friday with some slight variations. Only a few are open on Saturdays. The following are the most common high street banks and building societies, with central contact points. Web sites are often the quickest way of accessing information about the range of services available and many have branch locators too.

- **Abbey National**, 0645 724724, www.abbeynational.co.uk
- **Alliance and Leicester**, 0845 303 3000, www.alliance-leicester.co.uk
- **Barclays**, 0345 550022, www.barclays.co.uk
- **Co-operative**, 0345 21212, www.co-operativebank.co.uk; operates an "ethical banking" policy that promises not to invest in oppressive regimes or companies which cause environmental destruction or experiment on animals.
- **First Direct**, 0800 24 2424, www.firstdirect.com, a telephone and online banking service.
- **Halifax**, 0845 605 5010, www.halifax.co.uk
- **Lloyds/TSB**, 0845 3000 116, www.lloydstsb.com
- **HSBC**, 0800 520420, www.hsbc.com
- **National Westminster (NatWest)**, 0845 601 3355, www.natwest.com
- **Nationwide Building Society**, 0345 302010, www.nationwide.com; the largest remaining building society.
- **Royal Bank of Scotland**, 0207 833 2121, www.royalbankscot.co.uk
- **Sainsbury's Bank**, 0500 405060, www.sainsburys.com

CREDIT CARDS

Again, all the high street banks offer Visa or MasterCard credit cards. Note: whereas Visa and MasterCard are nearly always accepted, American Express and Diner's Club sometimes aren't. Many large stores like Marks & Spencer and John Lewis offer charge cards, which you can pick up details about in-store.

- **American Express**, 020 7834 5555, www.americanexpress.co.uk
- **Barclaycard**, 0345 573706, www.barclaycard.co.uk
- **Diner's Club**, 0800 460800, www.dinersclub.com
- **Morgan Stanley Dean Witter**, 0800 028 8990
- **People's Bank (MasterCard/Visa)**, 0500 551055
- **RBS Advanta (Visa)**, 0800 077770

MONEY TRANSFER

Money can be transferred abroad through a **Moneygram,** which can be sent through many post offices in this country. Ask at the post office counter or phone Moneygram on 00800 8971 8971. You also can send money through Western Union either over the phone using your credit card, or as a cash transaction through their many agents in local shops. Check the *Yellow Pages* or *Thomson Local* for an office near you, or do the whole thing by phone by calling the **Western Union** link-line on 0800 833833. Either service promises to have your money available at its destination within 10 to 15 minutes; fees depend on the amount you send.

CURRENCY EXCHANGE

Most large branches of high street banks offer bureau de change facilities which buy and sell currency for a fee. Larger post offices also provide this service. If you want a foreign currency, it is usually a good idea to order it over the phone or in person before you are going to need it. While most banks will have an adequate stock of the most popular tourist currencies, you may have to wait for a few days for others. Rates of exchange should be displayed and tend to be fairly similar from bank to bank. Some travel agents, for instance Thomas Cook, also offer currency exchange, though their fees tend to be higher. If possible, avoid the bureau de change kiosks you find in tourist areas, as their rates are very poor.

BANK HOLIDAYS

The following are England and Wales' bank holidays (Scotland and Northern Ireland have some different ones). On these dates banks, post offices, schools, and many workplaces are closed. Traditionally this applied to most shops and businesses as well—increasingly though, shops, especially the large chains and supermarkets, are now open for restricted hours on bank holidays.

- 1 January—New Year's Day
- Good Friday
- Easter Monday
- First Monday of May—May Day Bank Holiday
- Last Monday of May—Whit Bank Holiday
- Last Monday of August—August Bank Holiday
- 25 December—Christmas Day
- 26 December (or the following Monday if this falls on Saturday or Sunday)—Boxing Day

COUNCIL TAX

Council tax is payable to the borough in which you are resident. It pays for the services the council provides, from social services to refuse collection. The level is calculated by the value of the property you live in (regardless of whether the property is owned or rented), and varies between boroughs. Some landlords will include council tax in rent, others won't. You can pay the tax all at once or in monthly instalments by a range of payment options. Details will be included with your bill. For more information contact the council tax department of your local authority through the central switchboard number listed under the borough profiles.

VAT

VAT stands for value-added tax, and is added to the price of most goods and services in the UK. The few exceptions include kids' clothes, shaving gear, and books. For the majority of purchases, VAT, which currently runs at 17.5%, is already included in the price displayed. For major services or bulk orders, quotations are sometimes given at a price prior to it being added in which case the code "exclusive of VAT" should appear somewhere.

INCOME TAX

The Inland Revenue, the body that administrates and collects tax in the UK, treats you as a resident if you have come to live here permanently or if you will be here for three years or more. You are considered a UK tax payer if your stay here is for more that 182 days in a tax year (a tax year runs from 6th April until the following 5th April), in which case you are required to pay the UK income tax on all your earned income, and a capital gains tax. The

UK has double taxation agreements with a number of countries, including the USA, Canada, Australia, New Zealand, South Africa, and Ireland, which may entitle you to tax relief. Hopefully your employer will be able to help you out with these matters, but any queries regarding your tax position should be addressed to your tax office—look in the *Yellow Pages* under "Government Offices." For general enquiries phone the Inland Revenue on 020 7667 4001 or visit their web site, www.inlandrevenue.gov.uk.

EUROPEAN SINGLE CURRENCY

The European Single Currency, launched in January 1999 by the European Union, is part of the Economic and Monetary Union process that has a single European market as its goal. The term "euro" refers to the unit of currency. Currently there are 12 countries that have fixed the value of their local currencies to that of the euro, which is in turn controlled by the European Central Bank. In these countries the euro is now the official currency although as yet only non-cash (e.g. credit card) transactions can be conducted in it. National currencies will remain in sole cash use until January 2002 when euro notes and coins will be brought into circulation. The old currencies will then be phased out in a matter of months, leaving the euro as the single currency in these 11 countries. Monetary union with greater Europe is a sensitive political issue in Britain, and so far Britain is one of three member states not to have joined the currency. While Britain is expected to join eventually, it won't be until some point after 2002.

TIPPING

There are few hard and fast conventions regarding tipping in Britain, and if it is any consolation natives are as confused as anyone about when to tip and when not to. In restaurants, service is usually not included in the bill you receive at the end of your meal, and as a general rule, you should leave about a 12.5% tip, although it's up to you to decide how happy you were with the service. However, in some restaurants an "optional" service charge, up to 15%, *is* added to your bill as a matter of course; others add a service charge for parties of more than a certain number. While uncommon, you can deduct this if you are dissatisfied with the service. Bar staff usually are not tipped unless you are in a very upmarket bar or hotel. Taxi drivers should be tipped about 10% to 15%, especially if they have helped with bags and so on, although again it's largely a matter of your discretion.

UTILITIES

THESE ARE THE NECESSITIES YOU'LL WANT TO HAVE SORTED OUT AS soon as possible when you move into a new home. In many rental situations utilities will not be an issue: you will pay an "inclusive" rent which covers gas, electricity, water charges, and sometimes, council tax (for a definition of this see **Money Matters**). While this is the most convenient way of dealing with bills, you may run the risk of over paying. In the case where utilities are not part of your monthly rental payment you will be taking over the accounts of the previous occupants, so it will be a simple matter of phoning the respective companies to change the account to your name. Most utility companies will give you a discount if you opt to pay by direct debit, so be sure to ask if this is available when setting up your accounts.

GAS

Gas tends to the preferred source of energy for cooking and especially for central heating, as it is generally cheaper and more efficient than electricity. In the spring of 1998, the domestic gas market was opened up to competition, allowing domestic consumers to choose their gas suppliers—there are already over ten suppliers from which to choose. Previously **British Gas** was the only domestic supplier, and the majority of households are still buying gas from them. If the previous occupant(s) of your house or flat was with British Gas and the supply is still connected, phone them with your address and postcode, and if possible a meter reading from the date you moved. In the unlikely event that the supply was turned off, phone a couple of days before moving in to ensure reconnection. The only time you are likely to encounter problems is if the previous occupant(s) left a debt, in which case you may have to prove you aren't them! If your new household is not with British Gas, they should still be able to determine which company supplies your home, and you should then contact that company direct.

British Gas bills are issued quarterly and details of how to pay and payment plans are listed on them. Some rental properties have British Gas prepayment charge cards. In order to maintain your supply you will need to take the card to a designated shop, post office, or British Gas showroom and pay to have it charged. Phone British Gas to find out where you can get your card charged.

The new gas companies are now making it easy for you to switch away from British Gas, but beware of the extravagant claims these gas suppliers make. All will claim to be the cheapest and will offer a list of figures to prove it, however, the best deal will depend on volume of use, so be sure to do your research.

- **British Gas**, 0845 955 5510, www.gas.co.uk
- **Transco** 24-hour gas emergency line, if you smell gas or have a leak phone immediately (from your neighbor's phone) on **0800 111 999**.

ELECTRICITY

The electricity market was opened up to competition over the course of 1998 and 1999. There wasn't a national supplier of electricity before this, but regional companies had monopolies in their given locales. You now have the option of choosing your supplier. For those happy to stay with the same electric company as the previous tenants, follow the same path as for gas—phone the current provider with your address and a meter reading from the date you moved in. Again, the supply already will be connected in most properties, but act in advance if it is not.

Some rental properties operate a prepayment key meter system whereby you purchase the electricity you use in advance by charging a key at an electricity showroom, designated post office or shop. Coin meters, which used to be common in rental accommodation for both gas and electricity, fortunately are rare now and are best avoided as they charge at a very prejudicial rate.

- **Eastern Energy**, includes east and north London, 0800 731 3313
- **London Electricity**, covers the majority of the London area, 0800 096 5010
- **Southern Electric**, Ealing, Hounslow and outer west London, 0800 117116

ENERGY EFFICIENCY

There are lots of things you as an individual can do to help conserve the world's valuable energy resources and keep your bills down. For starters, use low energy light bulbs, invest in adequate insulation and ensure your heating system is well maintained. For expert guidance on these matters, call the **Energy Advice Centre** network on 0800 512012.

WATER

If your property has a water meter (only those built in the last ten years are likely to), you will be billed for the amount of water you use. For the remainder of properties without a meter you will receive a quarterly bill at a flat rate, based on the size and value of your property. You can request a meter that will be fitted without cost to you, which makes sense if you are a single person in a large property.

* **Thames Water**, 0645 200800, www.thameswater.com; emergencies: 0845 920 0800

TELEPHONE

Having a phone installed will help you get everything else in your new home set up. In your local London area you'll most likely have a choice between **British Telecom** (**BT**) or a cable phone company, both of which give you the full range of local, national, and international services. BT is still the most popular. For a property where a BT phone line already exists, the hook-up fee is £10, however, installation of a new line will set you back over £100. You can also rent equipment, arrange an answering service and choose additional features such as call waiting and call forwarding. BT may ask to see proof of address and/or identity if you had no previous account with them.

Cable companies offer increasingly competitive service with cheaper line rental and often lower call tariffs. Not all parts of London are wired yet, but the proportion is increasing all the time.

* **British Telecom**, to have a phone line installed, for account queries and other telephone enquiries dial 150; dial 151 to report a fault; finally dial 100 for any difficulty with making a call. If you are phoning these numbers from a network other than BT you may need to add 0800 800 to the beginning.
* **Cable London**, 020 7911 0911, www.cablelondon.co.uk

TOP UP TELEPHONE SERVICES

For those who make a lot of overseas calls it is possible to have a service added to your existing BT or cable account, which offer cheaper rates to national and international destinations. These services are offered by:

* **First Telecom**, 0800 458 9920
* **Primus Global/PlanetTalk**, 0800 036 0002
* **Alpha Telecom**, 0800 279 0000

CALL CHARGES

Rates charged by phone companies vary and take into account time, distance, and tariffs. In addition, you can expect higher rates for calls to and from mobile phones. Both mobile phone and pager numbers have been standardised to begin with "07." All landline area codes start with "01" or "02." Other codes useful to know are:

- **080**; calls made to numbers beginning with this code are free.
- **084**; these numbers are charged at the local rate wherever you are in the UK.
- **087**; these numbers charged at the national rate.
- **09**; designates premium rate services, which cover a range of things from information lines to adult services, and are charged at a more expensive rate than normal.

DIALLING ABROAD

From Great Britain, the access code for all foreign countries is 00. You must then dial a country code before the actual number. So for a New York number you would ring "00," then "1" followed by "212" and finishing with the local seven-digit number. If you experience any problems dialling overseas, call the international operator on 155.

- **Australia**, 61
- **Canada**, 1
- **Ireland**, 353
- **New Zealand**, 64
- **South Africa**, 27
- **United Kingdom**, 44
- **USA**, 1

MOBILE (CELLULAR) PHONE AND PAGING SERVICES

It's nigh on impossible to avoid the mobile phone revolution. At the moment you have a choice between analogue (offered by Vodafone and Cellnet only) and digital phones, but after 2005 they say all phones will be digital. The five companies listed below offer various package deals that take into account how much and what time of day you'll use your phone. If you intend to use your phone sparingly, a "pay as you go" service may make more sense. Phones can be bought on every high street from authorised dealers. To contact the national providers direct see below:

- **Cellnet**, 0800 405 030, www.btcellnet.net
- **One 2 One**, 0500 500 121, www.one2one.co.uk
- **Orange**, 0800 801 080, www.orange.co.uk
- **Vodafone**, 0800 101 112, www.vodafone.co.uk
- **Virgin**, 0845 6000 600, www.virginmobile.com

Pagers also can be bought on any high street, with paging services offered by BT and other companies that advertise in the national press.

CONSUMER COMPLAINTS—UTILITIES

If you receive substandard service, the first step is to complain to the customer service department of the relevant company. If you are unhappy with their response, a regulatory body (or, in the case of gas and electricity, two bodies) exists to oversee each of the privatised utilities:

- **Gas and Electricity**: **EnergyWatch** (The Gas and Electricity Consumers' Council), 0845 906 0708, www.energywatch.org.uk; **Ofgem**, Consumer Affairs, 6th Floor, 16 Palace Street, London, SW1, 0800 887 777, www.ofgem.gov.uk
- **Water**: **Ofwat**, 4th Floor (South), High Holborn House, 52-54 High Holborn, London, W1V, 0845 758 1658, www.ofwat.gov.uk
- **Telephone**: **Oftel**, 50 Ludgate Hill, EC4M, 020 7634 8700, www.oftel.gov.uk

ONLINE SERVICES

To get hooked up to the internet you'll need to choose an internet service provider (ISP). There are hundreds of these and their services are widely advertised in the press. Once you're online, you'll find the amount of information you can access is increasing exponentially all the time. As a matter of course, most businesses and organisations in London have web sites and can be contacted by e-mail.

Listed below are some of the most popular ISPs. All provide different levels of service and most have different subscription packages to suit your surfing needs. Your choice is likely to be affected by call charges, the amount of access you need, whether or not you want a content provider (one which has its own chat rooms and pages), the availability of technical support and general performance, and overall price. For up to date listings and reviews of service providers browse the wide selection of computer magazines available in newsagents and supermarkets.

INTERNET SERVICE PROVIDERS

- **AOL**, 0800 279 1234, www.aol.com
- **BT Internet**, 0800 800001, www.btinternet.com
- **Demon Internet**, 0845 272 2999, www.demon.net
- **ClaraNet**, 0800 358 2828, www.clara.net
- **Global Internet**, 0870 909 8041, www.global.net.uk
- **PlusNet**, 0870 705 8000, www.plus.net

- **Freedom to Surf**, 01727 811530, www.freedom2surf.net
- **Libertysurf**, 0870 730 6466, www.libertysurf.co.uk
- **Which?Online**, 0800 138 8080, www.which.net

FREE INTERNET SERVICE PROVIDERS

Free internet access is becoming more popular all the time. There are plenty of companies offering free unlimited access to the web, but beware of hidden costs such as high call charges. For the latest news on whose offering what, check out the web site, www.net4nowt.com.

- **Freeserve**, 0870 872 0099, www.freeserve.com
- **Virgin Net**, 0500 558800, www.virgin.net

REFUSE COLLECTION AND RECYCLING

All boroughs operate a weekly refuse collection service. You must leave your rubbish in black plastic bin bags in a designated spot outside your home, in a wheelie-bin or metal dustbin in the front yard of a property, or in communal rubbish bin areas. To find out the day your rubbish is collected phone the central council number (listed in the **Borough Profiles**) and ask to be put through to the refuse collection department. Alternatively, ask your neighbours. The council will collect bulkier items like discarded furniture at no charge—again go through the council switchboard to request this service.

Over four million tonnes of rubbish is discarded by Londoners every year. Appallingly only about seven percent of this is recycled. The rest winds up in landfill sites or incinerators. London is rapidly running out of space to dump its trash so recycling is becoming ever more necessary as well as desirable. Some boroughs now make separate collections for recyclables such as paper and glass, but the availability of these schemes varies widely. Borough recycling facilities are more often in the form of banks for paper, bottles and cans (and occasionally cloth). They can often be found in large supermarket car parks as well as other established drop-off points throughout the city. Call your council for more details or check the front pages of the *Thomson Local* and *Yellow Pages*. The central council dump ("tip") in your borough will often provide more extensive recycling facilities for things such as Christmas trees or car batteries, which should not be thrown out with ordinary household waste. Again the address can be obtained from your local council. It is against the law to pour motor oil down the drain, and if you need guidance on its disposal contact the **Oil Bank Line**, 0800 663366. For general recycling advice call **Waste Watch Wasteline** on 0870 243 0136, or visit www.wastewatch.org.uk.

TELEVISION

TV LICENCE

If you own or rent a television, the law states you must have a TV licence—otherwise you face prosecution. Licences can be obtained from TV Licensing via the Post Office, or phone them free on 0800 328 2020. Licences cost £104 (the money funds the BBC), one will suffice for all sets in a household and it's transferable if you change addresses, as long as they're notified. The cost of a licence for a black and white TV is less.

NATIONAL CHANNELS

To receive the five national channels all you need is a television set and an aerial. Most properties have a plug-in socket connected to an aerial on the roof. If not, a set-top aerial may be sufficient. In some areas good reception is hard to get this way and you may want to have an aerial installed on the roof yourself, at a cost of about £100. You'll find the names of installers in the *Yellow Pages* or *Thomson Local*. The five main channels are BBC1, BBC2, ITV, Channel 4 and Channel 5. The ITV network is split into different regional companies—London's is Carlton. TV schedules are widely reprinted in newspapers and magazines. If you are having problems with TV reception and don't want to pay for an aerial, the alternative is to go for cable or satellite television.

CABLE, SATELLITE AND DIGITAL TV

Cable, satellite, and digital TV services offer a huge selection of channels in addition to the five channels listed above. Many sports events, such as big boxing bouts or football matches, are only available if you subscribe to these services. The monthly subscription charge starts at about £19 for the most basic package that includes upwards of 30 channels and pay-per-view facilities. Movies and sports channels are available at a different cost. London's cable telephone and cable television companies are one and the same, so they usually offer deals to encourage you to sign up for both services. To get satellite TV you'll need to buy and install a dish, and subscribe to Sky TV (part of the Fox network), which is the only service available. Digital TV is the latest thing and is rapidly gaining in popularity. To get digital you need a mini-dish or set-top box, which is usually free when you sign up with a service.

- **Cable London**, 020 7911 0911, www.cablelondon.co.uk
- **Sky**, 08702 404040, www.sky.com; offers satellite and digital services.
- **ONdigital**, 0870 600 9696, www.ondigital.co.uk

RADIO STATIONS

London has plenty of radio stations, both licensed and unlicensed. Pirate stations have been a feature of British radio broadcasting since the heyday of Radio Caroline in the 1960s and they continue to plug gaps in the market. Many established licensed stations started out as pirate stations. Whatever your taste in music or talk, you'll find it on London's airwaves. The national BBC radio stations offer a benchmark of high standards, with unrivalled news and current affairs on Radio 4 and excellent sports coverage on Radio 5 Live.

FM

- Radio 2, classic rock and pop, easy listening, 89.1
- Radio 3, classical music, plays, 91.3
- Radio 4, talk, features, plays, current affairs, 93.5
- London Live, pop music, London traffic reports every 30 minutes, news, talk, 94.9
- Capital FM, chart music, traffic updates, 95.8
- Choice, soul music. 96.9
- News Direct, 97.3
- Radio 1, contemporary pop music, 98.8
- Kiss, dance music, 100
- Classic FM, 100.9
- Jazz FM, 102.2
- Greek, 103.3
- XFM, independent/alternative music, 104.9
- Magic, easy listening, torch songs, 105.4
- Virgin, contemporary mainstream rock and pop, 105.8
- Heart, adult-orientated rock and pop, 106.2

AM

- London Turkish Radio, 1584
- Capital Gold, classic pop 50s to 80s, 1548
- Sunrise, Asian, 1458
- Premier Radio, Christian talk, 1332/1305
- Virgin, contemporary and classic pop and rock, 1215
- LBC, talk, 1152
- Talk, sport, 1089/1053
- Ritz, country, 1035
- Liberty, 1970s music, 963/972
- Radio 5 Live, sport, live comment/talk, news, 909/693

- Radio 4, alternative schedule to FM, 720/198
- BBC World Service, 648
- Spectrum, ethnic, gay, 558

DRIVER'S LICENCE AND AUTOMOBILE REGISTRATION

The minimum age requirements for holding a driver's licence in Britain are 17 years for cars and motorcycles, 18 years for medium-sized goods vehicles and 21 for lorries and buses.

Overseas **visitors** carrying full car/motorcycle driving licences may drive any category of vehicle shown on their licence for up to a period of 12 months, from the date of entering Britain.

RESIDENTS—DESIGNATED COUNTRIES

New residents from a number of designated countries including Australia, Hong Kong, New Zealand, and Zimbabwe, holding a full valid license from their country of origin are allowed to drive small vehicles for 12 months from the time they became resident. To ensure continued driving entitlement, a Great Britain licence must be obtained before the end of this period. If you don't do this, you must stop driving, although you may apply to exchange your licence at any time within five years of becoming a resident. New residents are not entitled to drive medium or large class vehicles until they have swapped their licences for British equivalents. To exchange your licence, you'll need to complete a D1 application form (available from Driver and Vehicle Licensing Agency (DVLA) or post offices). The rules specify that you must have a permanent address in Great Britain and that the licence you are exchanging must be current at the time of application.

RESIDENTS—FROM NON-DESIGNATED COUNTRIES (INCLUDING USA AND CANADA)

Ordinary licence holders (car/motorcycle) can drive the category of vehicle detailed on their native licence for up to 12 months. To carry on driving after this point, you must obtain a provisional GB (Great Britain) licence and you must pass a driving test before the 12 months is up. Usually, when learning to drive in Great Britain and in possession of a provisional licence you would be subject to various conditions including supervision and display of "L" (for learner) plates. These conditions do not apply if you are in possession of an overseas licence. However if you do not pass the test during the 12 months, you will revert to being provisional licence holder and these rules will apply. To get a provisional driving licence you need to fill out a D1 application form (available from DVLA or post offices), to be returned to the DVLA.

New residents may not drive large vehicles until the relevant driving test has been passed in Britain. Drivers must pass a motor car (category B) test before going on to apply for provisional licence for larger vehicles.

For further information or application forms, call **DVLA Customer Enquiries** on 01792 772151, between 8:15 a.m. and 4:30 p.m., Monday-Friday.

VEHICLE REGISTRATION, TAX, AND MOT

All resident vehicles must have a registration document from the DVLA giving details of ownership and specifications of the vehicle. With the purchase of a vehicle, notification must be given to the DVLA so that a registration document can be issued. Legal operation of vehicles in the UK requires insurance, a displayed Vehicle Excise Duty disc (known as a tax disc), and for automobiles over three years old, a MOT road-worthiness certificate. (MOT stands for Ministry of Transport, which no longer exists—it is now the Department of Transport, Environment and the Regions.) MOT tests are performed at garages that are designated test centres. Motor insurance can be bought from many banks and building societies as well as from hundreds of companies you'll find listed under "Insurance Agents" in the *Yellow Pages* and *Thomson Local*. Tax discs can be purchased from the post office once you've acquired the necessary vehicle registration document, the insurance certificate, and, if necessary, the MOT certificate.

PARKING, TOWING

Parking is a major headache for Londoners with cars. The preponderance of terraced streets, which were built before cars existed, makes for insufficient space for the residents of any given street, let alone visitors. The most common parking restrictions are designated by lines along the edge of the road. Single yellow lines signify at least some parking restrictions, though you may stop to let someone out or pick someone up. Double yellow lines usually mean no parking at any time except to let someone in or out. Red lines indicate "red routes" that are designed to keep traffic flowing; never stop along these except at designated loading bays—posted street signs will give full details regarding parking restrictions.

In order to find a parking space in the centre of town, your most reliable, if not cheapest, option is to go to a **National Car Parks** (**NCP**) multi-storey car park, which charges at an hourly rate. NCP car parks are clearly sign posted. In many parts of London, both in the city centre and in local residential areas, there are additional restrictions on parking. Some areas have parking meters that charge by the hour. Local areas frequently operate resident only parking where permits are administered and issued by the council. You can contact the parking division through the central switchboard number (given in the **Borough Profiles**) to find out more about local schemes. If your car is parked illegally it is liable to be ticketed (a notice will be placed under your windscreen wiper and will include details of how to pay the fine), or even clamped and towed away—an even heftier fine awaits you in this instance. The borough in which your car was parked illegally will be the one to contact if it has been towed or clamped.

* **NCP Infoline**, 020 7404 3777

MOTORING ORGANISATIONS

These organisations offer breakdown coverage:
* **Automobile Association (AA)**, 0800 444999, www.theaa.com
* **Environmental Transport Association**, 0800 212810, www.eta.co.uk
* **Green Flag**, 0800 001391, www.greenflag.co.uk
* **Royal Automobile Club (RAC)**, 0800 550550, www.rac.co.uk

IDENTIFICATION

There is no universal identification card in existence in the UK. When asked to provide proof of identity for official purposes some of the things people use include driver's licence, passport, birth certificate, credit card, and official letters (from a bank or utility company for example). When asked to show proof of your address, say in the case of joining a library or video shop, the latter will usually suffice.

REGISTERING TO VOTE

British citizens and citizens of the Republic of Ireland are entitled to vote in elections in Britain. In order to exercise your right to vote your name must appear on the electoral register or roll, which is published annually on 16 February. To qualify you must be over 18 years old and living at your address by 10 October in the year prior to the publication of the register. Each year the local council sends out registration forms, which must be filled out and returned to secure voting rights. Get in touch with your local council if you have any queries.

PASSPORTS

You can pick up a UK Passport Agency application pack from any main post office. The pack includes all the relevant information about who can apply for a UK passport, the application process, the costs involved and the documents and references which must be provided. For urgent applications, go in person with your completed application to the London Office at Clive House, 70 Petty France, SW1H, open from 8:15 a.m. until 4 p.m. This office is specifically for urgent personal applications so go prepared to queue and, if possible, take evidence of your need to travel. For information phone 0870 521 0410. Note that only British citizens, British Dependent Territories citizens, British Nationals, British Overseas citizens, British Subjects and British Protected Persons are eligible to apply for a UK passport.

VITAL STATISTICS

The registration of births, deaths, and marriages takes place on a local authority level within London. Please refer to the front of the *Yellow Pages* or phone the central council number for your borough (listed here under **Borough Profiles**). In cases of births and deaths, medical staff will be able to advise you of procedures.

LIBRARY

All you need to do to join your local library is fill out an application and provide proof of your name and address. A library card is valid for all borough libraries. The addresses of local libraries are listed at the end of each borough profile. Most libraries will try to order books for you if they do not have them, or reserve books which are out on loan. Membership of the British Library on the Euston Road, a superb academic resource, is currently free but requires a recommendation from a university source.

NEWSPAPERS AND MAGAZINES

For such a large city, London has surprisingly few city-wide publications. Instead there are many local weekly newspapers on sale at newsagents that provide neighbourhood news and listings. Freesheets, truncated versions of such publications, are often posted through letterboxes. London's main, city-wide daily is the *Evening Standard* which, in addition to local, national, and international news stories, carries reviews, features and financial pages. Over the years various attempts, all unsuccessful, have been made to break the *Standard*'s stranglehold on the market. In addition there is *Metro*, a free daily given out at Tube stations during the morning rush hour. It was launched by the same company as the *Standard* as a pre-emptive strike against potential competitors. *Metro*'s content is a slimmed down version of the *Standard*'s with national and local news, short features and listings. The popular weekly magazine *Time Out* started out as a listings magazine, and its listings remain the best and most comprehensive to be found, but it is widely read for its features and celebrity interviews too. *What's On In London* is a straightforward listings magazine. *The Big Issue* is sold on the streets by the homeless and ex-homeless and gives respected coverage of community issues like policing, housing, and the environment, as well as listings and reviews. There are dozens of freesheets which are given out at Tube stations or which can be picked up at stands on the street. Among them are *LAM, Southern Cross, Footloose* etc., which are aimed at newcomers to London and often have interesting articles and suggestions for those just arrived in town. It is worth remembering that as all the national daily papers are based in London, they pay a lot of attention to London news stories and events. *The Voice* is the largest national black community newspaper that again tends to be biased towards London.

CITY WEB SITES

- **www.londontown.com**; the London Tourist Board's official internet site for London with everything from tourist attractions and accommodation to financial services and travel.
- **www.thisislondon.com**; *Evening Standard's* web site with particularly strong entertainment listings.
- **www.timeout.com**, *Time Out's* web site.
- **www.london-calling.co.uk**, current listings of entertainment and culture in the capital.

MAIL DELIVERY

Mail delivery in Britain is handled by one of the few remaining nationalised companies, the Royal Mail. Mail can be sent either by first class or second class post. First class does not guarantee next day delivery but it greatly enhances the chances. Using a full postcode is advisable; for **postcode information**, ring 0345 111222 or visit www.royalmail.com. In addition to regular deliveries at home and abroad, the Royal Mail offers a range of premium services which insure the contents of your mail, guarantee delivery and so on. Parcelforce handles the delivery of parcels. To find out about any of these services ask at your local post office or call the **Post Office customer helpline** on 0345 223344. In most areas mail is delivered twice every day, usually in the morning and then again in late morning, but times vary significantly. If you experience any problems, contact the **Royal Mail** on 0345 740740, or write to the Customer Service Centre, Royal Mail, FREEPOST, 6 St. Pancras Way, London, NW1 1AA.

PET LAWS AND SERVICES

If you're considering bringing a pet with you to the UK you need to bear in mind that any pet brought into the UK is subject to a mandatory quarantine period of six months. This is a measure designed to keep rabies out of the country, and as such it has been entirely successful. But many people have now come to the conclusion that the system is overly harsh. If your move to the UK is permanent, by all means bring the family pet. However, horror stories of ill-treatment and, occasionally the death of pets in custody, suggest that if your move is temporary it might be advisable to leave your pet in the care of someone in your home country. The UK's ultra-strict quarantine laws have come under a lot of scrutiny recently and a more flexible system is being developed.

The Dangerous Dogs Act of 1992 states that certain breeds of dogs (pit bulls, rottweilers, etc.) are classed as dangerous and must be muzzled in public. Local council bylaws cover dog owners' responsibilities. The rules are generally simple: keep your dog on a leash in built-up areas and do not allow them to foul the footpath. Your dog may come off its leash in most open areas such as parks and recreation grounds, except where there are signs up to the contrary (some children's play areas are dog-free zones for instance). There is no legal requirement for you to clean up after your dog, but it obviously makes for a much nicer and safer environment for us all if you do. Most parks have dog waste bins—use them!

Abandoned or lost dogs, and some cats, usually end up in Battersea Dogs Home (number listed below). They offer adoptions of these dogs or cats, which are vaccinated and micro-chipped. The Cats Protection League also picks up abandoned or stray cats and kittens, and has local branches that are listed in the *Yellow Pages* and *Thomson Local*. Note that some housing developments and many landlords have a no pets rule.

Local veterinary surgeries can be found listed in the phone directories. Veterinarian bills are notoriously high. One way of circumventing this is to take out pet insurance. This costs about £10 a month and is available through agencies that advertise in the national press. The Peoples Dispensary For Sick Animals (PDSA) operates several free clinics in London intended for those who can't afford vet bills—again look in the phone book for contact details. The Royal Society for the Prevention of Cruelty to Animals (RSPCA) has local animal hospitals where casualties, both domestic and wild, can be taken. They can be contacted on the number below.

- **RSPCA**, 24-hour helpline, 0870 5555 999
- **Battersea Dogs Home**, 4 Battersea Park Road, SW8, 020 7622 3626

SAFETY

As is the case in all the major cities of the world, crime and the fear of crime are major issues for the residents of London. Most property theft is opportunistic and risks to your belongings can be minimised by taking sensible precautions. Window locks are advisable, especially if you live on the ground floor. Buy a burglar alarm if you can afford it—visible security is a deterrent. Neighbourhood Watch Schemes operate in some areas whereby residents make a point of looking out for suspicious activity in their area. Stranger on stranger crimes are usually muggings. It's best not to use cash machines late at night, especially if you're on your own and there are few people about. If you feel you are being watched or followed, try to make your way purposefully to a more populated street. In busy areas the risk of falling victim to pickpockets and bag snatchers is higher. Place valuables in inside pockets or carry your bag securely. Unfortunately the current licensing laws in Britain mean that most pubs shut at 11 p.m. This can mean large numbers of drunken people converging on the streets and Tubes at the same time. The good news is that these outdated licensing laws are slowly changing with more late licences being granted to city centre venues. But if you are out and about around 11 p.m., try to avoid groups of aggressive or drunk people. Random violent crime or hate crime is rare but unfortunately does occur, but happily, due to strict laws, the likelihood of guns being involved is small. If you are a victim of crime, report it to the police as soon as possible. Go to the nearest police station or call 999 for immediate assistance or if you are witness to a crime. **Victim Support** can be reached on 0845 303 0900. In the event that you can provide information about a crime but do not want to give your name, call **Crimestoppers** free on 0800 555555.

A S YOU SETTLE IN AND GET ORGANISED YOU'LL WANT TO TAKE care of some general services, including registering with a doctor and dentist—before an emergency occurs—finding out about package delivery services, and perhaps tracking down a housekeeper. Also included here are resources for people with disabilities, including a section on getting around the city, and organisations and helplines. At the end of the chapter is a resource section on lesbian and gay life.

First get hold of some telephone directories where you'll find many suppliers and services. To order a free copy of the *Yellow Pages* ring 0800 671444 or go to www.yell.co.uk; the *Thomson Local* hotline is 01252 555555, www.thomweb.co.uk. Both the *Yellow Pages* and the *Thomson Local* list businesses by category. The *British Telecom (BT) Business and Services Phone Book*, which you receive free if you are a BT customer, lists companies alphabetically by name and is the only directory to cover the whole of the London postal district. You can also access directory information (at no cost) over the phone through *Talking Pages* on 0800 600900 or *Scoot* on 0800 192192; online go to www.scoot.com.

HEALTHCARE

In Britain, a basic level of healthcare is guaranteed by the **National Health Service (NHS)** offering free medical treatment to those "ordinarily resident" in the UK, though there are charges for dental treatment and prescriptions. Although not defined by law, "ordinarily resident" usually is taken to mean someone who has been living legally in the country for at least six months. Be aware that although treatment is free, the wait for some non-urgent operations through the NHS or for services such as psychotherapy can be months. Britain has reciprocal health agreements with many European countries which means visitors from those countries can access free treatment if the need arises during their stay. If you do not come from one of the countries covered by such an agreement, and your stay is for less than six months, then private medical insurance is advisable. However, emergency treatment is given free to residents and visitors alike. For information on NHS service provision and general health and treatment queries contact the **Health Information Service** on 0800 665544. For questions about NHS eligibility, contact the **Bilateral Health Agreement** on 020 7210 5318.

In order to receive general medical services through the NHS, you'll need to **register with a local General Practitioner** (GP) in your local area—usually defined as within a mile or so of your home. Doctors can refuse to register someone if they choose (though they rarely do). You are not bound to this physician, and you can switch doctors if necessary. Specific rules vary according to which health authority you live in—call the Health Information Service (see above) for more guidance. You should not have much difficulty registering but you should be aware that some practices are over-subscribed, especially in the inner-city areas, and waiting times for appointments can be long.

Registering with a dentist as an NHS patient also depends on filling the "ordinarily resident" criteria. Under the NHS you will be charged at least £5 for a dental examination and 80% of the cost of treatment (children, pregnant women, and some other groups are exempt from charges). In addition some dentists in private practice take NHS patients. Choosing a good dentist is largely a matter of luck but workmates or friends may have recommendations.

For immediate advice or information on any symptom or health concerns, call **NHS Direct** on 0845 4647. This service is available 24 hours a day.

MEDICENTRES

If you have not registered with a doctor or find it difficult to get an appointment at a convenient time, you might want to visit a medicentre. These are private, walk-in clinics that provide on-the-spot diagnosis and prescriptions for a basic fee of £40. Some medicentres are open at weekends. A whole host of other medical services are available too at various prices. There are clinics at Euston, Victoria, and Waterloo mainline stations, and Oxford Street Plaza. They are open for longer hours than most doctors' surgeries, no appointment is necessary for an initial consultation. For more information call 0870 600 0870, www.medicentre.co.uk.

EMERGENCIES

Dial 999 to summon an ambulance if you are at the scene of an accident or if someone falls ill in public; likewise to call the police or fire services. If you or a member of your family are taken ill at home, contact your doctor—if the surgery is shut, an emergency number will be given on an answering machine. If you are not registered with a doctor, dial **999**.

RENTAL SERVICES

As London's market in rented property is weighted in favour of furnished flats, furniture rental stores are rare. For those buying a property or renting unfurnished, purchasing furniture on credit or second hand are ways to minimise the initial costs. However, one major high street chain, **Box Clever**, will rent out the full range of electrical goods: televisions, VCRs, washing machines, tumble dryers, refrigerators, and computers. There is usually a minimum rental period of about 18 months. The *Yellow Pages* lists Box Clever under "TV and Video Rental," and can also be consulted for listings of smaller, local firms. In addition there are two national network companies with freephone numbers:

- **Direct Vision Rentals**, 0800 585149
- **Capital Rentals**, 0800 458 6808

CONSUMER PROTECTION

Many service suppliers, be they travel agents or plumbers, are members of a trade association or professional body. Some of these associations regulate their members, which is some indication of quality work and good customer service, other associations are just a compiled list of members in that trade. They are all listed at the back of the *Yellow Pages* and should be contacted individually with enquiries about what membership means. The **Consumers' Association** provides advice and guidance on a wide range of consumer issues in the magazine *Which?* Call them on 0800 252100.

Each local authority in London has a **Trading Standards Office**, which should be able to take up any complaint you have regarding faulty, dangerous or wrongly-advertised goods. Contact your central council and ask to be put through to Trading Standards. Nationally the relevant body is the **Office of Fair Trading** who can direct you to help; call 0845 722 4499.

The **Advertising Standards Authority** exists to ensure advertisers do not mislead or offend. Write, giving details of your complaint, to ASA, 2 Torrington Place, London WC1E 7HW.

The **Citizens Advice Bureau (CAB)** offers free information and advice on a range of issues such as housing, employment rights, and consumer advice. There is a network of offices throughout London. You can usually turn up during drop-in times and wait your turn or phone for an appointment. Best to phone first to check opening times and to find out if you need to book an appointment. For details of your nearest CAB, look in the *Yellow Pages* under "Counselling and Advice" or get in touch with the **National**

Association of Citizens Advice Bureau at 115-123 Pentonville Road, London N1, 020 7833 2181, www.nacab.org.uk, www.advice.org.uk.

DOMESTIC SERVICES

Domestic cleaning companies, dry cleaners, and gardeners are listed in the directories under these categories, as well as often advertising their services in the local press. Note that there are dry cleaners on most major and minor high streets so delivery is not typical and those that do deliver are significantly more expensive.

PEST CONTROL

The capital's antiquated sewer system has given birth to the oft-quoted and very unsavoury urban myth that in London you are never more than a few yards from a rat. Rats, mice, cockroaches, fleas ... they are all apt to thrive in the urban environment. Hopefully you won't encounter any such unpleasantness, however, if you do, you can call the council's pest control department through your council switchboard or contact one of the pest control agencies listed in the directories. At no cost to you the council will deal with rodent or insect problems in gardens and communal areas, though there may be a waiting list. There is a charge for inside treatments.

PACKAGE DELIVERY

For same-day deliveries around London, there are several courier firms. These are listed in the phone books under "Courier Services" and "Delivery and Collection Services." The following are some of those that do international deliveries:

- **ParcelForce**, 0800 224466, www.parcelforce.com, ParcelForce services are the only ones available over the counter at Post Offices.
- **DHL**, 0345 100300, www.dhl.com
- **Federal Express**, 0800 123800, www.fedex.com/gb
- **UPS**, 0345 877877, www.ups.com

MOVING AND STORAGE

Moving and storage services are listed in the directories under "Removals" and "Storage." A good selection of these advertise in *Loot* and local papers. If you need a removals firm, be aware that in Britain this is an unregulated industry. The choice is whether to pay for a bona fide removals firm, which is a member of the British Association of Removers (a trade association) and so adheres to accepted standards of practice, or to find a much cheaper "man with a van." Members of the BAR must provide you with a "schedule of service" which puts in writing the details of the job to be undertaken. The BAR will also deal with complaints regarding its member companies. If you choose a firm which is not a member of BAR, you have little legal recourse if things go wrong. Always ask for an estimate of the total cost, and whether hourly charges include petrol and the amount of time it takes the driver to get to you. Contact the British Association of Removers, 3 Churchill Court, 58 Station Road, HA2, 020 8861 3331 for more details.

Storage service comes with varying degrees of professionalism and security. The following are some of the major chains with branches all over London, which offer a good range of self-storage options:

- **Abacus Self Storage**, 0800 122522; storage space ranging from 20 square feet to 10,000 square feet; 13 branches in the London area.
- **Abbey Self-Storage**, 0800 622244, www.abbey-self-storage.co.uk; offers small scale storage for tourists and backpackers as well as options for large-scale storage.
- **Acorn Storage Centres**, 0500 202700
- **Safe Store**, 0800 731 8787

RESOURCES FOR PEOPLE WITH DISABILITIES

There are nearly a million people with disabilities in London. Although services for disabled people are not as good as they could be, they are improving all the time. There are a number of highly active organisations dealing with all kinds of issues, from employment, mobility, and housing, to arts and leisure. More and more sections of the public transport network can be used by disabled people with the Jubilee line extension ushering in a new era of accessibility. Likewise, access to cinemas and theatres is getting easier, with venues like the Royal National Theatre offering wheelchair spaces, front seats for the visually impaired, induction loops (which clarify sound for hearing aid users) and sign language interpreted performances. Generally, the newer the building, the better its facilities. Phone your prospective venue or Artsline, 020 7388 2227, minicom, 020 7388 7373, for details. For a comprehensive guide on how to get the most out of London if you have a disability, buy a copy of *Access in London* by Couch, Forrester and Irwin.

GETTING AROUND

For general public transport information see the **Transport** chapter. Disabled people can take advantage of a door-to-door transport service called **Dial-A-Ride**. For more details, contact the operations centre serving your area:

- **North London**, 020 8829 1200
- **Northeast London**, 020 8498 8200
- **South London**, 020 8784 6016
- **Southeast London**, 01689 896333
- **West London**, 020 8970 0090
- **Central London**, 020 7266 6100

PARKING

The Orange Badge Scheme gives people with disabilities parking conces-
sions, enabling close access to their destination. Application forms are available from your local council. The scheme does not apply at off-street car
parks or in certain parts of central London. A leaflet, also available in Braille,
large print, and on tape, offers detailed terms and conditions, and can be
requested from the **Department of the Environment, Transport and
the Regions**. Write to the Disability Policy Branch, Mobility Unit, Zone
1/11, Great Minster House, 76 Marsham Street, London SW1P 4DR.

COMMUNICATION

Typetalk is a national telephone relay system available for the deaf, hard of
hearing, and speech impaired. It is run jointly by the **Royal National
Institute for Deaf People** (**RNID**) and British Telecom, and works
through operator relay. In order to have access to this service you will need
a textphone—a phone with a keyboard and a small screen—and, if necessary, a visual ringing device. You can then register at no cost with Typetalk
(see below). If you have a textphone you can also communicate directly
with other textphones, although not many organisations have these.
Textphone numbers are usually denoted as "minicom" numbers (after the
brand name of the phones) and are given in this book where they exist.
Advice about where to buy a textphone should be sought from the RNID.

Signers should note that British Sign Language (BSL) differs consider-
ably from American Sign Language as it uses both hands rather than one.
For more information contact RNID:

- **RNID (Royal National Institute for Deaf People)**, 19-23
  Featherstone Street, EC1Y, 020 7296 8000, minicom: 020 7296 8001,
  www.rnid.org.uk
- **Typetalk**, John Wood House, Glacier Building, Harrington Road,
  Brunswick Business Park, Liverpool L3 4DF, 0151 709 9494; fax: 0151
  709 8119; minicom: 0800 500888, office hours are 9 a.m. to 5 p.m.

ORGANISATIONS & HELPLINES

Most boroughs have a disability association in place to assist with the services in your area. Consult the *Yellow Pages* under "Disabled—Information and Services" for a complete list. The following are London-wide or national organisations with helplines:

- **Artsline**, 54 Charlton Street, NW1, 020 7388 2227; minicom: 020 7388 7373; information service on aspects of the arts by and for disabled people, including details on accessibility, sign language interpretations, touch exhibitions etc.
- **British Sports Association for the Disabled**, Solecast House, 13-27 Brunswick Place, N1, 020 7490 4919
- **Disability Alliance**, Universal House, 88-94 Wentworth Street, E1, phone/minicom: 020 7247 8776; Rights Line, 020 7247 8763, produces *Disability Rights Handbook*.
- **Disability Law Service**, Room 241, 49 Bedford Row, WC1, 020 7831 8031; free law and advisory service.
- **RADAR**, 12 City Forum, 250 City Road, EC1V, 020 7250 3222, minicom: 020 7250 4119; umbrella organisation working to remove barriers. Telephone information service.
- **RNIB (Royal National Institute for the Blind)**, 224 Great Portland Street, W1N, 020 7388 1266
- **SHAPE**, 356 Holloway Road, N7, 020 7700 8138, fax: 020 7700 8143, minicom: 020 7700 8144, runs a ticket scheme providing reduced rate tickets, drivers, escorts and a specialised booking service.
- **SPOD (Association to Aid the Sexual and Personal Relationships of People with Disabilities)**, 286 Camden Road, N7, 020 7607 8851

CAMPAIGNING ORGANISATIONS

For those looking to get involved in the active disabled civil rights movement, call or write to the **British Council of Organisations of Disabled People**, Litchurch Plaza, Litchurch Lane, Derby, DE24, 01332 295 551.

LESBIAN & GAY LIFE

After arriving in the capital it won't be long before you realise that lesbian and gay life is part of the everyday here. That is not to say that prejudice or discrimination doesn't exist, but it does mean that you should never have to feel alone or bereft of help. There's a flourishing sector of bars, clubs, and shops that cater to the urban gay lifestyle. The annual pride parade and festival attracts hundreds of thousands of revellers. There are concentrations of gay-owned and gay-friendly shops and bars in Soho, Covent Garden, and Earls Court, as well as lesbian and gay venues in all the inner boroughs and most of the outer ones. *Time Out* and the gay press (see below) list selections of bars and clubs, and once you're at one, you can pick up flyers and freesheets for others. If nightlife is not your bag, there are all manner of social groups covering a wide range of interests and concerns, from choirs to swimming teams to reading groups. See the **Volunteering** chapter for community organisations.

- *Attitude*, fashion conscious monthly men's magazine slanted towards gay lifestyle.
- *Boyz*, men's fun weekly freesheet with listings, gossip and lots of personal ads.
- *Diva*, a monthly national lesbian lifestyle magazine offering the best coverage of lesbian concerns, news, features, classified ads and bar/club listings, available from most bookshops and larger newsagents; www.gaytimes.co.uk.
- *Gay Times*, a monthly, male-orientated gay magazine which carries comprehensive listings, widely available in bookshops and newsagents; www.gaytimes.co.uk.
- *The Pink Paper*, a weekly nationally distributed free paper covering current lesbian and gay issues, it also carries extensive classified ads including accommodation offered and personals. Available in bookshops and newsagents.

ADVICE AND SUPPORT

For those needing personal and confidential support, there are a number of helplines:

- **London Lesbian & Gay Switchboard**, 020 7837 7324, offers advice, referral, general information; 24 hour.
- **National Aids Helpline**, 0800 567123, 24 hour
- **Gay & Lesbian Legal Advice Line** 020 7831 3535
- **Lesbian & Gay Employment Rights** (**LAGER**), 020 7704 8066 (lesbians), 020 7704 6066 (gay men), for advice and support on discrimination at work.

L ONDON IS A STIMULATING, VIBRANT, AND VARIED ENVIRONMENT in which to bring up a family, but it can also be a daunting one. For those moving here with a family in tow, one of your most pressing concerns will be to ensure that your children are happy, and finding good childcare and schooling will be a priority. This chapter offers a synopsis of the English education system and an overview of the childcare options available. Try to access as many official resources as possible, but remember that the best advice will often come from other parents with similarly aged children, as there is no substitute for their knowledge and experience.

DAY CARE

In the last few years childcare has moved up on the political agenda, with changes in European law filtering down to the national level, bringing enhanced maternity and paternity leave for working parents. There is increasing recognition of the pressures working parents face when trying to juggle home and work. Some particularly progressive workplaces have crèches (on-site day care) but this is still relatively rare. Many people rely on family and informal childcare networks, which arise from local baby, toddler and parents' groups. You can find details of such groups and activities advertised in borough libraries or the local press. Working parents who cannot call on the services of relatives or trusted friends often find a childminder or day nursery. Each council has an early years service that registers childminders and inspects day nurseries. Registration is not a cast-iron guarantee of a childminder's competence but it does mean references have been provided, they have been subject to police checks, and their premises have been inspected. Formal qualification or training is not required. Contact your local council for a list (council numbers are listed under the **Borough Profiles**). Day care nurseries are inspected regularly and must conform to certain safety guidelines—they can be found in the *Yellow Pages* or *Thomson Local*.

NANNIES

Probably the most expensive day care option is hiring a nanny—although if the right person is found this can be a rewarding experience for everyone involved. Currently there are no national registering requirements for nannies. You will find nannies advertising their services in local papers and magazines, and on notice-boards in libraries or at baby, toddler, and parents' groups. There is also a London-wide childcare listings magazine called *Simply Childcare* (see below). Parents in turn often advertise their need for a nanny through similar routes. One of the most popular ways of recruiting a nanny is to go through an agency. There are hundreds of these, but your best bet may be to go with an agency that is registered with the Federation of Recruitment and Employment Services. This has a code of practice, which at least gives you the assurance that the nannies have been interviewed and their references checked (although it's best to double-check references yourself). Going through an agency is an expensive prospect—fees of up to £1,000 is common—but, in terms of peace of mind and time saved, some find the price well worth paying. Nannies may offer various qualifications, the most common being the NNEB diploma (this stands for the National Nursery Education Board) signifying a completed two-year course at a College of Further Education. Diplomas may also come from three independent colleges: the Princess Christian, the Chiltern, and the Norland. Further education colleges also offer B-Tec and National Vocational Qualifications (NVQs) in childcare. A nanny costs less if you provide food and board; for a live-out nanny you can expect to pay around £250 a week. If you are struggling to meet such costs or only need part-time help, you might want to consider nanny-sharing: a nanny either looks after the children of two families together full-time, or else splits her time between the two.

- **Simply Childcare** is London's childcare listings magazine, to subscribe or find out more phone 020 7701 6111 or visit www.simplychildcare.com.

AU PAIRS AND MOTHER'S HELPS

Au pairs and mother's helps are usually hired to do some light housework and bear some childcare responsibilities. They are often English Language students from European countries. Au pair agencies can be found under "Nannies and Childcare" in the *Yellow Pages* or *Thomson Local*. As with nannies, you are strongly advised to double-check references before hiring.

PARENTING HELP

Playgroups and toddler groups are often great ways to get in touch with local parents. Aimed at children, ages two to four, playgroup centres allow parents to leave their children at a scheduled time, in the care of trained staff. Toddler groups operate on a less formal drop-in basis and parents or caregivers remain with their children, offering the chance for parents to get to know each other and swap information. There are also play-gyms, themed playgroups, and many other variations, so ask around.

When it comes to finding **sitters**, parents are pretty much left to their own devices as there are no national or local registering schemes. References from co-workers or friends are really the only way to go when looking for a competent and reliable babysitter. Again, local networks of parents often arrange to look after each other's children. Nanny agencies sometimes have babysitters on their books.

London has an excellent chain of bi-monthly magazines aimed at parents with young children: *Families North*, *Families South East*, *Families South West*, and *Families West/Families on Thames*. These publications contain well-informed articles on childcare issues and are full of lots of helpful suggestions and tips. They can be picked up free at local libraries and venues that provide services to babies and toddlers.

NURSERY SCHOOLS

State nursery schools are available either free or on a means tested sliding scale for children aged from about three (they must be potty-trained) to five years old. You may choose from all the council nurseries or nursery classes attached to primary schools within your local area. Ask around for recommendations and be sure to investigate each establishment for yourself as standards vary. Contact the local education authority, via the central council switchboard, for a list of nursery schools in your borough. Once you have decided on a school you like, act swiftly as the most popular fill up quickly.

Private nursery schools will sometimes take children as young as age one. Parents often put their child's name down for the most prestigious private nursery schools within weeks of their birth in order to try to maximise enrolment chances. For full lists, including Montessori schools and those run by religious organisations, look under "Nursery Schools" in the *Yellow Pages* or *Thomson Local*. Information can also be had from the **Pre-School Learning Alliance**, 69 King's Cross Road, WC1, 020 7833 0991, www.pre-school.org.uk.

SCHOOLS

For permanent residents or for those staying longer than six months, full-time education is compulsory for children between the ages of five and sixteen. When Tony Blair's Government came to power in 1997, its priorities were announced as "education, education and education," recognising the fact that providing the best education for Great Britain's kids has become something of a national obsession in recent years. Educational opportunities and test scores vary dramatically from area to area and from school to school, despite the presence of a National Curriculum which dictates what subjects are taught and how. Blair's initiatives have included targets for literacy and numeracy and new guidelines on everything from homework to sex education.

All schools, state run and private, are subject to inspections by a body called **Ofsted (Office for Standards in Education)** which has a policy of "naming and shaming" failing schools. A school with a good reputation is one of the factors that increases real estate values in a neighbourhood. In London the situation is particularly edgy. State schools in some boroughs have such a poor image that parents will do almost anything to find their kids a place in a school in another borough. Some parents opt for private or religious schools. Beleaguered teachers in inner-city state schools argue that special circumstances exist, such as high levels of poverty and a large proportion of children with English as a second language, and that more realistic approaches to assessing student achievement is needed. Whatever the case, you'll find no shortage of differing perspectives and opinions on the state of education in London.

STATE SCHOOLS

Britain educates its children through state schools which are broken down by age into primary (ages 5 to 11) and secondary (ages 11 to 16). Schools that serve primary age children are sometimes further broken down into infants and juniors.

At secondary school children study in five age groups ("years" or "forms") with the aim of passing General Certificates of Secondary Education, known as GCSEs, in their final fifth year. Most secondary schools also offer a sixth-form for 16 to 18 year olds who have chosen to stay at school to do "A-levels"—the qualifications needed to enable them to go to university. Separate sixth-form colleges also exist.

Primary state schools are run by the local education authority (part of the council) which will be able to provide you with a list of schools in your area and their performance tables. State secondary schools include both those that are run by the local education authority and those that have opted out of local authority control to become "foundation schools." Foundation status means they are funded through a direct grant from the Government's Department of Education and Employment. Before 1999 some of these foundation secondary schools operated a selective admissions policy choosing pupils either through exams or interviews, and often achieved higher standards as a result. The selective procedure also meant that children from further afield could win places at schools that were perhaps not the closest to them—allowing for the "middle-class drift" effect of parents trying to escape the schools nearest them. However, beginning in 1999, schools were no longer allowed to choose pupils in this manner. Now the only state schools that do select pupils on the basis of ability are those which specialise in a particular field such as music or sports. If you have a child of secondary school age it's a good idea to research your local state schools, both those within your borough and in adjacent boroughs. Each school has a catchment area—proximity to a school—and that will be the biggest factor in your child's chances of getting a place, after it's the presence of siblings. Single sex girls' secondary schools often achieve higher standards than mixed schools, and the popularity of girls' schools has left some co-ed schools heavily male-dominated. The annual Ofsted report, as well as annual performance tables that rank schools by test and exam results, are the guides most parents use when making the decision about where to send their children. You'll find performance tables and summaries of Ofsted reports in the press at the time of their publication, or they can also be ordered direct (see below). Many argue that these reports do not tell the whole story about a school and that it is best to make your own enquiries, and visit, visit, visit. There are schools with good standards to be found in boroughs with poor reputations.

PRIVATE SCHOOLS

About seven percent of children in Britain are privately educated. Schools for which fees are paid are known as "private," "fee-paying," or "independent" schools (those for under the age of 13 are also known as "preparatory"). Confusingly for Americans, these used to be called, and are still sometimes referred to as, "public" schools! Most private schools are day schools, though there are several famous English boarding schools such Harrow and Eton in and around London. Most private schools are single sex and choose pupils either by exam or interview or both. Competition for places in private schools in inner London is fierce.

The **American School in London** is a private school that offers an American curriculum. Situated in St. John's Wood, it accepts pupils from the age of four and up on a selective basis. Applications can be made up to a year in advance of entry. Contact The American School in London at 2-8 Loudoun Road, NW8 0NP, 020 7449 1221, fax: 020 7449 1350, www.asl.org.

For further information on all fee paying schools in London contact the **Independent Schools Information Service (ISIS)** on 020 7798 1500, www.isis.org.uk.

RELIGIOUS SCHOOLS

Denominational religious or "voluntary-aided" schools, both in the state and private sector, have always been an integral part of the school system in Britain, and are some of the most popular choices. They include Church of England, Catholic, Jewish, and Islamic schools. Because of perceived higher standards, religious schools in the state sector are often preferred over their non-denominational counterparts even by parents without strong religious affiliations themselves. The catchment area of religious secondary schools is usually wider than that of non-religious ones, and regular church attendance is often one of the criteria of entry.

RESOURCES

- Contact your local education authority via the council number given in the borough profiles for information on local schools, and for primary school performance tables.
- The **Department of Education and Employment** publications order line, 0845 602 2260, is the place to call for secondary performance tables.
- **Advisory Centre for Education** (**ACE**), 1b Aberdeen Studios, 22-24 Highbury Grove, N5, is an independent national advice centre which has an extensive publications list and also offers confidential advice over the telephone: 020 7354 8321 between 2 p.m. and 5 p.m. Monday-Friday.
- **Focus Information Service**, 13 Prince of Wales Terrace, London W8, 020 7937 0050, www.focus-info.org; membership gives newcomers access to a range of relocation resources including school information. See **Finding a Place to Live** for more information.
- **Ofsted** reports can be ordered from 020 7510 0180, or accessed on the internet at www.ofsted.gov.uk.

I N BRITAIN, POST SCHOOL EDUCATION, WHICH MAY BE SUBJECT TO entrance requirements, is available at universities, colleges, institutes of higher education, and further education colleges. When the term "higher education" is used, it is to designate courses more advanced than "A" level, referring to degree and graduate courses at universities. "Further education" is used to mean everything else.

UNIVERSITIES

If you're over 18 and want to come to Britain to study full-time, you will need to provide evidence of your qualifications and of your ability to fund your chosen course of study. Individual institutions set fees for overseas students. The minimum cost for a graduate or postgraduate degree is £4,500 for an arts course, £6,500 for science, and £11,500 for medicine. First degree courses generally last three years full-time. Applications must be made through the **Universities and Colleges Admissions Service (UCAS)**. You can get a free handbook and application form from UCAS, P.O. Box 67, Cheltenham, Gloucester, GL50 3SF, or from a British Council representative overseas.

Following are London's public universities. The **University of London (UL)** is a federation of different colleges, which are listed here individually as they function largely as separate entities. In addition, there are various institutes and schools affiliated with the University of London that provide short courses and continuing professional development as well as degree and further degree courses. For a full listing contact 020 7636 8000 or visit the UL web site at www.lon.ac.uk. For private colleges and universities look in the *Yellow Pages* or *Thomson Local* but note that these need not be registered with any official body and so standards are not guaranteed.

- **Birkbeck College**, University of London, Malet Street, WC1, 020 7631 6000, www.bbk.ac.uk; this college specialises in part-time degree courses for mature students. It also offers many short courses, diplomas and certificates at different venues around London.

- **City University**, Northampton Square, EC1, 020 7477 8000, www.city.ac.uk
- **Courtauld Institute of Art**, Somerset House, Strand, WC2, 020 7872 3526; the Courtauld has a permanent collection of impressionist and post-impressionist paintings.
- **University of East London**, Romford Road, E15, 020 8590 7722, www.nel.ac.uk
- **Goldsmiths College**, University of London, Lewisham Way, New Cross, SE14, 020 7919 7171, www.gold.ac.uk; particularly known for its Fine Art Department
- **University of Greenwich**, Bexley Road, SE9, 020 8331 8000, www.gre.ac.uk
- **London Guildhall University**, 133 Whitechapel High Street, E1, 020 7320 1616, www.lgu.ac.uk
- **United Medical and Dental Schools of Guy's and St. Thomas's**, Lambeth Palace Road, SE1, 020 7922 8013, www.umds.ac.uk
- **King's College London**, University of London, Strand, WC2, 020 7836 5454, www.kcl.ac.uk
- **Kingston University**, Kingston Hill, Kingston-upon-Thames, Surrey, KT2, 020 8547 2000, www.king.ac.uk
- **Imperial College**, University of London, Exhibition Road, SW7, 020 7589 5111, www.ic.ac.uk; specialises in science, technology and medicine.
- **Middlesex University**, Bounds Green Road, N11, 020 8362 5000, www.mdx.ac.uk
- **University of North London**, 166-220 Holloway Road, N7, 020 7607 2789, www.unl.ac.uk
- **Queen Mary and Westfield College**, University of London, 327 Mile End Road, E1, 020 7975 5555, www.qmw.ac.uk
- **South Bank University**, 103 Borough Road, SE1, 020 7928 8989, www.sbu.ac.uk
- **Thames Valley University**, St Mary's Road, W5, 020 8579 5000, www.tvu.ac.uk
- **University College London**, University of London, Gower Street, WC1, 020 7387 7050, www.ucl.ac.uk
- **University of Westminster**, 309 Regent Street, W1, 020 7911 5000, www.westminster.ac.uk

PART–TIME STUDY

London has a thriving evening class and part-time study sector which covers everything from music and dance through the arts and sciences to exercise and sport. Whether you're looking to work towards a qualification or just meet some new people, evening classes can be a great boon. More or less any subject that might interest you, from Flamenco to zoology, from wine appreciation to yoga, will have a class devoted to it somewhere in the capital. Courses are held in further education colleges and community centres throughout London. The best way to find out about times, places, and fees is to consult the course guides *Floodlight* (www.floodlight.co.uk) or *OnCourse*, both widely available in bookshops, newsagents and libraries. There is also the Open University that offers distance learning degrees and has no entry requirements. Call them on 020 7278 4411.

FOR SOME, SHOPPING IS REGARDED AS A NECESSITY AND SOMEWHAT of a nuisance; for others it can be a pastime, a luxury, or a vocation. Regardless of your shopping passion (or lack thereof) or whether you're on a budget or on a spree, London is sure to have the right stores for you, conveniently located. Because London evolved slowly, in little hamlets, there is a mini town centre in nearly every section of the city, which comes complete with a high street as its main shopping area, and often is accompanied by a more recently built mall. If what's available locally doesn't satisfy, then there are concentrations of shops in the West End, and large shopping centres elsewhere. Over the course of the 1990s high streets have become quite homogenous, and you will soon come to recognise the chains that are to be found on most of them: Boots the Chemist, Marks and Spencer (clothes and/or food), Virgin (music), The Body Shop (natural cosmetics), WH Smith (stationery, toys, music, books), River Island, Next, and Gap (clothes stores). At least one of the "big four" supermarkets (see below) is usually there, as well as a Burger King and/or McDonalds, and a coffee shop—Coffee Republic, Costa or Starbucks. Providing a bit more shopping variety are over 100 street markets dotted throughout London, which range from the specialised or obscure to the most general. In addition there is a thriving secondhand/charity shop sector offering retro clothes, antiques, and bric-a-brac.

When shopping for your new home, you can choose to do it quickly at the high street stores, or be more adventurous and seek out smaller designer shops or antique shops. To find your nearest high street chain, check the *Yellow Pages* or *Thomson Local* or call *Talking Pages* on 0800 600900.

Although hours of operation are extending annually, and stores in central London stay open until about 7 p.m., you will generally find high street shopping hours to be 9 a.m. to 5:30 or 6 p.m., Monday-Saturday. Some shops still do not open on Sundays and those that do tend to open later and shut earlier. Grocery stores and off-licences (liquor stores) are the major exceptions to these rules. Your local corner shop will probably be open until 10 or 11 p.m., and most supermarkets are usually open until 8 or 9 p.m., with some offering 24-hour service a couple of days a week. A few general stores such as B2s and Seven-Elevens, as well as some petrol stations, are open around the clock.

SHOPPING DISTRICTS

The West End boasts some of the most patronised shopping destinations in London. Visitors come from all over the country, indeed the globe. None of these areas are ever what you might call quiet, but be prepared for especially large crowds on Saturdays all year round and all the time in the run-up to Christmas.

- **Oxford Street**, W1, London's longest shopping street offers major chains like Marks and Spencer, plus department stores John Lewis and Selfridges (see below), the music stores Virgin Megastore and HMV, plus much more. The western end of Oxford Street is geared towards department and big name stores, whereas the eastern end is more downmarket with cheap leather goods, jeans and souvenir shops interspersed with high street names.
- **Regent Street/Carnaby Street**, W1; go to Regent Street for Liberty, one of London's earliest and most influential department stores, for Hamley's vast toy emporium, and for a good range of upmarket and mid-market boutiques. Carnaby Street was once the epitome of London's swinging sixties and, although not quite so cool now, it's still a good place to look for street and retro fashion, shoes, and tacky tourist stuff.
- **Covent Garden**, WC1; unless you love swarms of tourists, it may be best to avoid Covent Garden, which is crowded and disappointing. Head instead to Neal Street for trendy and sporty gear at stores such as Diesel, Mambo, and Red or Dead. It's the place to go for shoes and sneakers as there are a dozen or so shops devoted to foot wear. Long Acre and the parallel Floral Street are good for both high street and designer fashions. The streets off the Seven Dials junction have plenty of quirky and interesting shops specialising in such varied items as cheese, jazz records, and coffee. Neal's Yard is a little haven of vegetarian cafes and alternative remedies (and if all that shopping is stressing you out, you can get a drop-in back massage for £8).
- **Fulham Road**, SW3; running parallel to the King's Road this street offers the best in contemporary interior design at Jerry's Home Store (design with an American flavour), Divertimenti (everything you could ever want for the kitchen), and The Conran Shop (modern design for every room in the house).

- **Kensington High Street**, W8; offers a good range of high street and designer stores all within a relatively small area.
- **King's Road**, SW1; once the haunt of punks and posers, the King's Road is now a high-class shopping area with a great range of home stores including Heal's, Muji, and Habitat.
- **Knightsbridge**, SW1; the most exclusive and expensive designer shops, and Harrods, are here.
- **Whiteleys of Bayswater**, Queensway, W2, 020 7229 8844; in-town shopping centre with the added attraction of a multi-screen cinema.

Shopping districts for second hand items can be found at the end of the chapter under **Street Markets**.

MALLS

If you like to do all your shopping under one roof, take a trip to one of these enormous malls situated on routes out of London.
- **Bluewater**, Upper Thames Walk, Bluewater, Greenhithe, Kent DA9, 0845 602 1021, transport information: 0845 603 1031, open Monday-Friday 10 a.m. to 9 p.m., Saturday 9 a.m. to 8 p.m., and Sunday 11 a.m. to 5 p.m. Spectacularly designed, this king among malls has over 320 stores and restaurants, making it one of the largest in Europe. The unrivalled facilities of the Welcome Halls include parent/child rooms, comfortable seating, hire of pushchairs, lockers, and a cloakroom. Bluewater is easily accessible by bus and train.
- **Brent Cross**, London NW4, (intersection of the North Circular A406 and Hendon Way A41), 020 8202 8095, Monday-Friday, 10 a.m. to 8 p.m., Saturday 9 a.m. to 6 p.m. and Sunday 11 a.m. to 5 p.m. Despite its unprepossessing 1970s exterior, you'll find everything from super-markets to high street shops to department stores. An added attraction is the nearby branch of IKEA.
- **Lakeside Thurrock**, West Thurrock Way, West Thurrock, Grays, Essex, RM20, 01708 869933, Monday-Friday, 10 a.m. to 10 p.m., Saturday 9 a.m. to 7:30 p.m. and Sunday 11 a.m. to 5 p.m.; Essex's finest and one of the biggest malls in the country.

DEPARTMENT STORES

These labyrinthine shops will take all day to negotiate and explore. Many have in-store cafes.
- **Barkers of Kensington**, 63 Kensington High Street, W8, 020 7734 6090
- **Bentalls**, Bentalls Centre, Kingston, Surrey, 020 8546 1001
- **Harrods**, Brompton Road, Knightsbridge, SW1, 020 7730 1234; worth a

visit for its fame alone though you won't find many bargains! Its astonishing food halls, featuring delicacies from around the world, are famous.

- **Harvey Nichols**, 109-125 Knightsbridge, SW1, 020 7235 5000;
  "Harvey Nicks" is legendary for its classy fashions and upmarket clientele.
- **John Lewis**, Oxford Street, W1, 020 7629 7711; **Peter Jones**, Sloane
  Square, SW1, 020 7730 3434—both these department stores are part
  of the John Lewis Partnership group and offer a "never knowingly
  undersold" policy that refunds the difference if you discover an item
  you have bought there at a lower price elsewhere. Check out the electrical goods and kitchen departments.
- **Liberty**, 210-220 Regent Street, W1, 020 7734 1234; complete with
  its distinctive mock-Tudor frontage, is known for its fabric selection.
- **Selfridges**, 400 Oxford Street, W1, 020 7629 1234; offers a fabulous food
  hall, and a catacomb of departments devoted to different fashion
  designers.

HOUSEHOLD SHOPPING

APPLIANCES/ELECTRONICS/COMPUTERS & SOFTWARE

A vast number of independent shops on **Tottenham Court Road** sell all
manner of computer goods and electronics, often beating the high street
stores for price and range, but beware that if anything goes wrong with your
purchase, you may face a bit of a battle to get it put right. The high street is
perhaps not the best place to buy computers and accessories. Those in the
know tend to go straight to the manufacturers or to computer fairs—these
are listed in computer magazines. For branches of all the high street stores
look in the *Yellow Pages, Thomson Local* or call *Talking Pages*, 0800 600900.

- **Argos** is an in-store catalogue shop selling inexpensive electrical and
  household goods and toys, but is marred by its convoluted system of
  ordering, paying, and collecting goods, which involves queuing twice.
- **Currys**, **Dixons**, **and Tandy** are high street electrical goods stores
  which are all part of the same company offering similar ranges of washing machines, refrigerators, vacuum cleaners, computers, kettles, toast-
  ers, hi-fi, etc.
- **P.C. World** is one of the few dedicated high street computer retailers.
- **Gateway Computers**, 10 Bedford Street, WC2, 020 7497 6000
- **Richer Sounds**, 29 Bloomsbury Way, WC1, 020 7831 2888 and
  branches; "pile 'em high, sell 'em low" hi-fi separates.
- **Superfi**, 2-4 Camden High Street, NW1, 020 7388 1300, or mail order hot-
  line 0800 731 1821; offers a wide range of separates and all-in-one systems.
- **Tempo** is a high street chain, which is independent of the Currys and
  Dixons group. It carries a similar range but sometimes has better prices.

CARPETS, FLOORING & RUGS

The department stores all offer a selection of carpets, rugs and hardwood and laminate flooring. **John Lewis** in particular is worth a visit for quality floor coverings. **Habitat** stocks a wide range of rugs at reasonable prices. The carpet superstore most commonly found in retail parks or on high streets is **Allied Carpets**, which also offers a limited choice of hardwoods and laminates. There are dozens of independents and small chains of carpet and flooring retailers in the capital. Consult the *Yellow Pages, Thomson Local* or *Talking Pages,* 0800 600 900, for the ones in your area.

FURNITURE & HOUSEWARES

The northerly end of **Tottenham Court Road** has a wide variety of furniture retailers, particularly those specialising in futons and sofas. The stores below offer a wide range of furniture and other items for all the rooms in the house.

- **Cargo Homeshops**, 245-249 Brompton Road, SW3, 020 7584 7611; 209 Tottenham Court Road, W1, 020 7580 2895, and branches; has cheap and cheerful household goods and some furniture.
- **The Conran Shop**, 55 Marylebone High Street, W1, 020 7723 2223; 81 Fulham Road, SW3, 020 7589 7401; offers expensive but lovely designer furniture and housewares.
- **Habitat**, 196 Tottenham Court Road, W1, 020 7255 2545; 206 King's Road, SW3, 020 7351 1211 and branches; good deals on stylish furniture, kitchenware, lighting, bedding and bathroom fittings.
- **Heals**, 196 Tottenham Court Road, W1, 020 7636 1666; 234 King's Road, SW3, 020 7349 8400; offers designer furniture and housewares.
- **IKEA**, Brent Park, 2 Drury Way, North Circular Road, NW10, and Valley Park, Purley Way, Croydon, 020 8208 5601; popular and affordable Swedish flat-packed furniture and housewares. Good for every budget.
- **Purves and Purves**, 220-224 Tottenham Court Road, W1, 020 7580 8223; up to the minute furniture and interior design accessories.

HOUSEWARES

- **Bodum**, 71 King's Road, SW3, 020 7376 3825; 24 Neal Street, WC2, 020 7240 9176; Unit 22A, Whiteley's Centre, Queensway, W2, 020 7792 1213; modestly priced and strikingly designed kitchen accessories.
- **David Mellor**, 4 Sloane Square, SW1, 020 7730 4259; offers stylish kitchen gear.
- **Divertimenti**, 139-141 Fulham Road, SW3, 020 7581 8065 and 45

Wigmore Street, W1, 020 7935 0689; good selection of kitchen accessories and gadgets.

- **Jerry's Home Store**, 163-167 Fulham Road, SW3, 020 7581 0909; 80-82 Tottenham Court Road, W1, 020 7436 7177 and 4th Floor in Harvey Nichols, 109 Knightsbridge, SW1, 020 7245 6251; everything the homesick American might want, from bar stools to trash cans to foodstuffs such as maple syrup and Oreos.
- **Muji**, 157 Kensington High Street, W8, 020 7376 2484; 187 Oxford Street, W1, 020 7437 7503; 77 King's Road, SW3, 020 7352 7148 and branches; serene Japanese designs.
- **The Source**, Market Towers, 1 Nine Elms, 020 7819 2600; offers a great range of reasonably priced items.
- **Urban Outfitters**, 47 Beak Street, W1, 020 7434 1166; the best in contemporary design.
- **Woolworths**, branches throughout London provide a good source of cheap, colourful, and practical household items.

HARDWARE & GARDEN CENTRES

Both **B&Q** and **Sainsbury's Homebase** are do-it-yourself superstores with branches in many locations. They offer comprehensive ranges of fixtures, fittings, paint, wallpaper and hardware, and often have a garden centre attached. In addition to these two mega-stores which dominate the market, there are many local hardware shops which offer friendly and knowledgeable service. Dedicated garden centres tend to be located in slightly out-of-the-way places so check the *Yellow Pages*.

FOOD

SUPERMARKETS

You will find most people make regular stops at one of the "big four" supermarkets: **Tesco**, **Sainsbury's**, **Safeway** or **Asda**. Asda and Tesco tend to be the cheapest. **Waitrose** has fewer branches than any of the mains and is aimed at the higher end of the market. **Marks and Spencer Food Halls** have a wide range of ready meals that combine innovation with convenience. **Iceland** specialises in frozen food and is notable for having a good selection of competitively priced organic products.

Warehouse shopping is available at **Kwik Save**, **Costco**, **Savacentre**, and **Lidl**. See *Yellow Pages*, *Thomson Local* or call *Talking Pages*, 0800 600900 for a location near you.

HEALTH FOOD STORES

Branches of **Holland and Barratt** supply the high streets with health foods and there are many local independent health food shops too. Some of the larger health food shops are in the centre of town:

- **Alara Wholefoods**, 58-60 Marchmont Street, WC1, 020 7837 1172
- **Freshlands Wholefoods**, 196 Old Street, EC1, 020 7250 1708
- **The Grain Shop**, 269a Portobello Road, W11, 020 7229 5571
- **The Health Food Centre**, 11 Warren Street, W1, 020 7387 9289
- **Planet Organic**, 42 Westbourne Grove, W2, 020 7221 7171 and 22 Torrington Place, WC1, 020 7436 1929; the capital's biggest selection of fresh and packaged organic foods, plus an amazing juice bar and takeaway section.

ETHNIC FOODS

With Asian culture being such a big part of daily life in London, you are likely to find most ingredients you'll need for making curries and stir-fries at your local store. Southall (Middlesex) has perhaps the biggest range of all kinds of Indian and Pakistani food stores. For a concentration of Bangladeshi shops, make for Brick Lane (E1). Caribbean ingredients can be found all over but particularly good places to go for these are Brixton Market (SW9), Shepherd's Bush Market (W12), Rye Lane, Peckham (SE15), and the West Green Road, Tottenham (N15). For kosher foods try Stamford Hill (N15) in northeast London, and Golders Green and Finchley in the northwest. There's no shortage of Italian delicatessens either, notable ones include Camisa's at 61 Old Compton Street, W1V, 020 7437 7610, Carluccio's, 28 Neal Street, WC2, 020 7240 1487, and those in Clerkenwell (EC1). Chinatown in London's West End has the full gamut of Southeast Asian groceries and restaurants. Turkish and Cypriot stores on Harringay Green Lanes sell feta cheese, halloumi, great selections of olives and olive oil, fresh breads and piles of continental fresh fruit and vegetables. And finally, there is a Japanese Mall in north London called Yaohan Plaza, 399 Edgware Road, NW9, 020 8200 0009.

RESTAURANTS

Because of the number of restaurants in London and the fact that dozens are added to and subtracted from the count every month, we have made no attempt to list them here. As surely as curry has replaced fish and chips as the national dish, so Britain's erstwhile reputation for lousy food is being slowly but firmly cast off. From posh nosh to a quick bite, Londoners now have the luxury of cuisine from all over the globe on their doorstep. Highly recommended is the *Time Out Guide to Eating and Drinking*, which pretty much has the subject covered.

SPORTING GOODS

Nowadays many high street stores, such as **Cobra**, **Sports Division**, and **First Sport** stock very little other than brand-name trainers and athletic clothing. Those listed below have a more comprehensive range of sports equipment. For bike shops, see the **Cycling** section of **Sport and Recreation**.

- **Harrods Sports Department**, Brompton Road, Knightsbridge, SW1, 020 7730 1234; over one hundred sports are represented in the famous department store.
- **Lillywhites**, 24-36 Regent Street, SW1, 020 7915 4000
- **NikeTown,** 236 Oxford Street, W1, 020 7612 0800
- **Snow and Rock**, 188 Kensington High Street, W8, 020 7937 0872 and 150 Holborn, EC1, 020 7831 6900; specialists in skiing and rock climbing gear.
- **Wigmore Sports**, 81-83 Wigmore Street, W1, 020 7486 7761; specialists in racquet sports.
- **YHA Adventure Shop**, 14 Southampton Street, WC2, 020 7836 8541; gear for hiking and climbing.

SECOND HAND SHOPPING

On every high street you'll find charity shops benefiting all sorts of causes and which sell all kinds of used goods. Increasingly the best clothes are weeded out and sold at specialised vintage clothing stores. If you want to do a second hand shopping tour, or for that matter sell all your worldly goods, head for Notting Hill Gate (W11) where there is a series of shops known collectively as the **Music and Video Exchange**. This empire of second hand stores spreads along Pembridge Road and Notting Hill Gate and they buy, sell, and exchange just about everything. There are shops dedicated to records, computers, clothes, accessories, books, furniture, electrical goods and musical instruments. Another source is *Loot*, www.loot.com, London's daily classified ads paper. Bargains abound but you'll need to be quick off the mark.

Car boot sales (the British equivalent to America's garage sales) have become popular over the last decade. Here private individuals sell their unwanted items. These sales are usually on Saturday or Sunday mornings and are advertised in local papers.

VINTAGE AND RETRO CLOTHING

Check out Greenwich, Camden, Portobello, and Spitalfields markets listed below which are all excellent hunting grounds for vintage clothes. The **Holloway Road** (N7) is a good place to visit too as it has a couple of cheap and cheerful retro clothes shops catering to students at the nearby University of North London. There are also several shops in central London that have impressive ranges:

- **Yesterday's Bread**, 29 Fouberts Place, W1, 020 7287 1929
- **Oxfam Charity Shop**, 26 Ganton Street, W1, 020 7437 7338
- **Pop Boutique**, 6 Monmouth Street, WC2, 020 7497 5262

ANTIQUES

- **Portobello Road**, W11; the southern end of the market has antique shops and stalls.
- **Camden Passage**, Upper Street, N1; dozens of antique shops and stalls are packed in a tiny area with rich pickings of antique and period items. Most shops are open Tuesday to Saturday, 10 a.m. to 5 p.m. with stalls on Wednesday and Saturday open from 8 a.m. until 4 p.m.
- **Alfies Antique Market**, 13-25 Church Street, Marylebone, NW6; a popular market with traders, Alfies has a huge range of stalls to browse with lots of intriguing and unusual wares. Open Tuesday-Saturday, 10 a.m. to 6 p.m.

STREET MARKETS

London has hundreds of street markets, a tradition that goes back centuries and still holds strong. Here are some of the noteworthy:

- **Bermondsey Market**, SE1; this antique market is located on the corner of Long Lane and Bermondsey Street and is famed for its early start—earnest collectors get there at dawn. Open only on Friday between 5 a.m. and 2 p.m.
- **Berwick Street**, W1; here in the heart of town, between Soho and Oxford Street, there is a terrific array of fruit and vegetables on offer, plus cheese, herbs and spices. Oddly, the shops along the street mostly sell records. Hours are Monday-Saturday, 9 a.m. to 5 p.m.
- **Brick Lane**, E1; one of London's most historic markets, Brick Lane has its origins as a livestock market in the 18th century. Now the stalls sell just about everything: bicycles, tools, electrical goods, duvets, trainers, eggs, fruit, vegetables and leather jackets were all spotted on a recent visit. Hours are Sunday, 8 a.m. to 1 p.m.

- **Brixton Market**, Electric Avenue, SW9; the terrific selection of Caribbean foodstuffs including meat, fish and vegetables, is augmented by stalls selling incense and reggae records. Open daily.
- **Camden Market**, NW1, greatly expanded since the early 1980s when there were just two market sites, it's now a top tourist attraction, taking up the whole stretch of Camden High Street, from the Tube station to the top of Chalk Farm Road. Stalls and traders crowd along the side of the street and in the proliferating market sites around Camden Lock selling trendy clothes, jewellery, juggling balls, candles, and the whole gamut of new age paraphernalia. Some stalls are open daily, but the busiest days are Saturday and Sunday, 9 a.m. to 5 p.m.
- **Columbia Road**, E2; a must for those with green thumbs, this market has all manner of indoor and outdoor plants and shrubs, plus colourful and spectacular cut flowers. It's especially nice at Christmas for providing trees, holly, and other festive greenery to deck your halls. Open every Sunday, 7 a.m. to 2 p.m.
- **Greenwich Market**, SE10; Greenwich Market is the collective name of the market sites in the town centre. There's the Central Market in Stockwell Street, a flea market in Thames Street, Bosun's Yard in Greenwich along Church Street, selling food and unusual gifts, and Greenwich Antiques Market with second-hand records, books and clothes. Open Saturday and Sunday, 8 a.m. to 4 p.m.
- **Leadenhall Market**, EC3; set in the heart of the City next to the Lloyds Building, this market retains a Victorian flavour, and sells high quality fresh fish, game, cheese, fruit and vegetables. Open weekdays, 9 a.m. to 5 p.m., closed weekends.
- **Petticoat Lane**, E1; the Victorians abolished the actual street-name "Petticoat Lane," and renamed it Middlesex Street (to remove the indelicate reference to underwear). Obviously the re-naming didn't take. Today the market is notable more for its reputation as the archetypal East End street market than for its offered wares, which tend to be a rather bland assortment of clothes, luggage, and linens. Open Monday-Friday 10.30 a.m. to 2.30 p.m., Sunday, 9 a.m. to 2 p.m.; closed on Saturday.
- **Portobello Road**, W11; Portobello is another market which has expanded far beyond its original boundaries supplying a whole range of things, from antiques at the posh Notting Hill end, all the way down to bric-a-brac at the scruffier North Kensington end. Nestled under the elevated section of the Westway (A40) on Fridays and Saturdays you'll find stalls with retro clothes, records, and housewares. Hours are Monday-Saturday, 9 a.m. to 5 p.m. (closes 1 p.m. Thursday).
- **Spitalfields**, Commercial Street, E1; the striking Victorian purpose-built indoor marketplace was the site of London's largest wholesale fruit and

vegetable market until the beginning of the 1990s. Since then this excellent space has been put to new and innovative uses and includes a sports centre, numerous restaurants and some very trendy furniture shops, as well as a new market. Organic produce is the market speciality with everything from carrots and potatoes to wine, olives, and tofu. You'll find lots of other things too: original artworks, crafts, old and new clothes, books and records. Some stalls are here Monday to Friday, 11 a.m. to 3 p.m., but the best day is Sunday 10 a.m. to 4 p.m.; closed on Saturday.

- **Walthamstow Market**, High Street, E17; mentioned chiefly for its claim to be the longest street market in Europe, Walthamstow Market is great for cheap fruit and vegetables and bargain housewares. Open Monday-Saturday, 9 a.m. to 5 p.m.

THE SHEER NUMBER OF THINGS TO DO AND SEE IN LONDON CAN make it hard to know where to begin. The museums and galleries of central London are celebrated for their magnificent collections and they're all worth a visit, but don't overlook the smaller, more esoteric museums, which can be great fun and a lot less crowded. London is both a hotbed for new talent and a magnet for high-profile productions and tours. The city's music scene encompasses jazz, indie-rock, reggae, and anything else you can think of. The bands playing in small pub venues in Camden today may be the stars of tomorrow. London's club land is at the cutting edge, along with its accompanying fashion trends. On the more highbrow side of things there is West End theatre of course, and also a fine selection of fringe and subsidised theatre throughout the capital. If you're keen to sing, act or dance yourself there is a huge array of courses and classes in London from which to choose (listed in the publications *Floodlight* and *OnCourse*). Film is more popular than ever in the capital, and huge new multi-screen cinemas are opening all over town, bringing new standards in choice and comfort. Meanwhile London's fine repertory cinemas offer opportunities to see classic and cult films as well as independent or foreign language titles. There is even one cinema that shows *The Rocky Horror Picture Show* every Friday night. Included below is a selection of some of the most renowned and established galleries, museums, and tourist attractions.

First, a few suggestions about where to look for reviews and listings:

- ***Time Out*** is a popular, extensive, and opinionated weekly listings magazine that also covers London news, consumer issues, gossip and celebrity interviews; www.timeout.com.
- ***What's On in London***, listings
- **"Hot Tickets"** in the ***Evening Standard*** Thursday edition; their web site is also great for listings and reviews: www.thisislondon.com.
- On Saturdays, ***The Guardian*****'s "The Guide"** and the ***Independent's*** **"The Information"** sections provide comprehensive listings and

abbreviated recommendations and reviews: www.guardian.co.uk, www.independent.co.uk.
- The **London Tourist Board** has an extensive web site, www. LondonTown.com.

TICKETS

Tickets for most events and performances may be purchased either directly through the venue's box office or via a ticket agency. It's always sensible to get tickets as far in advance as possible for high profile or critically acclaimed shows, concerts or exhibitions, as they sell out quickly. When calling ahead, have a credit or debit card ready, and be prepared to pay a booking fee on each ticket—the only away to avoid this is to buy your tickets in person at the box office. The Tourist Information Centre listed above also sells tickets for shows. Going through a ticket agency will add another level of charges to the price. Some theatres (the Royal National Theatre among them) hold back some tickets until the day of the performance which are then sold in the morning on a first come first served basis—contact individual venues to see if this applies. On the south side of Leicester Square is the **Half-Price Ticket Booth**, which has some tickets for some West End shows at half price plus a service charge. You only can get these by queuing on the day of your chosen performance, purchases must be made in cash, and there is a limit of four tickets per person. The booth is open Monday-Saturday, noon to 6:30 p.m., Sunday from noon to 3 p.m. There is no phone contact number. Other major ticket agencies include:
- **First Call**, 0870 906 3700/020 7420 1000, www.firstcalltickets.com
- **TicketMaster**, 020 7344 4444
- **Stargreen**, 020 7734 8932

MUSIC

CLASSICAL & OPERA

The **South Bank Centre** is home to three concert halls which play host to a wide range of classical concerts: the **Royal Festival Hall**, **Queen Elizabeth Hall**, and **Purcell Room**. The box office can be reached on 020 7960 4242 or check out the South Bank web site, www.sbc.org.uk. Other sites include:
- **Barbican**, Silk Street, EC2, 020 7638 8891, home to the London Symphony Orchestra
- **St. Johns**, Smith Square, London SW1, 020 7222 1061
- **Wigmore Hall**, 36 Wigmore Street, W1, 020 7935 2141, specialises in chamber music

- **Royal Albert Hall**, Kensington Gore, SW7, 020 7589 8212, venue for the Proms every summer
- **Royal Opera House**, Covent Garden, WC2, 020 7304 4000
- **London Coliseum**, St. Martin's Lane, WC2, 020 7632 8300, home to the English National Opera which puts on operas translated into English
- **Spitalfields Market Opera**, 4-5 Lamb Street, E1, 020 7247 2558

CONTEMPORARY MUSIC

In addition to the places listed below, contemporary music artists also sometimes play at the Royal Albert Hall or at the venues in the South Bank Centre.

CONCERT HALLS AND ARENAS
Headlining rock and pop bands tend to play these large-scale venues. Tours are generally advertised in the arts or listings pages of the press.
- **Astoria W1**, 157 Charing Cross Road, W1, 020 7434 0403
- **Brixton Academy**, 211 Stockwell Road, SW9, 020 7771 2000
- **Earls Court Exhibition Centre**, Warwick Road, SW5, 020 7373 8141
- **Forum**, 9-17 Highgate Road, NW5, 020 7344 0044
- **Shepherd's Bush Empire**, Shepherd's Bush Green, W12, 020 7771 2000
- **Wembley Arena/Stadium**, Empire Way, Wembley, 020 8902 0902

SMALLER MUSIC VENUES
These are the established places to find alternative and up-and-coming bands. In addition to those listed, there are dozens of less well-known pubs and clubs that showcase live bands.
- **100 Club**, 100 Oxford Street, W1, 020 7636 0933
- **Dingwalls**, Middle Yard, Camden Lock, NW1, 020 7267 1577
- **Dublin Castle**, 94 Parkway, NW1, 020 7485 1773
- **Finborough Arms**, Finborough Road, SW10, 020 7373 3842
- **The Garage & Upstairs at the Garage**, 20-22 Highbury Corner, N5, 020 7607 1818
- **Half Moon Putney**, 93 Lower Richmond Road, SW15, 020 8780 9383
- **Hope & Anchor**, 207 Upper Street, N1, 020 7354 1312
- **Monarch**, 49 Chalk Farm Road, NW1, 020 7916 1049
- **Rock Garden**, The Piazza, Covent Garden, WC2, 020 7240 3961
- **ULU**, University of London Union, Manning Hall, Malet Street, WC1, 020 7664 2030
- **Underworld**, 174 Camden High Street, NW1, 020 7482 1932
- **The Venue**, 2a Clifton Rise, New Cross SE14, 020 8692 4077
- **Water Rats**, 328 Grays Inn Road, WC1, 020 7284 0077

JAZZ, BLUES & FOLK
Soho's jazz scene was legendary in the 1950s and '60s, and there are still plenty of jazzmen and women to be found playing and singing the night away. Once again this is only a partial selection of what's on offer.
- **Jazz After Dark**, Greek Street, W1, 020 7734 0545
- **Jazz Cafe NW1**, 5 Parkway, NW1, 020 7344 0044
- **Pizza Express Jazz Club**, 10 Dean Street, W1, 020 7439 8722; other Pizza Express restaurants also put on live jazz—check listings for dates.
- **Pizza On The Park**, 11 Knightsbridge, Hyde Park Corner, SW1, 020 7235 5273
- **Ronnie Scott's**, 47 Frith Street, W1, 020 7439 0747; London's most famous venue for jazz.
- **The Spitz**, Old Spitalfields Market, 109 Commercial Street, E1, 020 7392 9032
- **Wag Club**, 35-37 Wardour Street, W1, 020 7437 5534
- **Watermans Arts Centre**, 40 High Street, Brentford, Middlesex, 020 8568 1176

CLUBS
London's nightlife embraces everything from rap to glam rock, but house and garage are still the most popular grooves on the dance floor. The clubs listed here are some of the city's most legendary and long established. All have door charges, and different nights are dedicated to different musical or sexual tastes so phone for details or check listings.
- **The Arches**, 53 Southwark Street, SE1, 020 7207 0707
- **Bagley's Studios**, Kings Cross Freight Depot, off York Way, N1, 020 7278 2777
- **Bar Rumba**, 36 Shaftesbury Avenue, W1, 020 7287 2715
- **Camden Palace**, 1a Camden High Street, NW1, 020 7387 0428
- **Fabric**, 77 Charterhouse Street, London, EC1, 020 7490 0444
- **The Fridge**, Town Hall Parade, Brixton Hill, SW2, 020 7326 5100
- **Gossips**, 69 Dean Street, W1, 020 7434 4480
- **Hanover Grand**, 6 Hanover Street, W1, 020 7499 7977
- **Heaven**, Under The Arches, Craven Street, WC2, 020 7930 2020
- **Home**, 1 Leicester Square, W1, 0207 909 0000
- **HQs**, West Yard, Camden Lock, NW1, 020 7485 6044
- **LA2**, 157 Charing Cross Road, WC2, 020 7434 0403
- **The Leisure Lounge**, 121 Holborn, EC1, 020 7242 1345
- **Limelight**, 136 Shaftesbury Avenue, WC2, 020 7434 0572
- **Ministry of Sound**, 103 Gaunt Street, SE1, 020 7378 6528
- **Plastic People**, 37-39 Oxford Street, W1, 020 7439 0464
- **Scala**, 278 Pentonville Road, N1, 020 7833 2022

- **Sound**, 10 Wardour Street, W1, 020 7287 1010
- **Subterania**, 12 Acklam Road (under Westway), W10, 020 8960 4590
- **Turnmills**, 63 Clerkenwell Road, EC1, 020 7250 3409
- **Velvet Room**, 143 Charing Cross Road, WC2, 020 7439 4655

THEATRE

London is fabulous for theatre, offering everything from tiny venues in rooms above pubs to huge West End musicals and Broadway transfers. Many smaller productions need not be booked much in advance, unless a play has garnered particular press attention or has a big name in the cast. On the other hand, tickets for West End shows sometimes need to be acquired months ahead. Leaflets telling you what's on at the Royal National Theatre and Royal Court, as well as smaller theatres can usually be found in libraries and in the foyers of other venues. For the commercial West End theatres (of which there are about 40) see daily newspapers and listings magazines. Below are a selection of subsidised companies and fringe/community theatre venues of particular note:

- **Almeida**, Almeida Street, N1, 020 7359 4404, is famed for highly rated productions of classic highbrow plays. Such Hollywood names as Juliette Binoche and Kevin Spacey have trod the boards here.
- **Battersea Arts Centre (BAC)**, 176 Lavender Hill, SW11, 020 7223 2223
- **The Bush**, Shepherd's Bush Green, W12, 020 7610 4224; often stages plays by talented new writers.
- **Donmar Warehouse**, Thomas Neal's, Earlham Street, WC2, 020 7369 1732
- **Drill Hall**, 16 Chenies Street, WC1, 020 7637 8270; specialises in gay and lesbian orientated productions.
- **The Gate**, 11 Pembridge Road, W11, 020 7229 5387/229 0706; tiny, imaginatively used theatre space.
- **Hampstead Theatre**, Avenue Road, NW3, 020 7722 9301
- **King's Head**, 115 Upper Street, N1, 020 7226 1916, is one of London's best-loved pub theatres.
- **Lyric Hammersmith**, King Street, W6, 020 8741 2311, www.lyric.co.uk
- **Oval House**, 52-54 Kennington Oval, SE11, 020 7582 7680
- **Riverside Studios**, Crisp Road, off Queen Caroline Street, W6, 020 8237 1111
- **Royal National Theatre**, South Bank SE1, 020 7452 3000, www.nationaltheatre.org.uk; three auditoriums offer a wide ranging programme of revived classics and new plays.
- **Royal Court Theatre**, Sloane Square, SW1, 020 7565 5000; London's most notorious venue for groundbreaking and challenging productions.

- **RSC The Barbican & The Pit**, Barbican EC2, 020 7638 8891/628 2295, www.rsc.org.uk; the Royal Shakespeare Company's London home puts on Shakespeare plus other classics.
- **Shakespeare's Globe**, Bear Gardens, Bankside, Southwark SE1, 020 7401 9919; 16th and 17th century plays in a truly authentic setting. Summer only, due to the absent roof!
- **Theatre Royal, Stratford East**, Gerry Raffles Square, Stratford, E15, 020 8534 0310
- **Tricycle Theatre**, 269 Kilburn High Street, NW6, 020 7328 1000
- **Young Vic**, 66 The Cut, SE1, 020 7928 6363

READINGS, POETRY, STORYTELLING

- **Voice Box, Royal Festival Hall**, South Bank Centre, SE1, 020 7960 4242
- **Poetry Cafe**, 22 Betterton Street, WC2, 020 8960 9001
- **Troubadour Coffee House**, 265 Old Brompton Road, SW5, 020 8354 0660

BOOKSHOPS

Enthusiasts of the written word will be delighted to find in London both chummy local bookshops and vast book emporiums in the West End. Many bookshops also hold regular readings and signings by established as well as up and coming authors, many of them local—see press for details. In addition to the established bookshop chains there are many specialist and second-hand bookshops in London, of which only a fraction are listed here. Dedicated bookshop browsers should make for the Charing Cross Road where they will find bookshops of every conceivable variety. Books on the best seller lists are available in supermarkets and branches of **WH Smith** and **John Menzies**.

GENERAL BOOKSHOPS

- **Borders Books, Music and Cafe**, 203 Oxford Street, W1, 020 7292 1600; 120 Charing Cross Road, WC2, 020 7379 6838; these book superstores offer several floors of books, stationery and CDs, with cafes on site.
- **Hatchards Booksellers**, 187 Piccadilly, W1V, 020 7439 9921
- **Waterstones**, 203-206 Piccadilly, W1 020 7851 2400; 82 Gower Street, WC1E, 020 7636 1577; 121-125 Charing Cross Road, WC2H, 020 7434 4291, and branches; the Gower Street store in Bloomsbury is excellent for academic and specialised books—there's an information desk on each floor and the staff will do their best to help you. There is a Coffee Republic cafe in the basement too. The six-floor Piccadilly

branch, reportedly the largest bookstore in Europe, has trumped all competitors by having a restaurant, The Red Room, and a bar, in addition to a coffee shop and a few books!

SPECIALIST BOOKSHOPS

- **BMJ Bookshop**, BMA House, Tavistock Square, WC1, 020 7383 6244; specialising in medical books
- **Books for Cooks**, 4 Blenheim Crescent, W11, 020 7221 1992
- **The Children's Book Centre**, 237 Kensington High Street, W8, 020 7937 7497
- **The Cinema Bookshop**, 13-14 Great Russell Street, WC1, 020 7637 0206
- **Crime In Store**, 14 Bedford Street, WC2, 020 7379 3795
- **Forbidden Planet**, 71-75 New Oxford Street, WC1, 020 7836 4179; science fiction books, comics, merchandise and videos
- **Gay's The Word**, 66 Marchmont Street, WC1, 020 7278 7654; the big bookshops all have gay sections but this stalwart still has the biggest range of lesbian and gay books and magazines in the capital.
- **Murder One**, 71-73 Charing Cross Road, WC2, 020 7734 3483
- **Politico's**, 8 Artillery Row, London SW1, 020 7828 0010, www.politicos.co.uk; the only specialist political bookshop in the country (it also sells coffee).
- **Silver Moon Women's Bookshop**, 68 Charing Cross Road, WC2, 020 7836 7906; offers a vast selection of books by and about women; helpful staff will order anything in print.
- **Sportspages**, Caxton Walk, 94-96 Charing Cross Road, WC2, 020 7240 9604, www.sportspages.co.uk
- **Stanfords**, 12-14 Long Acre, WC2, 020 7836 1321; large map and travel bookshop
- **Travel Bookshop**, 13 Blenheim Crescent, W11, 020 7229 5260; now famous as the model for Hugh Grant's bookshop in the film *Notting Hill*.

USED BOOKS

Other good hunting grounds apart from Charing Cross Road and Bloomsbury include Stoke Newington Church Street (N16), Spitalfields Market (E1), Greenwich Market (SE10), and the South Bank (SE1), where there is a mini book market on the bank of the Thames outside the National Film Theatre.
- **Any Amount of Books**, 62 Charing Cross Road, WC2, 020 7836 3697
- **Book and Comic Exchange**, 14 Pembridge Road, W11, 020 7229 8420
- **Gloucester Road Bookshop**, 123 Gloucester Road, SW7, 020 7370 3503
- **Magpie Bookshop**, 53 Brushfield Street, E1, 020 7247 4263
- **Skoob Books Ltd.**, 15 Sicilian Avenue, WC1, 020 7404 3063

CINEMA

If size is what you're after then Leicester Square is where you'll find the biggest picture houses with Warner West End and the Odeon often hosting national premieres. For these and local movie houses which show mainstream releases check listings, or phone *Scoot*, 0800 192192, for current programme information at any cinema in the country. In addition you can access programmed details or book at any Odeon cinema by ringing 0870 5050 007 or go to www.odeon.co.uk. Gathered together here are the independent and art house cinemas:

- **Barbican Screen**, Barbican Centre, Silk Street, EC2, 020 7638 8891
- **BFI IMAX Cinema**, South Bank, SE1, 020 7902 1234; located slap bang in the middle of one of the busiest roundabouts in town, the IMAX screen is an enormous 20 by 26 metres.
- **Curzon Soho**, 93-107 Shaftesbury Avenue, W1, 020 7439 4805, although part of a chain this cinema showcases the more unusual new releases and has excellent bar and cafe facilities, making it a nice place to hang out.
- **Goethe Institute**, 50 Princes Gate, Exhibition Road, SW7, 020 7411 3400; German films
- **ICA Cinematheque**, Nash House, The Mall, SW1, 020 7930 3647
- **Institut Francais**, 17 Queensberry Place, SW7, 020 7838 2144/2146; French films
- **Lux Cinema**, 2-4 Hoxton Square, N1, 020 7684 0201; London's newest and most dedicatedly obscure arthouse cinema.
- **National Film Theatre**, South Bank, SE1, 020 7928 3232; a cine-lovers dream with imaginative programming, a film bookshop and themed film festivals. Membership confers priority booking and ticket reductions. For details call 020 7633 0274.
- **Phoenix**, High Road, East Finchley, N2, call 020 8883 2233 for information and 020 8444 6789 for booking.
- **Prince Charles Cinema**, Leicester Place, WC2, 020 7437 8181; this cinema shows releases that are a couple of months old for a very cheap admission price. It's a great place for cult classics too, from *Sing-A-Long A Sound of Music* nights to the weekly screenings (Fridays) of *The Rocky Horror Picture Show*.
- **Pullman Everyman**, Hollybush Vale, NW3, 020 7431 1777; renovated to a high standard with a bar, bookshop and comfy seats.
- **Rio Cinema**, Kingsland High Street, Dalston E8, 020 7254 6677; charming local cinema.
- **Ritzy Cinema**, Brixton Oval, Coldharbour Lane, SW2, 020 7737 2121; independent multi-screen with something for everyone.

- **Riverside Studios Cinema**, Crisp Road, Hammersmith, W6, 020 8741 2255
- **Watermans Arts Centre**, 40 High Street, Brentford, Middlesex, 020 8568 1176

DANCE

The South Bank Centre and many theatres host dance events from time to time so check listings.
- **Sadler's Wells Theatre**, Rosebery Avenue, EC1, 020 7863 8000, is the capital's only large dedicated dance theatre. It's been refurbished to a high standard and offers an exciting programme of modern dance and performances by the Royal Ballet.
- **Peacock Theatre**, Portugal Street, WC2, 020 7863 8222
- **The Place Theatre**, 17 Duke's Road, WC1, 020 7387 0031, www.the-place.org.uk; small but established contemporary dance venue
- **Royal Opera House**, Covent Garden, WC2, 020 7304 4000; major ballet productions

COMEDY

Comedy clubs have burgeoned in popularity since the establishment of the Comedy Store and the first Jongleurs in the 1980s. These clubs launched a generation of British comedians including French and Saunders, Ben Elton, Rik Mayall, Ade Edmundson, and Alexi Sayle. Up-and-coming stand-up comedians are to be found at the pubs and clubs, while the more famous stars of TV sketch shows go on tours playing at larger theatres. A selection of the more established venues is listed below; others can be found listed in the press.
- **Banana Cabaret**, The Bedford, 77 Bedford Hill, Balham SE12, 020 8673 8904
- **Bound & Gagged**, Tufnell Park Tavern, Tufnell Park Road, N7, 020 8450 4100
- **Bound & Gagged Palmers Green**, The Fox, 413 Green Lanes, N13, 020 8450 4100
- **Camden Lock Tavern**, 35 Chalk Farm Road, NW1, 020 7387 9304
- **Canal Cafe Theatre**, The Bridge House, Delamere Terrace, W2, 020 7289 6054
- **Comedy Cafe**, 66 Rivington Street, EC2, 020 7739 5706
- **Comedy Spot**, The Spot, 29 Maiden Lane, WC2, 020 7379 5900
- **Comedy Store**, 1a Oxenden Street, SW1, 020 7344 0234
- **Downstairs at the Kings Head**, 2 Crouch End Hill, N8, 020 8340 1028

- **Hackney Empire**, 291 Mare Street, E8, 020 8985 2424
- **Jongleurs Battersea**, The Cornet, 49 Lavender Gardens, SW11, 0870 787 0707
- **Jongleurs Bow Wharf**, 221 Grove Road, E3, 0870 787 0707
- **Jongleurs Camden Lock**, Dingwalls Building, Middle Yard, Chalk Farm Road, NW1, 0870 787 0707
- **Soho Laughter Lounge**, The John Snow, 39 Broadwick Street, W1, 020 7437 1344
- **Tut & Shive Cabaret**, The Tut & Shive, 235 Upper Street, N1, 020 7359 7719

MAJOR ART GALLERIES

National collections are housed in the Tate Britain, the Tate Modern, the National Gallery, and the National Portrait Gallery (entry is free to all of these). Regular, large-scale, temporary exhibitions of major artists and movements are also held in these galleries and the others listed. The admission charge is usually around £8. If you're in the mood for trawling small upmarket galleries, these are numerous in the West End, along Cork and Dering streets. In the East End there is a vibrant gallery scene exhibiting the prodigious talent of London's young artists in all sorts of interesting spaces. Check newspaper and magazine listings for up-to-date information.

- **Barbican**, Barbican Centre, Silk Street, EC2, 020 7638 8891; changing modern exhibitions
- **Dulwich Picture Gallery**, College Road, SE21, 020 8693 5254; London's original public art gallery, displays an impressive collection of fine art.
- **Hayward Gallery**, South Bank Centre, SE1, 020 7960 5226; changing exhibitions
- **Institute for Contemporary Arts (ICA)**, The Mall, SE1, 020 7930 3647; changing exhibitions of modern art
- **National Gallery**, Trafalgar Square, WC2, 020 7839 3321, offers a permanent collection of fine art spanning Europe from the Renaissance until Post-Impressionism.
- **National Portrait Gallery**, St. Martin's Place, WC2, 020 7306 0055; view likenesses of heroes and villains, good, bad, and beautiful, through the ages.
- **Royal Academy**, Piccadilly, W1, 020 7300 8000; changing exhibitions of fine and modern art
- **Saatchi Gallery**, 98a Boundary Road, NW8, 020 7624 8299, phone for opening hours; this is where you'll find the most controversial and outrageous contemporary art.

- **Serpentine**, Serpentine Gardens, Hyde Park, W2, 020 7402 6075; changing exhibitions.
- **Somerset House**, Strand, WC1, 020 7845 4600; houses the Courtauld Gallery (Impressionists and Post-Impressionists); Gilbert Collection (gold and silver work); Hermitage Rooms (changing exhibitions of art and artefacts on loan from the State Hermitage in St Petersburg).
- **Tate Britain**, Millbank, SW1, 020 7887 8000; permanent collection of British art of all eras
- **Tate Modern**, Bankside, SE1, 020 7887 8000; a disused power station converted into an immense and stunning gallery space. The Tate Modern opened to great acclaim and popular interest in 2000 and houses a wealth of twentieth century art.
- **Whitechapel**, Whitechapel High Street, E1, 020 7522 7878; changing exhibitions

MUSEUMS—MAJOR

London's museums are some of the finest in the world. All of the following have entrance charges except the British Museum, but many grant free admission towards the end of the afternoon so phone for details.

- **British Museum**, Great Russell Street, WC1, 020 7323 8000; antiquities from Ancient Egypt, Greece, the Roman Empire and all periods of British history. Changing exhibitions of art from around the world. The famous round Reading Room of the British Museum, which used to house the British Library, is now open to the public as a reference library. It is surrounded by a new huge covered piazza strikingly designed in steel and glass.
- **Design Museum**, Butlers Wharf, Shad Thames, SE1, 020 7940 8790; the design secrets of everyday objects
- **Imperial War Museum**, Lambeth Road, SE1, 020 7416 5000; permanent collections of wartime paraphernalia from aircraft to medals; plus changing exhibitions focussing on different aspects of modern warfare and its impact.
- **Museum of London**, London Wall, EC2, 020 7600 3699, 24-hour information line, 020 7600 0807; offers a fascinating tour through London's past and present.
- **National Maritime Museum**, Romney Road, Greenwich, SE10, 020 8858 4422; atmospheric setting for the history of a sea-faring nation
- **London Transport Museum**, The Piazza, Covent Garden, WC2, 020 7836 8557; how London keeps moving—then and now, with lots of buses and trams on which to clamber about.
- **Natural History Museum**, Cromwell Road, SW7, 020 7942 5000; inspiring collections covering the earth's history, the development of

species and ecology; includes the Earth Galleries where you can experience a simulated earthquake.

- **Science Museum**, Exhibition Road, SW7, 020 7942 4455; an inspiring and imaginative museum dedicated to scientific discovery and innovation.
- **Victoria & Albert Museum**, Cromwell Road, SW7, 020 7942 2000; English fashions and household interiors through the ages

MUSEUMS—SPECIALIST

These are a few of London's many fascinating off-beat museums and collections. Opening times can be a bit erratic so it's sensible to phone before setting out. Unless otherwise stated, there is an admission charge.

- **Cabinet War Rooms**, King Charles Street, SW1, 020 7930 6961; the government's wartime hideout has been carefully preserved and a map chart still shows the exact positions of allied forces on VE day.
- **Cuming Museum**, 155-57 Walworth Road, SE1, 020 7701 1342; a treasury of all sorts of objects and curiosities which span the centuries; includes items relating to ancient Egypt, to the kings and queens of England, and to personalities such as Charles Dickens and Michael Faraday. Free admission.
- **Fan Museum**, 12 Crooms Hill, Greenwich, SE10, 020 8858 7879; yes, really!
- **Freud Museum**, 20 Maresfield Gardens, NW3, 020 7435 2002; Sigmund Freud: the man, the theories and *that* couch
- **Geffrye Museum**, Kingsland Road, E2, 020 7739 9893; view the history of English domestic interiors, including a recently opened 20th century gallery. Free admission.
- **Horniman Museum**, 100 London Road, Forest Hill, SE23, 020 8699 1872; an exploration of African lands, a music room and an aquarium are among the permanent exhibits at this south London museum. Free admission.
- **House of Detention**, Clerkenwell Close, EC1, 020 7253 9494; the story of one of London's oldest, busiest, and dankest prisons—not for the faint-hearted!
- **Jewish Museum Camden**, Raymond Burton House, 129-131 Albert Street, NW1, 020 7284 1997; collection of ceremonial art, plus changing exhibitions
- **Kew Bridge Steam Museum**, Green Dragon Lane, Brentford, Middlesex, 020 8568 4757; come here for great big engines that are set in motion at the weekends.
- **The Old Operating Theatre**, 9A St. Thomas Street, SE1, 020 7955 4791; a painstaking restoration of a Victorian operating theatre.

- **Ragged School Museum**, 46-50 Copperfield Road, E3, 020 8980 6405; this local museum reviews the lives of the children who attended Dr. Barnardo's Ragged School in Victorian times. Free admission.
- **Sir John Soane's Museum**, 13 Lincolns Inn Fields, WC2, 020 7405 2107; the ultimate Victorian collector amassed hoards of objects and oddities from around the world. Free admission.
- **Theatre Museum**, Russell Street, WC2, 020 7943 4700

TOURIST ATTRACTIONS

These are the most popular tourist honey-pots. Your kids or friends visiting from back home may clamour to be taken to these attractions and a great time may be had by all. But lines are likely to be long, especially in summer, and prices are high—you have been warned.

- **British Airways London Eye**, South Bank, SE1, 0870 5000 600; also known as the millennium wheel, this giant Ferris wheel affords a unique vantage point over London. Its panoramic views take in Battersea Power Station, the Houses of Parliament and Canary Wharf. Tickets for a ride in one of its glass pods are available in advance by phone. Turn up in person at the on-site box office for tickets less than a week ahead or to try to get tickets on the day.
- **London Aquarium**, County Hall, Westminster Bridge Road, SE1, 020 7967 8000
- **London Dungeon**, Tooley Street, SE1, 020 7403 7221; offers a gory exhibition charting torture and punishment throughout the ages, not suitable for young children.
- **London Planetarium**, Marylebone Road, NW1, 020 7935 6861
- **Madame Tussauds**, Marylebone Road, NW1, 020 7935 6861; perennially popular waxwork museum whose long lines try the patience.
- **Tower of London**, Tower Hill, EC3N, 020 7709 0765; nearly a thousand years of London's history to explore at the best example of a medieval fortress in Britain. Plus the crown jewels.
- **St. Paul's Cathedral**, St. Paul's Churchyard, EC4, 020 7236 4128; Christopher Wren's greatest achievement and an icon of London.

CULTURE FOR KIDS

Many theatres stage productions for kids, especially during the school holidays. Likewise some cinemas have special matinees. The museums and tourist attractions listed above are often suitable for children, with popular choices being the Natural History Museum (dinosaurs), the London Aquarium (sharks), and the Science Museum which, as well as offering terrific interactive displays, organises science night sleepovers for birthday parties. The big museums all organise kid-friendly workshops, events and fun during the school holidays too. Our four-legged friends at London's zoos and city farms are always firm favourites. For more ideas consult the **Parks and Open Spaces** and **Sport and Recreation** chapters—often parks, in conjunction with local authorities, run "one o'clock clubs" aimed at pre-school aged kids. These offer indoor and outdoor activities and are fully staffed, though children must be accompanied by an adult.

THEATRE AND PERFORMANCE

In addition to the theatres below which have regular kids' slots, many other venues put on special programmes for children during the school holidays, check listings magazines for details.

- **Battersea Arts Centre (BAC)**, 176 Lavender Hill, SW11, 020 7223 2223, runs a summer school for kids up to the age of fifteen, with arts, crafts, drama, and dance among the attractions.
- **Chats Palace Arts Centre**, 42-44 Brooksby's Walk, E9, 0208 533 0227, Saturday afternoon programmes encompass drama, clowns, storytelling and classes in dance and music.
- **Greenwich Theatre**, Crooms Hill, Greenwich, SE10, 020 8858 7755/8858 3800
- **Jackson's Lane Community Centre**, Archway Road, N6, 020 8340 5226, offers lots of holiday play-schemes with such exciting activities as circus skills and video-making.
- **Lauderdale House**, Waterlow Park, Highgate Hill, N6, 020 8348 8716/341 2032
- **Little Angel Theatre**, 14 Dagmar Passage, Cross Street, N1, 020 7226 1787
- **Lyric Hammersmith**, King Street, Hammersmith, W6, 020 8741 2311
- **Polka Theatre**, 240 The Broadway, Wimbledon, SW19, 020 8543 4888
- **Puppet Barge Theatre**, Little Venice, Blomfield Road, W9, 020 7249 6876
- **Theatre Royal, Stratford East**, Gerry Raffles Square, Stratford, E15, 020 8534 0310
- **Tricycle Theatre**, 269 Kilburn High Road, NW6, 020 7328 1000
- **Unicorn Arts Theatre**, 6 Great Newport Street, WC2, 020 7836 3334, offers acting workshops for four year olds and up.
- **Warehouse Theatre**, Dingwall Road, Croydon, 020 8680 4060
- **Watermans**, 40 High Street, Brentford, 020 8568 1176
- **Wimbledon Theatre**, The Broadway, SW19, 020 8540 0362

EXHIBITIONS

- **Bethnal Green Museum of Childhood**, Cambridge Heath Road, E2, 020 8980 2415
- **Pollock's Toy Museum**, 1 Scala Street, W1, 020 7636 3452
- **Thames Barrier Visitor Centre**, Unity Way, Eastmoor Street, SE18, 020 8854 1373; apart from the spectacle of the flood barrier itself, there are working models and hands-on exhibitions exploring the river's history and environment.

See the **Sport and Recreation** chapter for more child-friendly outings.

EVERYONE KNOWS THAT EXERCISE IS GOOD FOR YOUR HEALTH AND helps relieve stress. Over the past decade there has been a great expansion in the number of private fitness clubs and gyms to be found on the high street—so there's no excuse for not keeping that body beautiful! With the large amount of green space around the capital and the many parks within it, outdoor sporting facilities in London are excellent too. Getting involved in communal sporting activities can be a great way to meet people. Whether you have a passion for playing sports or love to watch, the capital has plenty to keep you active and occupied.

PROFESSIONAL SPORTS

AMERICAN FOOTBALL

American football is not big in Britain, but the country is represented in the NFL Europe by the **England Monarchs**. Visit their web site at www.monarchs.co.uk for game details.

BASKETBALL

NATIONAL BUDWEISER BASKETBALL LEAGUE
For the latest basketball news and results go to www.bbl.org.uk
- **London Leopards**, Brentwood Leisure Centre, Doddinghurst Road, Brentwood, Essex, 01277 230231, www.leopardsbasketball.com
- **London Towers**, Crystal Palace National Sports Centre, Ledrington Road, SE19, 020 8776 7755, www.london-towers.co.uk

The **women's league** is represented by the **London Heat**, Lee Valley Sports Centre, Quartermile Lane, E10, 020 8519 0017.

CRICKET

Cricket is the quintessential gentle English summer sport, which neverthe-less stirs up great passions. The season starts in April and stretches through the summer.

- **Lord's**, St. John's Wood Road, NW8, 020 7289 1611; the Middlesex County Cricket Club plays here. This historic ground also houses a small museum about the history of English cricket.
- **Oval**, Kennington Oval, SE11, 020 7582 6660; home to Surrey County Cricket Club and where many international matches are played.

FOOTBALL (SOCCER)

Football (calling it soccer won't win you any friends) is the national game and a national obsession. If you have the inclination, following "the beautiful game" allows you to take part in one of Britain's, and indeed Europe's biggest communal pastimes. English professional football is played in the F.A. Carling Premiership, which has 20 teams, and the minor Nationwide League, which is divided into three divisions. London has 13 professional football clubs of which five currently belong to the Premiership. These Premiership teams com-pete against other top-level teams such as Manchester United and Liverpool. The remaining seven London clubs are part of the Nationwide League. Such is football's popularity that tickets for Premiership games, which will set you back anything from £12 to £50, are often sold out well before the day of a match. Book ahead by phone using a credit card or buy in person at the grounds. For dedicated fans, season tickets are available. Tickets for lower divi-sion matches are much cheaper, as low as £5 for standing room (Premiership grounds are all-seaters with no standing room) rising to about £20 for the best seats, and are nearly always available on match day. The football season extends from September to May. Although most games are played on Saturday afternoons with a 3 p.m. kick-off, or on midweek evenings, days and times of matches sometimes vary to meet the demands of television coverage. In addition to competition within England, the best clubs from the Premiership also compete at the international level. They play in cup compe-titions against the best clubs from other leagues in Europe. There is also a team representing England as a whole made up of the best players in the country. The English team competes against other national teams in occa-sional championships such as the World Cup and the European Cup.

F.A. CARLING PREMIERSHIP CLUBS

- **Arsenal**, Arsenal Stadium, Avenell Road, N5, 020 7704 4000, www.arsenal.co.uk

- **Chelsea**, Stamford Bridge, Fulham Road, SW6, 020 7385 5545, www.chelseafc.co.uk
- **Fulham**, Craven Cottage, Stevenage Road, SW6, 020 7893 8383, www.fulhamfc.co.uk
- **Tottenham Hotspur**, White Hart Lane, High Road, N17, 020 8365 5000, www.spurs.co.uk
- **West Ham**, Boleyn Ground, Green Street, E13, 020 8548 2748, www.whufc.co.uk

NATIONWIDE LEAGUE CLUBS
- **Barnet**, Underhill Stadium, Westcombe Drive, Barnet, EN5, 020 8441 6932
- **Brentford**, Griffin Park, Braemar Road, Brentford, Middlesex, 020 8847 2511, www.brentfordfc.co.uk
- **Charlton Athletic**, The Valley, Floyd Road, SE7, 020 8333 4010, www.charltonathletic.co.uk
- **Crystal Palace**, Selhurst Park, Whitehorse Lane, SE25, 020 7771 8841, www.cpfc.co.uk
- **Leyton Orient**, Matchroom Stadium, Brisbane Road, E10, 020 8926 1111
- **Millwall**, The Den, Zampa Road, SE16, 020 7232 1222, www.millwallfc.co.uk
- **Queen's Park Rangers**, Loftus Road, South Africa Road, W12, 020 8740 0503/020 8743 0262, www.qpr.co.uk
- **Wimbledon**, Selhurst Park, Whitehorse Lane, SE25, 020 8771 8841, www.wimbledon-fc.co.uk

GOLF

- **Sunningdale**, Ridgemount Road, Sunningdale, Ascot, Berkshire, 01344 621681
- **Wentworth**, Wentworth Drive, Virginia Water, Surrey, 01344 842201

HORSE RACING

The horseracing year is divided into flat racing, which takes place between April and September, and National Hunt racing (races with jumps), from October to April.
- **Ascot**, High Street, Ascot, Berkshire, 01344 22211
- **Epsom**, Epsom Downs, Epsom, Surrey, 01372 470 470
- **Kempton Park**, Staines Road East, Sunbury-on-Thames, Surrey, 01372 470 047
- **Sandown Park**, The Racecourse, Portsmouth Road, Esher, Surrey, 01372 470 047
- **Windsor**, Maidenhead Road, Windsor, Berkshire, 01753 865234

MOTOR RACING

- **Brands Hatch**, Fawkham Longfield, Kent, 0990 125250
- **Wimbledon Stadium**, Plough Lane, SW17, 01256 333277

RUGBY

There are two different sorts of rugby played in Britain—Rugby Union and Rugby League. Rugby Union is professional, has 15 players on each team, the season runs from September to May and games are played on Saturday afternoons. Rugby League, with 13 players on each team, is far more popular in the north of England than it is down south, and is traditionally amateur, though it has been brought up to the professional level in recent years. International rugby and cup finals are played at **Twickenham Stadium**, Rugby Road, Twickenham, Middlesex, 020 8892 8161.

RUGBY UNION CLUBS
- **Blackheath**, Rectory Field, Charlton Road, SE3, 020 8858 1578
- **Harlequins**, Stoop Memorial Ground, Langhorn Road, Twickenham, Middlesex, 020 8410 5000
- **London Irish**, The Avenue, Sunbury-on-Thames, Surrey, 01932 783034
- **London Scottish**, Athletic Ground, Kew Foot Road, Richmond, Surrey, 020 8332 2473
- **London Welsh**, Old Deer Park, Kew Foot Road, Richmond, Surrey, 020 8940 2368
- **Richmond**, Athletic Ground, Kew Foot Road, Richmond, Surrey, 020 8940 8155
- **Rosslyn Park**, Upper Richmond Road, Priory Lane, Roehampton, SW15, 020 8876 1879
- **Saracens**, Vicarage Road, Watford, Hertfordshire, 01923 496009
- **Wasps**, Loftus Road, South Africa Road, W12, 020 8902 4220

RUGBY LEAGUE
- **London Broncos**, Stoop Memorial Ground, Langhorn Road, Twickenham, Middlesex, 020 8410 5000

TENNIS

The jewel in Britain's tennis crown is, of course, the Wimbledon fortnight. If you're a fan of the game don't miss the opportunity to experience these historic championships. Tickets for the big matches on the show courts are hard to come by. A primitive but fair system exists—drawing names out of the hat! Phone the All England Club (below) for details. During the first week of matches you can turn up and queue for a ticket on one of the show courts, or you can gain entry to the outer courts at any time to see un-seed-ed players and doubles matches. For a greater chance of seeing a big name without the queues try the Queen's Club Stella Artois Tournament which takes place at the beginning of June.

- **The Championships, Wimbledon**, All England Club, SW19, 020 8944 1066
- **Stella Artois Tennis Championships**, Queen's Club, W14, 020 7413 1444

PARTICIPANT SPORTS & ACTIVITIES

London has clubs and courses for just about every conceivable sport, of which those listed below are just a small selection. Call **Sportsline** on 020 7222 8000 if you're having trouble finding what you're looking for, or to find out about local cricket, football, and rugby teams. The weekly guide *Time Out* has a useful sports section that lists informal teams and activities. Library and college notice boards are good places to look too. Local author-ity-run leisure centres are listed under the borough profiles and are the best places to look to for badminton, squash, gym, and swimming facilities. The fees to use these are generally quite modest and you can usually get further reductions through the purchase of a borough leisure card. All the bor-oughs have slightly different schemes but generally a one-off fee will entitle you to reduced rate entry to all the borough's facilities. Many of the addi-tional leisure facilities below have several tiers of membership and varying session fees, so phone for details. Don't forget to ask about reduced rates for children, senior citizens and students.

For classes in indoor sports and activities like martial arts and yoga con-sult *Floodlight* or *OnCourse* to find details of courses, prices and locations.

PARKS AND RECREATION GROUNDS

Local parks often have playing fields, tennis and basketball courts, which are free. Parks are managed by local authorities so if you have any queries phone your local council number listed in the borough profiles and request the parks and leisure department.

ATHLETICS/TRACK & FIELD

Some of the most extensive track and field facilities in the capital are listed below. The big event in the running calendar is the **Flora London Marathon**, which takes place annually in April. Call 020 7620 4117 for details.

- **Barnet Copthall Stadium**, Great North Way, Hendon, NW4, 020 8457 9900
- **Croydon Sports Arena**, Albert Road, SE25, 020 8654 3462
- **Crystal Palace National Sports Centre**, Ledrington Road, SE19, 020 8778 0131
- **New River Stadium**, White Hart Lane, N22, 020 8881 2323
- **Paddington Recreation Ground**, Randolph Avenue, W9, 020 7798 3642
- **Queen Elizabeth Stadium**, Donkey Lane, Enfield, Middlesex, 020 8363 7398
- **Parliament Hill Fields**, Highgate Road, NW5, 020 7435 8998
- **Terence McMillan Stadium**, Maybury Road, E13, 020 7511 4477
- **Tooting Bec Track**, Tooting Bec Road, SW17 (no phone)

AUSTRALIAN RULES FOOTBALL

- **British Australian Rules Football League**, P.O. Box 6237, London, W12 9GA, 020 8992 5569, www.barfl.co.uk

BASEBALL

Baseball is not a very well organised sport in Britain, with teams and leagues springing up only to disappear again. The web site www.baseballsoftballuk.com will give you details on how to get involved with baseball currently being played in London.

BOWLING

- **GX Superbowl**, 15-17 Alpine Way, E6, 020 7511 4440
- **Hollywood Bowl**, Leisure Way, Finchley High Road, N12, 020 8446 6667
- **Rowans Tenpin Bowl**, 10 Stroud Green Road, N4 2DF, 020 8800 1950

BUNGEE JUMPING

If throwing yourself off a very high crane with only a piece of elastic around your ankles is your idea of fun, then you won't want to miss the opportunity of doing it over the Thames.
- **UK Bungee Club**, Chelsea Bridge Tower, Adrenalin Village, Queenstown Road, SW8, 07000 286433

CHESS, BRIDGE

The Chess World Championship was held in London in 2000. For fans of the game there is always plenty happening. The best place to get information about area chess clubs is from the London Chess Centre (details below). Staffed by experts, this should be the first stop for anyone interested in the game. It's a mine of information about **bridge** too. As UK chess clubs can be a bit stuffy, the casual player may be happier going to weekend tournaments—there is a thriving weekend quickplay tournament circuit here. Most fall and winter weekends, on either a Saturday or Sunday, you can show up in the morning, pay a small fee (around £10), and play in a "Swiss style" tournament. These are extremely competitive and gruelling, but very good fun!

- **London Chess and Bridge Centre**, 369 Euston Road, NW1, 020 7388 2404, www.chesscenter.com

CLIMBING

Don't let the minor fact that there are no rocks in London stop you from climbing.

- **The Castle Climbing Centre**, Green Lanes, N4, 020 8211 7000; fax: 020 8211 7000; Britain's biggest indoor rock climbing facility is housed in a spectacular Victorian folly—a pumping station built in the shape of a Scottish castle. Beginners courses available.
- **Mile End Climbing Wall**, Cordova Road, E3, 020 8980 0289; caters to all levels.

CYCLING

- **Herne Hill Velodrome**, Burbage Road, SE24, 020 7525 1540
- **Lee Valley Cycle Circuit**, Temple Mills Lane, E15, 020 8534 6085; open from March until October.
- **London Recumbents**, Rangers Yard, Dulwich Park, College Road, SE21, 020 7928 4785 and Staff Yard, Battersea Park, SW11, 020 7223 2533; have fun with recumbent multi-seater bikes in these two south London parks; kids' activities and cycle training also organised.
- **Original Bike Hire Company**, Richmond Bridge Boathouse, Surrey, 0800 013 8000

CYCLE SHOPS

The central London bike shops listed below offer sales and repairs and have knowledgeable staff. There are dozens more good bike shops in outlying areas of London. The London Cycling Campaign magazine, The London Cyclist (www.lcc.org.uk), is great for finding out about local cyclist groups, campaigns, activities, and sponsored rides.

- **Bikefix**, 48 Lambs Conduit Street, WC1, 020 7405 1218
- **Bike Park**, 11 Macklin Street, WC2, 020 7430 0083 and The Courtyard,

151 Sydney Street, SW3, 020 7565 0777, www.bikepark.co.uk; bike storage facilities.
- **Brixton Cycles**, 435-437 Coldharbour Lane, SW9, 020 7733 6055, www.brixtoncycles.co.uk
- **Cycle Surgery**, 9 Steward Street, Spitalfields, E1, 020 7375 3088, www.cyclesurgery.com; bike hire available too.
- **Evans**, 77 The Cut, SE1, 020 7928 4785
- **Mosquito Bikes**, 123 Essex Road, N1, 020 7226 8841, www.mosquito-bikes.co.uk
- **Psycho**, 553 Battersea Park Road, SW11, 020 7223 7549; specialise in mountain bikes.
- **Wheelie Serious**, 2 Nottingham Court, off Shorts Gardens, WC2, 020 7836 1752, www.wheelie-serious.com

For more on cycling in London see the **Transport** chapter.

DANCE

In addition to the dedicated dance class venues listed here, many other courses are offered in local centres around the capital; check *Floodlight* or *OnCourse* for details.
- **DanceWorks**, 16 Balderton Street, W1, 020 7629 6183, offers a wide range of dance courses.
- **Pineapple Dance Studio**, South Langley Street, WC2, 020 7836 4004

FENCING

The British Fencing Association web site, www.britishfencing.com holds details of the many smaller London clubs dedicated to the art.
- **The Fencing Academy**, Suite One, 37b New Cavendish Street, W1, 0800 096 0505; fax: 020 7625 2626; www.fencingacademy.org

FISHING

For information about fishing licences and where you can go to fish in London, contact the **London Anglers' Association** on 020 8520 7477.

FOOTBALL (SOCCER)

From workplace teams to amateur leagues, football is played obsessively at all levels in every corner of London. The **London Football Directory**, online at www.nikelondon.co.uk, is an excellent online resource for finding local park teams.

GOLF

While never fashionable, golf is always popular. A comprehensive list of upwards of 50 golf clubs in and around Greater London can be found at www.golfeurope.com.

PRACTICE AND LESSONS
- **Knightsbridge Golf School**, Lowndes Square, SW1, 020 7235 2468
- **Regent's Park Golf and Tennis School**, Outer Circle, Regent's Park, NW1, 020 7724 0643

GOLF COURSES
- **Airlinks**, Southall Lane, Hounslow, Middlesex, 020 8561 1418
- **Brent Valley**, Cuckoo Lane, W7, 020 8567 1287
- **Central London Golf Centre**, Burntwood Lane, SW17, 020 8871 2468
- **Chingford**, Bury Road, E4, 020 8529 5708
- **Lee Valley**, Picketts Lock Lane, N9, 020 8803 3611
- **Muswell Hill**, Rhodes Avenue, N22, 020 8888 2044
- **Richmond Park**, Roehampton Gate, Richmond Park, SW15, 020 8876 3205
- **Stockley Park**, off Stockley Road (A408), Uxbridge, Middlesex, 020 8813 5700

HORSE RIDING

- **Belmont Riding Centre**, Belmont Farm, The Ridgeway, NW7, 020 8906 1255
- **Ealing Riding Centre**, 17-19 Gunnersbury Avenue, W5, 020 8992 3808
- **Hyde Park Stables**, 63 Bathurst Mews, W2, 020 7723 2813
- **Wimbledon Village Stables**, 24 High Street, SW19, 020 8946 8579

ICE SKATING

- **Alexandra Palace Ice Rink**, Alexandra Palace Way, N22, 020 8365 2121; in addition to ice skating, you may also want to get involved in ice hockey here with one of the teams organised by Haringey Greyhounds Ice Hockey Club.
- **Broadgate Ice Rink**, Broadgate Circus, Eldon Street, EC2, 020 7505 4068; the only outdoor ice rink in the capital, open from October until the beginning of April.
- **Lee Valley Ice Centre**, Lea Bridge Road, E10, 020 8533 3154

- **Michael Sobell Leisure Centre**, Hornsey Road, N7, 020 7609 2166
- **Queens Ice Skating Club**, 17 Queensway, W2, 020 7229 0172
- **Streatham Ice Rink**, 386 Streatham High Road, SW16, 020 8769 7771

IN-LINE SKATING

- **Skate Attack**, 95 Highgate Road, NW5, 020 7267 6961; offering skate hire from £10 an hour and tuition from £20.
- **Slick Willies**, 41 Kensington High Street, 020 7937 3824; in-line skate rentals for £10 an hour, perfect for use in nearby Hyde Park.

MARTIAL ARTS

- **The Academy**, 16 Hoxton Square, N1, 020 7729 5789
- **The London Aikido Club**, 60a Windus Road, N16, 020 8806 3219, www.londonaikido.demon.co.uk
- **National Tai Chi Chuan Association**, 36 Queens Road, E11, 020 8556 6393

SCUBA DIVING

- **Scuba Training**, The Scuba Store, 204 Fulham Palace Road, W6, 020 7381 5000; as well as selling all the gear, Scuba Training runs courses at two pools in Putney and Chelsea.
- **Seymour Leisure Centre**, Seymour Place, W1, 020 7723 8336; home of the British Subaqua Club.

SKIING & SNOWBOARDING

There's rarely any real snow to speak of in London, but the upside is that these dry ski slope facilities are open all year round:

- **Bromley Ski Centre**, Sandy Lane, St. Paul's Cray, Orpington, Kent, 01689 876812
- **Beckton Alpine Centre**, Alpine Way, Beckton, E6, 020 7511 0351
- **Hillingdon Ski Centre**, Gatting Wall Park Road, Hillingdon, Middlesex, 01895 255183

SNOOKER & POOL

These are very popular pastimes and there are plenty of places to play in the capital. Look under "Snooker and Pool Centres" in the *Yellow Pages* or "Snooker, Billiards and Pool Halls" in *Thomson Local*, but don't forget that loads of pubs have pool tables where you can play for 50p.

SOFTBALL

Softball is a fast-expanding participant sport in Britain, with ten leagues in London organised into over 300 teams, all of which play co-ed slow-pitch. There are a smaller number of single sex and fast pitch teams. You can reach the **London Softball Federation** on 020 7453 7035, or look up www.baseballsoftballuk.com.

TENNIS

There are dozens of local tennis clubs in London, for more information check the web site: www.tennis.org.uk.
* **Islington Tennis Centre**, Market Road, N7, 020 7700 1370
* **Regent's Park Golf and Tennis School**, Outer Circle, Regent's Park, NW1, 020 7724 0643

WATERSPORTS

Since its demise as a working river, the Thames has become a playing one. Rowing, sailing, canoeing, jet skiing and water skiing are just some of the possibilities.
* **Capital Rowing Centre**, Polytechnic Boathouse, Ibis Lane, off Hartington Road, W4, 020 8742 1997
* **Docklands Sailing and Watersports Centre**, Westferry Road, E14, 020 7537 2626
* **Lee Valley Watersports Centre**, Banbury Reservoir, Harbet Road, E4, 020 8531 1129
* **Princes Club**, Clock House Lane, Bedfont, Kent, 01784 256153
* **Royal Docks WaterSki Club**, Gate 16, King George V Dock, Woolwich Manor Way, E16, 020 7511 7000
* **Thames Tradesmen Rowing Club**, Chiswick Boathouse, The Promenade, Duke's Meadows, W4, 020 8994 9470
* **Surrey Docks Watersports Centre**, Rope Street, SE16, 020 7237 5555

HEALTH CLUBS

As mentioned above, many local authority-run sports centres have gyms. Before you can use these you will usually have to pay a nominal fee (around £5 to £10) to undertake an induction course lasting a couple of hours. Then there is a charge to use the gym each time thereafter, with rates dependent on the time of day. For private gyms in outer London check the *Yellow Pages* under "Health Clubs and Fitness Centres" or *Thomson Local* under "Health Clubs, Gymnasiums and Beauty Centres." The health club chain **Holmes Place** has branches all over London; its excellent facilities include pools, fully equipped gyms, saunas, women only sessions and even childcare. Other large central London fitness centres are:

- **Central YMCA Club**, 112 Great Russell Street, WC1, 020 7343 1700; known as a good value club, this centre runs dozens of fitness classes. Alongside its gyms, are a pool and squash, badminton, volleyball and basketball courts. A trial day membership is £15; full membership prices are on a sliding scale.
- **Jubilee Hall Leisure Centre**, 30 The Piazza, WC2, 020 7836 4835; reasonable rates for extensive gym, racquet sports courts, alternative health clinic and health food restaurant.
- **The Oasis**, 32 Endell Street, WC2, 020 7831 1804; no membership needed to take part in the wide array of exercise classes, or to use the great gym and swimming pools, but joining will get you discounts.
- **Porchester Centre**, Queensway, W2, 020 7792 2919; pools and gym facilities.
- **The Sanctuary**, 12 Floral Street, WC2, 020 7240 9635; women only health club offering pool, steam room and beauty treatments.

SPORT AND RECREATION FOR KIDS

Get them away from the TV for a while!

- **Docklands Sailing and Watersports Centre**, Westferry Road, E14, 020 7537 2626; school holiday courses in sailing and canoeing, eight years and up.
- **Football Coaching**, Arsenal Football Club, Arsenal Stadium, Avenell Road, N5, 020 7704 4140; evening, weekend and holiday sessions.
- **Islington Boat Club**, 16-34 Graham Street, N1, 020 7253 0778; canoeing and boating for ages nine to eighteen.
- **MCC Indoor School**, Lord's Cricket Ground, NW8, 020 7432 1014; cricket coaching for age groups eight years and up.
- **Silver Blades**, 386 Streatham High Road, SW16, 020 8769 7771; your toddler can take his or her first step on ice here and there are "fun skate" courses for all ages.
- **Surrey Docks Watersports Centre**, Rope Street, SE16, 020 7237 5555; school holiday courses in dinghy sailing, canoeing and windsurfing, eight years and up.
- **Sutton Junior Tennis Club**, Rose Hill, Sutton, Surrey, 020 8641 6611; court hire and coaching for members
- **Thames Young Mariners**, Riverside Drive, Ham, Surrey, 020 8940 5550; courses for kids in kayaking, canoeing, sailing and power boating, eight years and up

ZOOS AND CITY FARMS

London has two major zoos, Chessington (with the massive World of Adventure theme park) and Regent's Park. Many local parks have small animal enclosures. City farms or petting zoos are designed to give inner-city kids a taste of animal husbandry and country life—you probably won't have to travel far to find one and admission is usually free or very cheap.

- **Chessington World of Adventures**, Leatherhead Road, Chessington, 01372 729560, www.chessington.com; attractions for all young ages, including Beanoland and white-knuckle rides such as the Vampire and Samurai.
- **Regent's Park Zoo**, Regent's Park, NW1, 020 7722 5909
- **College Farm**, 45 Fitzalan Road, Finchley, N3, 020 8349 0690
- **Corams Fields**, 93 Guildford Street, WC1, 020 7837 6138
- **Deen City Farm**, 39 Windsor Avenue, Merton Abbey, SW19, 020 8543 5300
- **Freightliners Farm**, Paradise Park, Sheringham Road, Holloway, N7, 020 7609 0467
- **Hackney City Farm**, 1a Goldsmiths Row, E2, 020 7729 6381
- **Kentish Town City Farm**, Cressfield Close, off Grafton Road, NW5, 020 7916 5420
- **Mudchute Park & Farm**, Pier Street, Isle of Dogs, E14, 020 7515 5901
- **Newham City Farm**, King George Avenue, Custom House, E16, 020 7476 1170
- **Spitalfields Farm Association**, Weaver Street, E1, 020 7247 8762
- **Stepney Stepping Stones Farm**, corner of Stepney Way and Stepney High Street, E1, 020 7790 8204
- **Thameside City Farm**, 40 Thames Bridge Road, Barking, Essex, 020 8594 8449
- **Vauxhall City Farm**, 24 St. Oswalds Place (entrance in Tyers Street), Lambeth SE11, 020 7582 4204

THEME PARKS

Children love the grandness and variety of these places. The (hefty) admission charges include all rides, so plan to spend at least a few hours in order to get your money's worth.

- **Legoland**, Windsor Park, Windsor, Berkshire, 0990 04 0404; situated west of London and open from mid-March to end of October. Includes rides, activities, and a whole landscape created from Lego bricks.
- **Thorpe Park**, Staines Road, Chertsey, KT16, 0870 4444 466; popular water rides, plus performances and a farm on site.

THE ENTHUSIASM OF VICTORIAN TOWN PLANNERS FOR BLENDING green spaces into the landscape of London, along with the tradition of enclosing bits of land as hunting-grounds for royalty, means Londoners have a lot more green on their horizon than many other city dwellers. In addition to the formally designated parks mentioned here, most neighbourhoods will have some kind of recreation ground, dog walking area, or children's playground nearby. These are of varying quality, some too small and near busy roads to be very pleasant, whilst others may be wino hangouts. You should be able to quickly assess how popular and safe a particular open space is by checking its daytime activity level and state of repair. London also has many garden squares, little peaceful oases, sometimes open only to residents. Their existence is a remnant from the 17th century when land would be leased out to property developers with the proviso that a central communal space be incorporated into the building plans. In otherwise heavily built up places like Bloomsbury and central Islington these provide welcome spaces for students and office workers in which to eat or study outside.

When exploring parks and gardens be aware of others. Dogs owners, although not obliged to by law, should clean up after their canines. (For a guide to what the capital has to offer our four-legged friends track down a copy of *Dogs' London* by Mary Scott.) Seclusion is obviously appealing but do avoid deserted places when you're on your own. For the most aesthetically pleasing experience it's worth seeking out some of the largest and best maintained parks of London.

The **royal parks** of London benefit from sustained care and investment, making them attractive and clean. Slap bang in the middle of things is **Hyde Park**, the biggest of the royal parks extending over 340 acres, and straddling the boroughs of Westminster and Kensington and Chelsea. Opened to the public at the beginning of the 17th century it was sold in 1652 for the princely sum of £17,000. The new owner was castigated at the time for charging one shilling for coaches to enter, and sixpence for horses! Suffice it to say these tolls have since been dropped. On the south-eastern side of the park are stretches of rolling lawn leading to a big lake, the Serpentine, which was formed by the damming of the Westbourne, one of London's many hidden rivers. There are boats to hire, and plenty of open space for picnics or just lazing in the sun. In the middle of the 19th century the Crystal Palace was erected between the park's main roads, Rotten Row and the Carriage Road, to house the Great Exhibition of 1851. This pinnacle of Victorian engineering was built using 4,000 tons of iron, 400 tons of glass and 30 miles of guttering and was tested by squads of sol-diers who were ordered to stamp up and down to check its strength. Unfortunately, after being painstakingly dismantled and rebuilt south of the river, the Crystal Palace was completely destroyed by fire in 1936 leaving only the legend and the name. In the northeastern corner of Hyde Park is Speakers' Corner, this much vaunted emblem of free speech is where assembled loons and zealots harangue the tourists every Sunday. If that's not your idea of fun, the Serpentine Art Gallery can be visited for a spot of cutting edge culture. For homesick Americans there are baseball games played here on the weekends.

Hyde Park melds with **Kensington Gardens** on its western edge, where there is a round pond and Kensington Palace, a royal residence. There is a memorial garden to the late Princess of Wales in this generally peaceful and uncluttered park. **Regent's Park**, to the north of Westminster, is another beautifully laid out royal park, complete with manicured lawns, an open-air theatre, and a boating lake, it is also home to the London Zoo. Located across Prince Albert Road, which runs around the northern bound-ary of Regent's Park, is **Primrose Hill**. This steep hill is great for flying kites and affords terrific views over the cityscape. The other two royal parks, **St. James's Park** and **Green Park** are smaller and tend to get rather crowded in summer but are still pleasant enough for a stroll or a jog. **Holland Park** has incorporated the remains of the old Holland House and has two gal-leries, a cafe, a posh restaurant and a theatre. There is a Youth Hostel within its grounds attracting many international visitors. It also offers wooded areas, a Japanese garden, a sculpture garden, and glimpses of animal life, including rabbits and peacocks.

On the borders of inner city boroughs Tower Hamlets and Hackney is **Victoria Park**, a splendidly spacious park with ponds, playgrounds, and playing fields. Interestingly it was the first park in the capital to be designed with local residents rather than royalty in mind. Also giving a breath of fresh air to the northeastern end of town is **Clissold Park** in Stoke Newington. Once an adjunct to a private estate, it retains features such as a herd of deer, goats, rolling grassland, and duck ponds, as well as Clissold House, the old manor house which is now a funky cafe. A small selection of animals and a mini adventure playground ensure that it is popular with the kids. The enormous **Hampstead Heath** serves north London, and is perhaps the most appealing park in London. Its 789 acres offer something for everyone. Panoramic views over the city can be taken in from the high ground of Parliament Hill. Legend has it that it is so named because Guy Fawkes and his cohorts planned to watch parliament burn from here after planting their bomb. Due to an unforeseen consequence of Victorian prudery, the park boasts single-sex bathing ponds which are now very popular with lesbians and gay men (the Heath is also known generally as a gay men's cruising ground). There is also the beautifully atmospheric 18th century Kenwood House where a series of outdoor classical music concerts is held in summer. North of the Heath, **Highgate Wood** is a charming place in which to wander ancient woodland. Also in the north of London is **Alexandra Palace Park**, known affectionately as the "Ally-Pally." The view is terrific from here. If you want to pick out landmarks in more detail there are coin operated telescopes. In addition to the permanent attractions of an ice rink and a pub with a terrace, a special children's funfair is open during the summer months. Further afield **Golders Hill Park** in NW11, has flamingos and other exotica, **Trent Country Park** out in Enfield offers 413 acres of grassland, woodland, lakes, and farm animals. There are similar attractions to be explored at **Fryent Country Park** in Brent.

In the central section of south London outdoor bathing is possible at the lido in Brixton's popular **Brockwell Park**. On the southern banks of the Thames, **Battersea Park** was the second park in London originally intended for use by the masses. It has a kid's zoo, a Victorian ornamental boating lake, and London's largest adventure playground. **Clapham Common** is the quintessential urban park with room for everyone: dog-walkers, joggers, idlers or cruisers. There are four ponds (one dedicated to model boats), football pitches, a children's playground, and two refreshment points—one a functional outlet for ice-cream and soft drinks, the other a brightly painted sixties throwback vegetarian cafe.

In the southeast of the city head for **Greenwich Park**, created as a deer park in 1433 by Henry VI. A cluster of tourist attractions like the Cutty Sark and the Maritime Museum are close at hand. The Royal Observatory, with the meridian line passing through it, is atop the park's hill where you can also experience fantastic views of the river, Docklands, and the Greenwich peninsula. **Burgess Park** in Camberwell, SE5, has a garden with plants and trees from all over the globe. **Crystal Palace Park**, SE20, offers ever-popular dinosaur models in its creaky Victorian Theme Park along with a mini-fair, mini-steam train, maze, and pony and traps—all great for kids. It also houses a concert bowl. In outer southeast London **Oxleas Wood**, the formation of which dates back to the ice age, **Castle Wood, Jackwood**, and **Shepherdess Woods**, form part of a green chain stretching 15 miles from the Thames Barrier to New Beckenham.

Look at any map of the city and you will immediately see that south-west London has the highest proportion of green space by far, with **Putney Heath** and Wimbledon Common linking with the two-and-a-half-mile wide Richmond Park. **Wimbledon Common**, once a common area used by all and sundry for grazing cattle and sheep, is today a multifaceted place perfect for a short stroll over rolling lawns or a hike through the park's densely wooded areas. The Royal Wimbledon Golf Course is at the souther-ly end of the Common, and The Windmill Museum is in its northern half. Built around a windmill surviving from 1817, the museum introduces you to the intricacies of windmill technology. The impressive 2,470 acres of the royal **Richmond Park** incorporate two fishing ponds, a pond for model boats, herds of deer, and an astonishing 24 football pitches. While there you might well believe you've left the city completely. The **Royal Botanic Gardens** at Kew is one of the world's top botanical institutions spawning many imitations in other cities. The Victorian and modern glasshouses hold over 9,000 varieties of trees and 40,000 species of plants from all over the globe. There's an entrance fee, but it's worth it as there are galleries, a marine display and many other things to see. Over the river, **Syon Park**, owned by the Duke of Northumberland, offers a stately home with beauti-ful landscaped gardens, a butterfly house, the "Great Conservatory," a gar-den centre and two long lakes. **Brent River Park** (known locally as "the bunny park" after its animal enclosures which contain monkeys, wallabies, reptiles and, yes, a few bunnies), runs through parts of Ealing.

The creation of the **Thames Path** has helped make the river more accessible to walkers. You can walk all 180 miles of it from the Thames Barrier east of London to the river's source in Cricklade, Gloucestershire, if you're feeling particularly energetic. Within London there are many pleas-ant and interesting stretches such as those at Hammersmith and Richmond. Forty years ago the water of the Thames was too dirty to sustain any form of animal life except for the occasional eel. One of the happier results of its decline as a working river is that it now supports upwards of 100 species of fish and 350 different species of invertebrates.

London's canals, while still an underused resource, provide a fascinat-ing glimpse of London's industrial heritage. You can stroll along the tow-path of the **Regent's Canal** which starts at Limehouse Basin and works its way through scruffy bits of East London to gentrified Islington, through still derelict land at King's Cross to Camden Lock and on past Regent's Park. Alternatively take a boat trip from Camden Lock. Further west the **Grand Union Canal** takes in the idyllic community of Little Venice with its canal-side homes, before snaking through the industrial estates and tangle of rail-way lines north of Wormwood Scrubs; it becomes a picturesque prospect again as it reaches Ealing. A good place to start or finish an exploration of the waterways might be the **London Canal Museum**, located in a former Victorian ice house at 12-13 New Wharf Road, N1, 020 7713 0836, www.canalmuseum.org.uk.

Greater London is surrounded by a green belt that, in theory, is protected from developers in a bid to stop urban sprawl. So the margins of London offer loads more parks and woods to enjoy. **Epping Forest**, which butts up against the eastern edge of the city, is one of the easiest greenspaces to get to and best to get lost in.

For information on those parks with special sports facilities, see the **Sport and Recreation** chapter. Finally for nature buffs, **The London Wildlife Trust** organises walks that explore the urban habitats of some of the capital's surprisingly varied wildlife, including bats and foxes. Call them on 020 7261 0447, or check www.wildlifetrust.org.uk/london.

ONDON'S ABSORPTION OF MANY CULTURAL COMMUNITIES ALLOWS for most of the world's religious organisations to be represented somewhere in the capital. In addition to spiritual commitment, many places of worship in London are notable for their colourful histories or striking architecture. Listed below are central contact numbers where they exist, and selections of some of the main places of worship in central London. Consult your *Yellow Pages* or *Thomson Local* under "Places of Worship" or "Religious Organisations" for more extensive listings.

CHRISTIANITY

ANGLICAN (CHURCH OF ENGLAND)

- **Southwark Cathedral**, Montague Close, SE1, 020 7367 6700; there has been a church here since the 7th century, but the main tower visible today was constructed in 1689. The cathedral has fascinating additions, monuments, memorials, and furnishings dating from many different periods. John Harvard, of Harvard University fame, was born locally and baptised here in 1607. The Harvard Chapel in the north transept of the cathedral is dedicated to his memory.

- **St. Paul's Cathedral**, St. Paul's Churchyard, EC4, 020 7246 8348; the original cathedral on this site was founded in 604 AD by the first Christian king in England—Ethelbert. In the latter half of the 17th century, after a chequered history, Christopher Wren was commissioned to rebuild the crumbling Norman cathedral on the site. Wren's design has a magnificent dome topped off with a cross rather than a traditional steeple. It is worth spending a few hours exploring both the exterior and interior of this remarkable religious monument.

- **Westminster Abbey**, 20 Deans Yard, SW1, 020 7222 5152, www.westminster-abbey.org; in the 11th century a church was built on this site at the behest of Edward the Confessor. His successor William I was crowned here starting a tradition that most kings and queens of England have followed. In the 13th century the abbey was redesigned in the French gothic style, unusual for London. The task of finishing the abbey took many centuries, culminating in Nicholas Hawksmoor's West Towers, which were completed in 1745. The abbey's vast array of tombs and monuments makes it a huge tourist draw. Alongside memorials to royalty, the aristocracy, famous scientists, engineers, and musicians, Poets' Corner commemorates a whole tradition of English writers, from Geoffrey Chaucer to the Brontes to T.S. Eliot. In the nave is the tomb of the Unknown Warrior, the body of a nameless soldier brought back from France after the First World War.

BAPTIST

- **Bloomsbury Central Baptist Church**, 235 Shaftesbury Avenue, WC2, 020 7240 0544; John Gibson built this Norman-influenced church structure in 1845.

CONGREGATIONAL

- **Orange Street Congregational Church**, Orange Street, WC2, 020 7321 0373; this church is built on a site with a long history of religious associations. A Huguenot chapel stood here in the 17th century, which later became a Church of England chapel, where the Reverend Augustus Toplady, composer of the hymn "Rock of Ages," preached.

EASTERN ORTHODOX

- **All Saints Greek Orthodox Church**, Camden Street, NW1, 020 7485 2149; built in the first half of the 19th century by father and son team William and Henry Inwood in a style full of Greek influences. All Saints has been Greek Orthodox since 1948.
- **Greek Orthodox Cathedral of St. Sophia**, Moscow Road, W2, 020 7229 7260; this Byzantine Revival architecture dreamt up by John Oldrid Scott was built in 1877.
- **Russian Orthodox Cathedral in London**, 67 Ennismore Gardens, SW7, 020 7584 0096

EVANGELICAL

- **Evangelical Alliance**, Whitefields House, 186 Kennington Park Road, SE11, 020 7582 0228

GAY & LESBIAN

- **Lesbian and Gay Christian Movement**, Oxford House, Derbyshire Street, E2, 020 7739 1249

INDEPENDENT/INTERDENOMINATIONAL

- **American Church in London**, 79a Tottenham Court Road, London W1, 020 7580 2791; when completed in 1760 Whitefields Tabernacle, as it was known, was the biggest Methodist church in the world, seating up to 8,000 worshippers. It is now a multi-denominational church with Calvinist roots.

JEHOVAH'S WITNESS

- **The Kingdom Hall**, 11 Monmouth Road, W2, 020 7792 0332

LATTER-DAY SAINTS/MORMON

- **Church of Jesus Christ of Latter-Day Saints**, 64-68 Exhibition Road, SW7, 020 7584 7553

LUTHERAN

- **Lutheran Council of Great Britain**, 30 Thanet Street, WC1, 020 7383 3081

METHODIST

- **Methodist Central Hall**, Storeys Gate, SW1, 020 7222 8010

PENTECOSTAL

- **Elim Pentecostal**, Kensington Temple, Kensington Park Road, W11, 020 7727 4877

ROMAN CATHOLIC

- **Brompton Oratory**, Brompton Road, SW7, 020 7808 0900; one of the most historic Catholic churches in town, the Oratory is a beautiful Baroque building. Inside are marble statues of the apostles from Siena Cathedral and a grand Italian altarpiece.

- **St. James Catholic Church**, Spanish Place, 22 George Street, W1, 020 7935 0943; this cavernous late 19th century gothic church is a popular venue for society weddings.
- **Westminster Cathedral**, Clergy House, 42 Francis Street, SW1, 020 7798 9055; home to the Archbishop of Westminster, this major English Catholic cathedral was constructed at the beginning of the 20th century out of Portland stone and brick. Its interior has spectacular columns and mosaics featuring over 100 different kinds of marble.

SOCIETY OF FRIENDS (QUAKERS)

- **Bunhill Meeting House**, Quaker Court, Banner Street, EC1, 020 7251 0376; the grave of George Fox, founder of the Society of Friends, lies in nearby Bunhill Fields, one of London's most historic burial grounds.
- **Friends House**, 173-177 Euston Road, NW1, 020 7663 1000; this is the British headquarters of the Religious Society of Friends. As well as a meeting house and offices, it has an extensive library of Quaker literature and historical documents.
- **Westminster Meeting House**, 52 St. Martin's Lane, WC2, 020 7836 7204

UNITARIAN

- **Essex Unitarian Church**, 112 Palace Gardens Terrace, W8, 020 7221 6514
- **General Assembly of Unitarian & Free Church Christian Churches**, Essex Hall, 1-6 Essex Road, WC2, 020 7240 2384

WESLEYAN

- **Wesley's Chapel and House**, 49 City Road, EC1, 020 7253 2262; Wesley's chapel was opened in 1778 and, after falling into disrepair over the middle years of the 20th century, was restored during the 1970s. There is a museum in the crypt and John Wesley's house is open to the public.

ISLAM

The web site, www.muslimdirectory.co.uk, is a great resource for finding out about area mosques.

- **London Central Mosque and Islamic Cultural Centre**, Regent's Park, 146 Park Road, NW8, 020 7724 3363; the plans to build a major mosque in London date back to the 1920s, but it was not until 1978 that the building opened.

- **East London Mosque**, 82-92 Whitechapel Road, E1, 020 7247 1357

JUDAISM

There are Jewish congregations of many different descriptions in and around the London area—those listed below are just a fraction. For comprehensive listings of synagogues and events, and for news, views, and contacts in London's Jewish community, try the web site: www.jewish.co.uk.

ORTHODOX—UNITED SYNAGOGUE

The mainstream orthodox movement in the UK:
- **Chelsea Synagogue**, Smith Terrace, Smith Street, SW3, 020 7352 6046
- **New West End Synagogue**, Bayswater Road, W2, 020 7229 2631
- **St. John's Wood Synagogue**, Grove End Road, NW8, 020 7286 3838
- **West End Great Synagogue**, 32 Great Cumberland Place, W1, 020 7723 9333

REFORM

- **West London Synagogue**, 34 Upper Berkeley Street, W1, 020 7723 4404

LIBERAL

- **Liberal Jewish Synagogue**, 28 St Johns Wood Road, NW8, 020 7286 5181
- **West Central Liberal Synagogue**, The Monatagu Centre, 21 Maple Street, W1, 020 7636 7627

SEPHARDI/SPANISH AND PORTUGUESE

- **Bevis Marks Synagogue**, Bevis Marks, EC3, 020 7626 1274; completed in 1701 and the oldest in Britain, this East End Sephardi synagogue was built as a monument to symbolise the return of the Jewish people to England in 1656, after an exile of some four centuries.
- **Spanish and Portuguese Synagogue**, St. James Gardens, W11, 020 7603 7961

EASTERN TRADITIONS

BAHA'I

- **London Baha'i Centre**, 27 Rutland Gate, SW7, 020 7584 0843

BUDDHIST

- **Buddhapadipa Temple**, 14 Calonne Road, SW19, 020 8946 1357
- **Heruka Buddhist Centre**, 13 Woodstock Road, NW11, 020 8455 7563, e-mail: info@heruka.org

HARE KRISHNA

- **International Society for Krishna Consciousness**, 10 Soho Street, W1, 020 7437 3662

HINDU

- **Swaminarayan Hindu Mandir**, 105-119 Brentfield Road, NW10, 020 8965 2651

WHEN YOU'RE SETTLING INTO A NEW ENVIRONMENT, VOLUN-teering can be a satisfying way of meeting like-minded people and getting involved in your new community. In Britain volunteering is becoming more popular all the time, increasingly recognised as a fulfilling way of using free time and/or of gaining valuable experience. Volunteering opportunities are plentiful in London, where many national charitable organisations are based. In addition, there are plenty of neighbourhood initiatives set up to tackle the problems of homelessness or young people in distress. Local hospitals and health care providers are always in need of volunteers, so contact them direct if you are interested in this field. There is a national helpline listed below, which will be able to assist you if you need further information on any aspect of volunteering. A number of volunteer bureaux throughout the capital will direct you to the many places where your help is needed locally, or try the search box at www.do-it.org.uk.

About twice monthly *The Guardian* newspaper carries adverts for specific volunteering opportunities, in its Wednesday Society subsection. Assistance in charity shops or volunteers to staff helplines are particularly sought after. On the first Monday of every month the *Evening Standard* carries a regular volunteer page. What follows is a list of organisations and charities that are always seeking new volunteers.

VOLUNTEER PLACEMENT SERVICES

NATIONAL

- **National Centre For Volunteering**, Carriage Row, 183 Eversholt Street, NW1, 020 7388 9888, www.volunteering.org.uk
- **National Association of Hospital and Community Friends**, 2nd Floor, Fairfax House, Causton Road, Colchester, CO1 1RJ, 01206 761227

- **Women's Royal Voluntary Service**, Volunteering Department, Milton House, Milton Hall, Abingdon, Oxon, OX13, 01235 442900; Britain's biggest organisation of volunteers (women and men) working throughout the community to help those in need.

LOCAL

- **Hackney Agency for Volunteering**, 92 Dalston Lane, E8, 020 7241 4443
- **Islington Volunteer Centre**, 65-69 White Lion Street, N1, 020 7833 9690
- **Lambeth Volunteer Development Agency**, 160 Westminster Bridge Road, SE1, 020 7401 9941
- **Volunteer Action Camden**, 207-215 King's Cross Road, WC1, 020 7284 6550
- **Volunteer Action Tower Hamlets**, 179-181 Whitechapel Road, E1, 020 7377 0956
- **Volunteer Action Westminster**, 37 Chapel Street, NW1, 020 7723 1216
- **Volunteer Bureau, Kensington & Chelsea**, Canalside House, 383 Ladbroke Grove, W10, 020 8960 3722

SPECIFIC CAUSES

AIDS

- **Crusaid**, 73 Collier Street, N1, 020 7833 3939, www.crusaid.org.uk
- **Terence Higgins Trust Lighthouse**, 52-54 Grays Inn Road, WC1, 020 7831 0330, www.tht.org.uk
- **The Food Chain**, 25 Bertram Street, N19, 020 7272 2272, www.food-chain.org.uk

ANIMALS

- **People's Dispensary for Sick Animals**, PDSA Voluntary Office, Unit 9, City Business Centre, Hyde Street, Winchester, SO23 7TA, 0800 854 194, www.pdsa.org.uk
- **Royal Society for the Protection of Animals**, Causeway, Horsham, West Sussex, RH12 1HG, 0870 3335 999, www.rspca.org.uk
- **Royal Society for the Protection of Birds**, The Lodge, Sandy, Bedfordshire, SG19 2DL, 01767 680551, e-mail: volunteers@rspb.org.uk, www.rspb.org.uk

CHILDREN

- **Childline**, Studd Street, N1, 020 7239 1000, www.childline.org.uk; national helpline for children in trouble—trains volunteer counsellors.
- **Home-Start Islington**, 11-12 Highbury Crescent, N5, 020 7609 2192
- **Friends United Network**, 404 Camden Road, N7, 020 7609 5444

CRIME

- **Victim Support**, Cranmer House, 39 Brixton Road, SW9, 020 7735 9166

CRISIS

- **The Samaritans,** central recruitment line: 020 7287 0545; provides emotional support to those who are despairing or suicidal.

CULTURAL IDENTITY

- **National Coalition for Black Volunteering**, 35-37 William Road, NW1, 020 7387 1681

CULTURE AND THE ARTS

- **National Trust**, 36 Queen Anne's Gate, SW1, 0207 222 9251, www. nationaltrust.org.uk

ELDERLY

- **Age Concern**, Age Concern England, Astral House, 1268 London Road, SW16, 020 8765 7200, www.ace.org.uk

DISABLED ASSISTANCE

- **Disability Sport England**, 13 Brunswick Place, N1, 020 7490 4919, minicom: 020 7336 8721
- **Kith & Kids**, c/o Irish Centre, Pretoria Road, N17, 020 8801 7432; befriending schemes for children and young people with disabilities.
- **Winged Fellowship Trust**, Angel House, 20-32 Pentonville Road, N1, 0207 833 2594, www.wft.org.uk; enabling people with disabilities to go on holiday.

DEVELOPMENT

- **Oxfam Volunteering Hotline**, 0845 3000 311, www.oxfam.org.uk

ENVIRONMENT

- **British Trust for Conservation Volunteers**, 80 York Way, N1, 020 7278 4293/4294; www.btcv.org.uk
- **Friends of the Earth**, 26 Underwood Street, N1, www.foe.co.uk
- **Greenpeace**, Canonbury Villas, N1, 0207 865 8100, www.green-peace.org.uk
- **Tidy Britain Group**, Elizabeth House, the Pier, Wigan, WN3 4EX, 01942 824620, www.tidybritain.org.uk

HEALTH AND HOSPITALS

Something most of us can do which takes up very little time but helps save lives is give blood—phone 0845 7711 711, or visit www.bloodnet.nbs.nhs.uk for more information.

- **British Red Cross**, 9 Grosvenor Crescent, SW1, 020 7235 5454, www.redcross.org.uk
- **Cancerlink**, www.cancerlink.org; national network with many local groups and services
- **St. John Ambulance**, 1 Grosvenor Crescent, SW1, 020 7235 5231, www.sja.org.uk

HOMELESS SERVICES

- **Crisis**, 1st Floor, Challenge House, 42 Adler Street, E1, 020 7655 8323
- **Homeless Network**, Alliance House, 12 Caxton Street, SW1H 0QS; write enclosing a self-addressed, stamped (41p) envelope for a copy of *Time to Help*—a guide to volunteering opportunities for people wishing to help the homeless in London.

LESBIAN & GAY

- **Lesbian and Gay Switchboard**, P.O. Box 7324, London N1 9QF, 020 7837 7324, www.llgs.org.uk
- **Stonewall**, 46-48 Grosvenor Gardens, SW1, 020 7881 9440, www.stonewall.org.uk; lobbies for lesbian and gay equality.

LITERACY

- **Volunteer Reading Help**, High Holborn House, WC1, 020 7404 6204; targets children in schools who need additional help with reading.

MENTAL HEALTH

- **Mencap**, National Centre, 123 Golden Lane, EC1, 020 7454 0454
- **Mind**, www.mind.org.uk; volunteers work on mental health telephone information service.
- **SANE**, 199-205 Old Marylebone Road, NW1, 020 7375 1002

YOUTH

- **Barnardo's**, Tanners Lane, Barkingside, Ilford, Essex IG6 1QG, 020 8550 8822, www.barnardos.org.uk
- **Guide Association**, Commonwealth Headquarters (CHQ), 17-19 Buckingham Palace Road, SW1, 020 7834 6242, www.guides.org.uk
- **Scout Association**, Baden-Powell House, Queen's Gate, SW7, 020 7584 7030, www.scoutbase.org.uk
- **UK Youth**, 2nd Floor, Kirby House, 20-24 Kirby Street, EC1, 020 7242 4045, www.youthclubs.org.uk

G ETTING TO A POINT OF COMFORT AND EASE WITH THE PUBLIC transport system is essential in a city the size of London. Generally it's convenient and efficient—particularly when compared to getting around the city by car. In fact, many Londoners rely on some form of public transport, making it a big public policy issue too. You will soon notice that conditions of travel in the capital, both for drivers and those reliant on public transport, are a frequent topic of conversation and the butt of many jokes. Just consider the issues of trying to get about in the capital as the glue that binds Londoners together, and try to remember that patience is a virtue!

PUBLIC TRANSPORT

There is a 24-hour phone line offering timetable information, up-to-the-minute news about how services are running, and advice on the best way to travel within the city: **London Travel Information**, 020 7222 1234, minicom: 020 7918 3015, www.transportforlondon.gov.uk. Ring this number with questions about **all public transport** within the Greater London region.

THE LONDON UNDERGROUND

The London Underground system, universally referred to as "the Tube" and designated by a red circle with a horizontal line running through it, is one of the most comprehensive of any in the world. A mind-boggling 2.5 million journeys are made on it every day. The first line opened in 1863 and used steam engines to take passengers between Paddington and Farringdon. Electric trains were introduced in 1890. The Underground as we now know it was developed by an American, Charles Tyson Yerkes, who built the now-derelict generating plant in Lots Road, Chelsea. Running on over 260 miles of track, the system covers an area of 630 square miles. Although increasingly complicated due to annual extensions and additions of new lines, Tube users benefit from a very easy to understand map, which is often cited as a modern design classic. (Just don't imagine that it actually bears any resemblance to the true geography of the city!) You can pick up the essential **Tube map** from most stations or find it on the back of an *A-Z*. Or go online to www.thetube.com where you can research routes, schedules, and determine travel times.

The London Underground service is generally reliable and efficient, but problems do exist and delays are more common and severe than one would hope. Some lines, particularly the Northern Line (long dubbed "the misery line" by regular users), suffer from outdated rolling stock and stations in urgent need of renovation. The system is heavily biased towards north London, with a mere 32 stations out of almost 300 located south of the river. Tube services start at about 6 a.m. and finish around midnight. One final note: no smoking is allowed anywhere on the London Underground network. This rule is almost universally observed due to the 1987 fire at the King's Cross underground station, which tragically claimed the lives of 31 people—the cause was a discarded cigarette.

FARES

Much to the chagrin of Londoners, fares on the underground are more expensive than those of any other comparable world city, and they increase every January. The network is divided into six zones—fares are determined by your start zone, the zones you travel through, and your destination zone. Zone 1 covers most of the City and the West End, and is the most expensive one to travel into and around. In January 2001, a one-way journey between two stops in Zone 1 cost £1.50 (child 60p), between two stops in the same outer zone the price was 90p (child 40p). Travelling into Zone 1 from Zone 2 was £1.90 (child 80p) each way; £2.20 (child £1) from Zone 3. Children travel at reduced rates, but there are no fare reductions for students or senior citizens. You can buy tickets from automated ticket machines or from staffed windows in the stations. Note: if you are caught travelling without a valid ticket you may be liable for a £10 on-the-spot fine. In addition, all stations in Zone 1, and a large proportion of others, have automatic ticket gates through which you cannot pass without a ticket.

If you are travelling every weekday at peak hours, it's generally cheaper to buy a weekly, monthly or annual pass. Tube passes are accepted on buses and trains within London. For weekly, monthly, and annual passes you'll need a passport-sized photograph for a photocard. One-day travelcards (valid after 9:30 a.m. on weekdays and all day Saturday and Sunday) and weekend travelcards are available without a photocard, and give you the freedom to use the Tube, bus, and rail in specified zones. They're particularly good for exploring the city and, except for single one-way journeys, they are nearly always the best value option. Travelcards can be purchased from all Tube stations as well as from the many newsagents with a "pass agent" sign displayed. Rates for a one day or weekend travelcard vary, depending on the zones you need it to cover. If you're travelling with the kids you can get a one day family travelcard—the price depends on the number of adults and children in the group but works out to be less expensive than buying individual travelcards.

THE DOCKLANDS LIGHT RAILWAY (DLR)

The **DLR**, 020 7918 4000, www.dlr.co.uk, is a light rail system built in the 1980s to serve the new business district of Docklands. Initially its dinky, driverless trains were regarded as something of a novelty. Over the early- and mid-1990s the system came into its own, and is heavily relied upon by Docklands' growing number of workers. However, the realisation that the DLR would prove inadequate to cope with the ever expanding Docklands business community was the impetus for the final go ahead for the Jubilee line extension. The DLR now covers a large patch of east London and Docklands, intersecting with the Tube network at Bank, Tower Hill and Stratford.

TRAMLINK

After its successful reintroduction in Manchester and other major UK cities, this mode of transport made its first reappearance in London in over 40 years with the opening of the Tramlink light rail network in November 1999. The trams run on dedicated tracks and combine the best elements of bus and train—energy efficiency and no fumes. Tramlink covers suburban south London, linking Wimbledon, Croydon, New Addington and Beckenham. For more information call **Tramlink**, 020 8681 8300, www.croydentramlink.co.uk.

BUSES

Many people living in London avoid buses if they can, regarding them as mysterious and quixotic. However, with a bit of research and bravery, it may be that bus lines in your part of town prove to be a useful addition or cheaper alternative to the Tube. In some parts of the city ill served by the Tube, notably many areas of south London, public transport by bus becomes essential. All areas have local bus maps, which usually can be found at local libraries. In addition to the famous red two-deckers, buses in London now come in all sizes and colours, and are divided into two types:

driver-only buses and those with conductors. All buses can be boarded at designated stops by putting your hand out to indicate you want to get on. You enter driver-only buses through the front entrance, state your destination and pay the driver your fare. Buses with conductors are entered at the rear of the vehicle, and you state your destination and pay the fare to the conductor when he/she requests it, after finding your seat. Single bus fares are either 70p for a journey outside Zone 1, or £1 for a journey into or within Zone 1. Try to have some change ready when boarding a bus, £5 notes are usually fine, but many drivers and conductors will refuse to change anything larger. Travelcards are valid on buses, but you can also get passes just for buses. Senior citizens are entitled to a bus pass, which gives them free travel, and children travel at a reduced rate; there are no student discounts. The penalty is £5 for not being in possession of the correct ticket. Low-floor buses, which are easier for wheelchair users, the less mobile, and those with buggies to negotiate, operate on some routes.

Regular bus service ends somewhere between 11 p.m. and 12.30 a.m. From then on the only available public transport is **Night Buses**, which provide a limited service running between Trafalgar Square and points all over London. For details about routes and times get the free booklet "Buses for Night Owls" by phoning 020 7222 1234, or check online at www.transportforlondon.gov.uk. Night Bus fares are significantly higher than those for equivalent daytime routes, but all travelcards are valid on Night Buses.

RAIL

Prior to 1995 a nationalised company called British Rail (BR) operated all train services within mainland Britain. With privatisation came a multitude of companies offering different services on different lines. So while people still use the terms British Rail or BR as shorthand to designate all overland train services, there is actually no such thing. Train schedules are displayed in stations or can be accessed by phoning **London Travel Information**, 020 7222 1234, www.transportforlondon.gov.uk.

SERVICES WITHIN LONDON

There are a number of rail lines traversing London to and from the suburbs and the home counties. For residents of south London or Hackney these services are heavily used by commuters travelling into the City and the West End. For other areas too they can offer a handy by-pass of the Tube. Silverlink Metro, which runs the North London line, provides the only east-west rail link that doesn't involve going through the middle of town, linking stations in east London through a wide arc of north London over to Kew in the west.

MAINLINE STATIONS

London has a number of mainline stations that offer services to the rest of the country, and in the case of Waterloo International, to the continent via the Channel Tunnel Rail Link. For details about all mainline services, call **National Rail Enquiries** on 08457 484950, minicom, 0845 6050600. Online check out www.thetrainline.com or www.railtrack.co.uk (the latter does not offer online ticket sales).

- **Paddington Station**, W1, serves the west of England and Wales; the fabulous new Heathrow Express runs from here.
- **Liverpool Street**, EC1, offers service to Stansted Airport, Hertfordshire, Cambridgeshire and Essex.
- **King's Cross**, N1, offers service to the Northeast of England (including York and Newcastle) and the east coast of Scotland (Edinburgh, Aberdeen, Inverness).
- **St. Pancras**, N1, serves the Midlands and Luton Airport.
- **Euston**, NW1, offers service to the Northwest of England (Liverpool, Manchester) and west of Scotland (Glasgow); trains to Stansted Airport.
- **Victoria**, SW1, offers service to the South coast and the Gatwick Express.
- **Waterloo**, SE1, for trains to Kent, Surrey and Hampshire, plus the Channel Tunnel Rail Link to Paris and Brussels.

Charing Cross, Fenchurch Street, and Marylebone offer various commuter trains to outlying areas.

DISABLED PASSENGERS

Wheelchair accessibility (lift access to platforms), previously limited, is now available at a handful of Tube stations, and the situation is constantly improving. All new transport developments incorporate disabled access as a matter of course, and include lift access, step-free access, and both audible and visual information systems. The Docklands Light Railway and Tramlink are fully accessible, and the new stations on the Jubilee line offer lift access. Many trains are able to accommodate wheelchairs and all the major London mainline stations have accessible toilets. With 24-hours notice, train companies aim to guarantee assistance at larger stations to those who are in a wheelchair or need wheelchair assistance, or who are blind, partially sighted, deaf, or registered disabled. Phone National Rail Enquiries on 08457 484950 to make arrangements. Discount train fares are available to those who qualify for a Disabled Persons Railcard. For criteria and further information ask for an application form at any mainline station or write to the **Disabled Persons Railcard Office**, P.O. Box 1YT, Newcastle-upon-Tyne, NE99 1YT.

Travelling between stations is made possible by the fully accessible Stationlink bus service, which runs hourly in a loop connecting the mainline train terminals and Victoria Coach Station. The Airbus, 020 8400 6655/minicom 020 7918 3015, www.airbus.co.uk, which carries passengers between Heathrow and Victoria and King's Cross, is also wheelchair accessible. Special Mobility Buses operate a limited service in most parts of London and some regular bus routes now use "low floor" or "kneeling" buses that can be accessed by passengers in wheelchairs and those less mobile. All newly built buses have stopping signs, palm press bells, and colour-contrasted handrails. Contact the **Unit for Disabled Passengers, London Transport**, 172 Buckingham Palace Road, London SW1, 020 7918 3312, minicom, 020 7918 3876, for up-to-date information on all these services. The Unit is responsible for the Stationlink and Mobility Bus services, and publishes an invaluable guide called "Access to the Underground." Additional information is available in the form of leaflets, tapes, and Braille.

CAR OR MOTORCYCLE

Drivers new to Britain are strongly advised to buy a copy of "The Highway Code," available from most bookshops and larger newsagents, which offers a comprehensive account of the rules of the road. Remember, in Britain, unlike most of the world, we drive on the left. The speed limit in residential areas is 30 m.p.h. and the wearing of seatbelts in front and rear seats is compulsory. Riders of motorcycles, scooters or mopeds, and their passengers, must wear approved safety helmets.

The fact that traffic in London moves as slowly as it did during the time of horse and carriage doesn't seem to deter anyone from driving. In fact, traffic-jams and delays are the rule rather than the exception—the inevitable result of 140,000 cars driving towards the same centre every day. And, the "rush hour" has long since expanded to include most of the day and evening. The "school run" also plays havoc in many local areas as parents drop off their children at school before 9 a.m. and pick them up again around 3 p.m. (ironically the worry most parents cite as a reason for accompanying their children to school is traffic). Other things to look out for when driving around London include one-way systems and roundabouts. Road congestion in the capital and its resultant pollution is a major concern of the new Greater London Authority. Strategies will likely include some form of road tolling. While all London radio stations provide traffic information and bulletins, Capital Radio, on 98.5 FM, which has a helicopter, and London Live, on 94.9 FM, which has access to police traffic monitoring cameras, are the most reliable.

TAXIS AND MINICABS

Black cabs are the large distinctive taxis you see on London's streets. They are traditionally black but sometimes now are covered in advertising. In order to gain a licence, a driver must have passed "the Knowledge" which requires a lengthy study of London's streets. When the sign above the windscreen is lit up and displays the words "For Hire," or "Taxi" you are free to hail the cab. Black cabs can also be booked by phoning 020 7272 0272 or 020 7253 5000. Cabs have a meter and a minimum charge. Inside each one there is an individual registration number, which should be noted for any complaints. Many black cabs are wheelchair accessible. A Taxicard system, funded by the borough councils, provides disabled residents with discounts on taxi journeys (phone 020 7484 2929). The administrating body for black taxis is the Metropolitan Police. Any complaints should be addressed in writing to: the Assistant Commissioner of Police, Public Carriage Office, 15 Penton Street, London N1 9PU.

Licensed black cabs are the only taxis that can be hailed in the street, and while relatively expensive, the service generally is superior to the legions of private minicab firms. London was unique in the country in having an unlicensed minicab sector. This led to a huge number of firms operating, many with low standards of service. As of October 2001, all minicab firms are required to have a licence, and it's clear standards are improving. If you discover a local cab firm which is reliable and cheap, stick with it. Be aware, it is illegal for minicabs to tout for business on the street; they should always be prior booked or booked on the spot in a cab office. Never get into a cab without knowledge of the driver's firm. For cab firms check the *Yellow Pages* or *Thomson Local* under "minicabs."

CAR HIRE

In addition to the national companies listed below, there are numerous local car hire services operating, often with more competitive rates than the nationals. Look in the *Yellow Pages* or *Thomson Local*, or call *Talking Pages* on 0800 600900.

- **Alamo**, 0800 272300
- **Avis**, 0990 900500
- **Budget**, 0800 181181
- **easyRentacar**, www.easyRentacar.com
- **Eurodollar**, 0990 365365
- **Europcar**, 0345 222525
- **Hertz**, 0990 996699
- **Kenning**, 0541 567567
- **Thrifty**, 01494 442110

MOTORWAYS

Motorways are the largest roads in the UK, linking major towns and cities across the country. They (usually) have three lanes of traffic going in each direction, with no pedestrians or cyclists allowed. The motorway system aims to provide straightforward and regulated ways of travelling long distances— the equivalent of freeways in the United States. Stopping is not allowed except at designated service stations and the speed limit is 70 m.p.h. The M25 is the orbital motorway that rings Greater London. Other motorways which radiate outwards from London towards other major cities are:

- **M1** for northern England
- **M40** for Oxford and Birmingham
- **M4** for western destinations: Bristol, Wales and the southwest
- **M3** for southern England, through Hampshire to Southampton
- **M23** for Gatwick Airport
- **M20** for Kent and the Channel ports
- **M11** for Harlow, Stansted Airport and Cambridge

ROAD CLASSIFICATION

"A" roads are major routes. They include dual carriageways, which have two lanes in either direction, and where motorway speed limits apply. At certain points an "A" road may have three lanes in each direction, as is the case for a motorway; this is designated by an "M" in brackets. In addition to having a street name, an "A" road also is designated by a number. "B" roads are minor routes marked on maps by a "B" and a number. Generally, within London, "A" and "B" roads are known by their street names; once they reach the countryside they are more likely to be referred to by their numbers. Important London "A" roads, moving traffic in, out, and around town, include:

- **A406**, North Circular, a broad arc from the Chiswick Roundabout (start of the M4 motorway) around north London to East Ham and Barking.
- **A205**, South Circular, from Woolwich in the southeast of London through the southern halves of Greenwich, Lewisham, Southwark and Lambeth to Clapham Common and the A3. Note the North Circular and South Circulars do not meet.
- **A1**, from Angel and Islington north along Upper Street/Holloway Road to Highgate to meet the North Circular at Finchley and then progresses north.
- **A2**, Old Kent Road/Shooter's Hill Road, from Borough near Tower Bridge eastwards towards Kent.
- **A3**, from Elephant & Castle, southwest through Lambeth, Wandsworth to Wimbledon and beyond.

- **A4**, leading westwards from Piccadilly through Kensington, Hammersmith and Chiswick to become the M4 motorway.
- **A5**, runs north-west along Edgware Road/Maida Vale Kilburn High Road/Cricklewood Broadway and beyond.
- **A40**, runs across west London from Paddington.
- **A41**, Finchley Road/Hendon Way leading out of London to Watford.
- **A10**, a dead straight road running north from the City through Hackney to Tottenham and further north.
- **A102**(M), the Blackwall Tunnel.

CYCLING

Cycling is a healthier, cheaper, greener, and often faster alternative to the car. Once converted to pedal power, few go back. Unfortunately, many in London are initially put off by the perceived dangers of heavy traffic and pollution. For safety's sake a cycle helmet, fluorescent clothing or accessories, and good bike lights are certainly necessary. Some dedicated cycle routes do exist in London but as yet their coverage is patchy and ill-maintained. As bike travel gains in popularity, cyclists' needs are gradually being taken more seriously, and policy-makers are beginning to take notice. The good news: the London Cycle Network, with the backing of the government and the local authorities, aims to develop over 2000 km of cycle routes across London over the next few years. It is a good idea to find out how cycle friendly your local roads are and how confident you feel before you buy a bicycle. There are numerous local cycling clubs and networks so check in your nearest cycle shop or library for leaflets or notices. For general cycling advice and information contact the **London Cycling Campaign (LCC)**, 020 7928 7220, www.lcc.org.uk. Membership of the LCC will provide you with a regular magazine to keep you up-to-date on cycling issues and allows you to claim discounts at many bike shops throughout the capital (see **Sport and Recreation**).

BIKE PARKS

It costs about 50p a day to store your bike in these secure and dry surroundings.
- **Covent Garden**, 11-13 Macklin Street, WC2, 020 7430 0083, www.bikepark.co.uk; workshop and changing room on site.
- **Chelsea**, The Courtyard, 151 Sydney Street, SW3, 020 7565 0777, www.bikepark.co.uk; the site includes shop, shower facilities and coffee shop.

AIRPORTS

London is well served with airports: five are close by. (For details of cut-price airlines, see **Quick Getaways**.)

- **Heathrow**, reached via the Piccadilly Line, Airbus, and the new express train link from Paddington, is one of the world's busiest airport, 0870 000 0123, www.baa.co.uk.
- **Gatwick**, lying south of London, is popular for charter and holiday flights and is served by the Gatwick Express from Victoria and the Thameslink service from King's Cross, 0870 0002 468, www.baa.co.uk.
- **Stansted**, in Hertfordshire, is served by train links from Liverpool Street and Euston, 0870 0000 303, www.baa.co.uk.
- **Luton**, reached via King's Cross Thameslink, is in Bedfordshire, and is served by the cut-price airline Easyjet, which offers inexpensive flights to major destinations on the continent and elsewhere in the British Isles, 01582 405100, www.easyjet.com.
- **London City** is a small city centre airport near the City and Docklands, used mostly by business passengers. It can be reached via Silverlink train services or shuttle bus from Liverpool Street, Canary Wharf or Canning Town stations. At present London City offers two or three flights to the continent per day, 020 7646 0000, www.londoncityairport.com.

HUNDREDS OF HOTELS, GUESTHOUSES AND B&BS, RANGING FROM sparse lodgings to the most luxurious top international hotels, can be found on London's streets. The biggest clusters of hotels are in the tourist districts of Westminster and Kensington and Chelsea, but there's no shortage of places to stay elsewhere. Even though hotels and bed & breakfasts, especially those in these central areas, are expensive, we have tried to pick out some reasonably priced options in town.

Keep in mind that room rates vary by the season, and that summer is the most expensive, followed by the holiday periods of Christmas and Easter. All prices given are for a single room (add about 20% for a double). Generally accommodation can be booked by phone, using a credit or debit card. Usually a deposit is requested with a reservation, which will then be deducted from your final bill. If you don't fancy ringing hotels yourself, the **London Tourist Board's Telephone Accommodation Booking Service**, 020 7932 2020, can recommend a place that meets your requirements and will advise on hotels suitable for extended stay.

The following list of hotels is by no means complete. For a more exhaustive account with recommendations, there are numerous hotel guides available produced by the English Tourist Board, RAC, and AA (the AA has a web site that includes hotel recommendations, www.theaa.co.uk). A less expensive and perhaps more interesting option is "home-stay" where you room with a British family. Also included are budget options such as staying at a youth hostel or university dormitory.

BOOKING ONLINE

You can trawl the net for your ideal place or look for last minute vacancies and discounts at these web sites:

- **www.LondonTown.com**
- **www.ukhotelfinder.com**

- **www.ukhotelreservations.co.uk**
- **www.bookhotel.com**
- **www.budgethotel.co.uk**

BED & BREAKFASTS

There are many B&Bs in London that operate as temporary homes for homeless families (local authorities foot the bill), and the standards of such establishments are very poor indeed. Because of this, you should have some kind of recommendation to a B&B before making a reservation. The following are suitable for newcomers:

- **Barry House Hotel**, 12 Sussex Place, W2, 020 7723 7340; fax: 020 7723 9775; e-mail: bh-hotel@bigfoot.com; B&B from £42; near Paddington station and Hyde Park.
- **Dover Hotel**, 44 Belgrave Road, SW1, 020 7821 9085; fax: 020 7834 6425; e-mail: dover@rooms.demon.co.uk; web site: www.rooms. demon.co.uk; B&B from £40; small establishment near Victoria station and handy for the tourist trail.
- **Windsor House**, 12 Penywern Road, SW5, 020 7373 9087; fax: 020 7385 2417; B&B from £32; near Earl's Court so useful for Heathrow.
- **York House Hotel**, 27-28 Philbeach Gardens, SW5, 020 7373 7519/020 7373 7579; fax: 020 7370 4641; e-mail: yorkhh@aol.com; B&B from £33—Earl's Court.

HOTELS

INEXPENSIVE

It is rare to find a room in a reasonable hotel for less than £40 a night. The W2 postcode covering the Paddington and Bayswater neighbourhoods has the highest proportion of hotels under the £50 mark. There are also plenty in Earl's Court (SW5). Although not offering much in their immediate vicinities, these locations are convenient for getting to Heathrow and the West End. For other cheaper options look outside the central London area.

- **Avonmore Hotel**, 66 Avonmore Road, W14, 020 7603 3121; fax: 020 7603 4035; e-mail: avonmore.hotel@dial.pipex.com; B&B from £63; recently refurbished small, friendly hotel near Earl's Court Exhibition Centre and West Kensington Tube.
- **Beaver Hotel**, 57-59 Philbeach Gardens, SW5, 020 7373 4553; B&B from £40—Earl's Court.
- **Beverley House Hotel**, 142 Sussex Gardens, W2, 020 7723 3380, fax: 020 7262 0324; B&B from £53—Paddington.
- **The Bonnington in Bloomsbury**, 92 Southampton Row, WC1, 020

7242 2828, fax: 020 7831 9170, e-mail: sales@bonnington.com; B&B from £46; large hotel near Holborn and Russell Square.

- **Crescent Hotel**, 49-50 Cartwright Gardens, WC1, 020 7387 1515, fax: 020 7383 2054; B&B from £43; Georgian townhouse in pleasant Bloomsbury crescent with access to gardens and tennis courts; conveniently situated near Euston station.
- **The Delmere Hotel**, 128-130 Sussex Gardens, W2, 020 7706 3344, fax: 020 7262 1863; delmerehotel@compuserve.com; B&B from £74—Paddington.
- **Kensington Court Hotel**, 33-35 Nevern Place, SW5, 020 7370 5151; fax: 020 7370 3499; e-mail: kensington.court.hotel@visit.uk.com; B&B from £63; modern hotel with private parking near Earl's Court.
- **Kingsway Hotel**, 27 Norfolk Square, W2, 020 7723 5569; fax: 020 7723 7317; e-mail: kingsway.hotel@btinternet.com; B&B from £42—Paddington.
- **Lancaster Court Hotel**, 202-204 Sussex Gardens, W2, 020 7402 8438; fax: 020 7706 3794; bed only from £32—Paddington/Lancaster Gate.
- **Lord Jim Hotel**, 23-25 Penywern Road, SW5, 020 7370 6071; fax: 020 7373 8919; B&B from £25; reasonable rates for pretty hotel near Earl's Court.
- **The Mad Hatter**, 3-7 Stamford Street, SE1, 020 7401 9222; fax: 020 7401 7111; e-mail: madhatter@fullers.co.uk; B&B from £67.50; traditional style London inn near Blackfriars.
- **Manor Hotel**, 23 Nevern Place, SW5, 020 7370 6018; fax: 020 7244 6610; B&B from £26—Earl's Court.
- **Montana Hotel**, 67-69 Gloucester Road, SW7, 020 7584 7654; fax: 020 7581 3109; B&B from £67—Gloucester Road.
- **Wigmore Court Hotel**, 23 Gloucester Place, W1, 020 7935 0928, fax: 020 7487 4254; www.wigmore-court-hotel.co.uk; B&B from £40; good sized rooms at fair prices near Oxford Street shops and Marble Arch Tube.

MIDDLE RANGE

Many large chains of hotels come in at this price range such as the **Radisson** (www.radisson.com), **Posthouse** (www.forte-hotels.com), **Thistle** (www.thistle.co.uk), and **Hilton** (www.hilton.com). These all offer consistent standards and have branches in the West End, the City and near the airports.

- **Academy Hotel**, 17-25 Gower Street, WC1, 020 7631 4115, fax: 020 7636 3442; academyh@aol.com; bed only from £100; atmospheric Bloomsbury townhouses near University of London buildings and with highly rated restaurant, Alchemy, attached—Goodge Street.

- **The Basil Street Hotel**, Basil Street, SW3, 020 7581 3311; fax: 020 7581 3693; e-mail: info@thebasil.com; B&B from £160; country style hotel near Harrods—Knightsbridge.
- **Blooms Townhouse**, 7 Montague Street, WC1, 020 7323 1717, fax: 020 7636 6498; e-mail: blooms@mermaid.co.uk; B&B from £130; Georgian building in a genteel Bloomsbury setting—Russell Square.
- **Central Park Hotel**, 49 Queensborough Terrace, W2, 020 7229 2424; fax: 020 7229 2904; e-mail: cph@centralparklondon.co.uk; B&B from £95; large modern hotel between Queensway and Bayswater Tubes.
- **Chelsea Green Hotel**, 35 Ixworth Place, SW3, 020 7225 7500; fax: 020 7225 7555; e-mail: cghotel@dircon.co.uk; B&B from £150; small-scale luxury townhouse hotel near South Kensington Tube.
- **The Copthorne Tara**, Scarsdale Place, W8, 020 7937 7211; fax: 020 7937 7100; e-mail: tara.sales@mill.cop.com; B&B (double or twin rooms only) from £196; big corporate hotel with all modern conveniences—High Street Kensington.
- **Dolphin Square Hotel**, Chichester Street, SW1, 020 7834 3800; fax: 020 7798 8735; e-mail: reservations@dolphinsquarehotel.co.uk; B&B from £142; large hotel with private gardens and health club—Pimlico.
- **Forum Hotel London**, 97 Cromwell Road, SW7, 020 7370 5757; fax: 020 7373 1448; e-mail: forumlondon@interconti.com; web site: www.interconti.com; B&B from £193. Well-appointed hotel of nearly 1000 en suite rooms with choice of on-site restaurants and bars—Earl's Court.
- **Hotel Number Sixteen**, 16 Sumner Place, SW7, 020 7589 5232; fax: 020 7584 8615; e-mail: reservations@numbersixteenhotel.co.uk; B&B from £100; pleasantly situated award-winning hotel near major museums and South Kensington Tube.
- **The Jarvis Kensington**, 31-33 Queen's Gate, SW7, 020 7584 7222; fax: 020 7589 3910; bed only from £105; medium sized hotel near Gloucester Road which is part of a reasonably priced chain; there are other branches at Hyde Park, Regent's Park and Marylebone.
- **My Hotel Bloomsbury**, 11-13 Bayley Street, WC1, 020 7667 6000; fax: 020 7667 6044; e-mail: guest_services@myhotels.co.uk; B&B from £193; Conran designed newcomer, this is a trendy hotel near Tottenham Court Road which offers a gym, library, restaurant and champagne bar.

LUXURY

- **Brown's Hotel**, Albemarle Street and Dover Street, W1, 020 7493 6020; fax: 020 7493 9381; e-mail: brownshotel@brownshotel.com; web site: www.brownshotel.com; B&B from £350; institution in the

heart of Mayfair—Green Park.
- **The Dorchester**, Park Lane, W1, 020 7629 8888, fax: 020 7409 0114; e-mail: reservations@dorchesterhotel.com; B&B from £370—Hyde Park Corner.
- **The Landmark, London**, 222 Marylebone Road, NW1, 020 7631 8000; fax: 020 7631 8080; e-mail: reservations@thelandmark.co.uk; web site: www.landmarklondon.co.uk; bed only from £316; the most luxurious London has to offer, near Marylebone station and Regent's Park.
- **Le Meridien Waldorf**, Aldwych, WC2, 020 7836 2400; fax: 020 7836 7244; B&B from £320; air-conditioned rooms, restaurants, bars and conference suites in the heart of Covent Garden's theatre land.
- **London Hilton**, 22 Park Lane, W1, 020 7493 8000; fax: 020 7208 4136; email: sales_park_lane@hilton.com; bed only from £400; the Hilton's flagship hotel which kick started Sonny and Cher's career by turning them away in the 1960s. Near Hyde Park Corner, the luxurious bedrooms have splendid views over London.
- **The Metropolitan**, Old Park Lane, W1, 020 7447 1000; fax: 020 7447 1100; e-mail: sales@metropolitan.co.uk; B&B from £283; one of London's most fashionable hotels with a bar to be seen in and a Japanese restaurant on-site.
- **The Ritz**, 150 Piccadilly, W1, 020 7493 8181; fax: 020 7493 2687; e-mail: enquire@theritzhotel.co.uk; www.theritzhotel.co.uk; B&B from £650; traditional, atmospheric and very expensive—Green Park.
- **St. Martins Lane**, 45 St. Martin's Lane, WC2, 020 7300 5555; fax: 020 7300 5501; B&B from £205; luminously designed by Philippe Starck, this dramatic new hotel has an amazing array of bars and restaurants, a gym and beautiful rooms. Great location near Covent Garden and Leicester Square.

SUMMER ONLY

- **Bankside House**, 24 Sumner Street, SE1, 020 7633 9877; fax: 020 7574 6730; e-mail: bankside-reservation@lse.ac.uk; B&B from £30—Southwark
- **Butlers Wharf Residence**, 11 Gainsford Street, SE1, 020 7407 7164; fax: 020 7403 0847; B&B from £30—London Bridge/Tower Hill
- **Imperial College**, Imperial College Conference Centre, Watts Way, Prince's Gardens, SW7, 020 7594 9525 / 020 7594 9511; fax: 020 7594 9504; e-mail: reservations@ic.ac.uk; B&B from £35—South Kensington.
- **King's College London**, for all contact: 020 7928 3777; fax: 020 7928 5777; e-mail: vac.bureau@kcl.ac.uk; B&B from £19.50; space available at the following:
  - **Great Dover Street Apartments**, 165 Great Dover Street, SE1—London Bridge/Borough

- **Hampstead Campus**, Kidderpore Avenue, NW3—Finchley Road
- **King's College Hall**, Champion Hill, SE5—Denmark Hill
- **Stamford Street Apartments**, 127 Stamford Street, SE1—Waterloo
- **Wellington Hall**, 71 Vincent Square, SW1—Victoria/St. James's Park
- **LSE Residence High Holborn**, 178 High Holborn, WC1, 020 7379 5589; fax: 020 7379 5640; e-mail: high.holborn@lse.ac.uk; B&B from £28—Holborn
- **Rosebery Avenue Hall**, 90 Rosebery Avenue, EC1, 020 7278 3251; fax: 020 7278 2068; e-mail: rosebery@lse.ac.uk; B&B from £26—Angel
- **Regents College**, Inner Circle, Regent's Park, NW1, 020 7487 7495; fax: 020 7487 7602; e-mail: markhamt@regents.ac.uk; bed only from £26—Baker Street
- **Sir John Cass Hall**, 150 Well Street, E9, 020 7739 7440; fax: 020 7729 5570; e-mail: enquiries@sirjohncass.demon.co.uk; B&B from £16—Bethnal Green
- **University of Westminster**, for all contact: 020 7911 5799; fax: 020 7911 5141; e-mail: comserv@westminster.ac.uk; bed only from £25; space available at the following:
  - **Alexander Fleming Halls of Residence**, 3 Hoxton Market, N1—Old Street.
  - **Furnival House**, Chomeley Park, N6—Archway
  - **International House**, 1-5 Lambeth Road, SE1—Waterloo/Lambeth North
  - **Marylebone Road Hall of Residence**, 35 Marylebone Road, NW1—Baker Street
  - **Wigram House**, 84-99 Ashley Gardens, Thirleby Road, SW1—Victoria
- **Walter Sickert Hall City University**, Graham Street, N1, 020 7477 8822, fax: 020 7477 8823; e-mail: i.gibbard@city.ac.uk; B&B from £30—Angel

YOUTH HOSTELS

The **Youth Hostel Association** (**YHA**) offers budget and standardised accommodation, which is popular with young backpackers. Though their facilities are basic, with shared dormitory-style rooms, they are clean and well-located. Some have family rooms available so contact the individual hostel for details. There is a central reservations number for all the London Youth Hostels, 020 7373 3400, fax 020 7373 3455, web site: www.yha.org.uk, or you can contact each one directly. Prices are around a very reasonable £20 per night:

- **City of London Youth Hostel**, 36 Carter Lane, EC4, 020 7236 4965; fax: 020 7236 7681; e-mail: city@yha.org.uk—St. Paul's/Blackfriars.
- **Earl's Court Youth Hostel**, 38 Bolton Gardens, SW5, 020 7373 7083; fax: 020 7835 2034; e-mail: earlscourt@yha.org.uk—Earl's Court.
- **Hampstead Heath Youth Hostel**, 4 Wellgarth Road, NW11, 020 8458 9054/7196; fax: 020 8209 0546; e-mail: hampstead@yha.org.uk— Golders Green.
- **Holland House Youth Hostel**, Holland House, Holland Walk, W8, 020 7937 0748; fax: 020 7376 0667; e-mail: hollandhouse@yha.org.uk— High Street Kensington.
- **Oxford Street Youth Hostel**, 14 Noel Street, W1, 020 7734 1618; fax: 020 7734 1657; e-mail: oxfordstreet@yha.org.uk—Oxford Street.
- **Rotherhithe Youth Hostel**, Salter Road, SE16, 020 7232 2114; 020 7237 2919; e-mail: rotherhithe@yha.org.uk—Rotherhithe.
- **St. Pancras Youth Hostel**, 79-81 Euston Road, NW1, 020 7388 9998; fax: 020 7388 6766; e-mail: stpancras@yha.org.uk—Euston/King's Cross.

HOME STAY AGENCIES

These agencies arrange accommodation in private host homes. Prices are given per night, in addition to which a deposit is payable in advance. A minimum stay of at least two nights is usually required.

- **At Home In London**, 70 Black Lion Lane, W6, 020 8748 1943; fax: 020 8748 2701; e-mail: info@athomeinlondon.co.uk; www.athomein-london.co.uk; from £30
- **Best Bed & Breakfast London**, P.O. Box 2070, W12, 020 8742 9123; fax: 020 8749 7084; e-mail: bestbandb@atlas.co.uk; www.best-bandb.co.uk; from £25
- **Homes Away**, Doolittle Cottage, 38 Oakdale Road, E18, 020 8530 2271; fax: 020 8530 2271; e-mail: homesaway@hotmail.com; from £20
- **Host and Guest Service**, 103 Dawes Road, SW6, 020 7385 9922/020 7385 3434; fax: 020 7386 7575; e-mail: acc@host-guest.co.uk; from £16.50
- **London Bed & Breakfast Agency Limited**, 71 Fellows Road, NW3, 020 7586 2768; fax: 020 7586 6567; e-mail: stay@londonbb.com; from £22
- **London First Choice Bed & Breakfast**, 111 Hill Rise, Greenford, Middlesex UB6, 020 8575 8877; fax: 020 8933 5778; e-mail: reserve@lfca.co.uk; from £30
- **London Homestead Services**, Coombe Wood Road, Kingston upon Thames, Surrey KT2, 020 8949 4455; fax: 020 8549 5492; e-mail: lhs@netcomuk.co.uk; from £15
- **Uptown Reservations**, 41 Paradise Walk, SW3, 020 7351 3445; fax:

020 7351 9383; e-mail: enquiries@uptown.co.uk; from £70
- **Welcome Assured**, 1 Hillcrest Avenue, Edgware, Middlesex HA8, 020 8958 3996; fax: 020 8905 4747; from £24

APARTMENTS

Renting a whole house or apartment is another option for a short stay. If you are arriving with your family in tow this can be a more convenient and affordable option (as long as you don't mind fixing your own breakfast). Prices vary based on location, size, and quality of apartments, as well as with the season. The following agencies offer a wide selection of properties. The prices given are per week and the range given encompasses the lowest prices during the slow season to the highest at peak season.

- **Acorn Management Service**, Sutherland House, 70-78 West Hendon Broadway, NW9, 020 8202 3311; fax: 020 8202 6797; from £322 to £1,040
- **Adelaide Marine Ltd.**, Adelaide Dock, Endsleigh Road, Middlesex, UB2, 020 8571 5678; fax: 020 8571 5126; houseboats from £450 to £1,200
- **Apartment Services London**, 2 Sandwich Street, WC1, 020 7388 3558; fax: 020 7383 7255; from £175 to £1,500
- **Aston's Budget & Designer Studios**, 31 Rosary Gardens, SW7, 020 7590 6000; fax: 020 7590 6060; from £455 to £1,155
- **Citadines**, 7-21 Goswell Road, EC1, 020 7766 3800; fax: 020 7766 3766; from £574 to £1,015
- **Craven Garden Lodge**, 5-10 Craven Hill Gardens, W2, 020 7402 0393/020 7402 0396; fax: 020 7262 7179; e-mail: lero@cravenlodge.swinternet.co.uk; from £350 to £1,350
- **Dolphin Square Hotel**, Chichester Street, SW1, 020 7798 8890; fax: 020 7798 8896; e-mail: reservations@dolphinsquarehotel.co.uk; from £490 to £2,520
- **Grundy, Lytton & Partners**, 2 Violet Hill, NW8, 020 7624 1165; fax: 020 7625 4552; from £200 to £1,000
- **NGH Apartments Ltd**, Nell Gwynn House, Sloane Avenue, SW3, 020 7589 1105; fax: 020 7589 9433; e-mail: reservations@nghapartments.co.uk; from £440 to £1,320
- **Royal Court Apartments**, 51-53 Gloucester Terrace, W2, 020 7402 5077/0800 318798; fax: 020 7724 0286; royalcourt@dial.pipex.com; from £560 to £1,575

THERE'S NEVER ANY SHORTAGE OF THINGS TO DO IN LONDON BUT sometimes you may get the urge to leave the hurly-burly behind and escape to a gentler place. One of the benefits of living in the capital city is that access to the rest of Britain is relatively easy, as road, rail, and air networks radiate outwards from here. So if you're looking to spend a night or two away don't feel constrained to stay within the Southeast. Mainland Britain is quite small, and by car you can reach the Scottish border within about seven hours; by rail Edinburgh is just over four hours away, and by air much less. Other towns and cities have a great deal to offer in the way of culture, heritage and nightlife. For more ideas visit the **Britain Visitor Centre** at 1 Regent Street, SW1, just off Piccadilly Circus, Monday-Friday, 9 a.m. to 6:30 p.m. and weekends 10 a.m. to 4 p.m.; July to September its extended Saturday hours are to 9 a.m. to 5 p.m. For weekend breaks Western Europe is easily accessible. You can get the train from London direct to Paris or Brussels, and there are several cut-price airlines that offer bargain flights to destinations throughout Europe.

For information about all trains within the United Kingdom ring **National Rail Enquiries** on 08457 484950. www.railtrack.co.uk.

GREAT BRITAIN

THE NATIONAL TRUST

Founded in 1895 the National Trust is a charity with the aim of preserving Britain's heritage. It owns upwards of 300 historic buildings, stately homes, and gardens throughout the country, which are open to the public and perfect for day trips. The Trust also owns and preserves stretches of open countryside and coastline that are free to visit. Descriptions of all the property the National Trust looks after can be found in the *National Trust Handbook*, which is available in bookshops. Membership of the Trust entitles you to reduced or free admission to its properties. To join contact The National Trust, P.O. Box 39, Bromley, Kent, BR1 3XL, 020 8315 1111.

THE SOUTHEAST

Oxford and **Cambridge** are famous university towns and are popular day trip destinations, taking an hour or so by train (from Liverpool Street or King's Cross for Cambridge and from Paddington for Oxford). Punt on the rivers and experience the dreamy atmosphere of their historic university buildings.

As the birthplace of William Shakespeare, the picturesque town of **Stratford on Avon** is on many must-see lists. After visiting Anne Hathaway's house and other sights which claim a tenuous link with Will, you can catch a performance of one of his plays at the Royal Shakespeare Company, Stratford. Call 01789 295623 for programme details. Trains go to Stratford from Liverpool Street station.

A day trip to the seaside is an annual outing for many Londoners. Many of the resorts near London veer towards the tacky, but if toffee apples, kiss-me-quick hats, and funfairs are what you're after then **Southend** and **Clacton** on the Essex coast are within easy reach by rail from Liverpool Street. If you fancy a day by the sea in a town with a bit more going on, **Brighton**, which boasts grand hotels lining the seafront, and the striking 18th century Brighton Pavilion, might be for you. Many come for the hopping nightlife, and there is a trendy shopping district called "The Lanes," as well as amusement arcades on the Palace Pier, and a nudist beach. Take care though, Brighton's beach is not sand, but rather uncomfortable shingle! Thameslink trains depart from Victoria or King's Cross. Trains also leave Victoria for the more traditional resorts of **Worthing**, **Hastings**, and **Eastbourne** on the Sussex coast. Over the past decade beaches in Britain have become notorious for being dirty. Those few which have passed hygiene tests have been awarded blue flags. If you want to swim or surf it's certainly advisable to head for these. Check the web site www.tidybritain.org.uk for a list.

CORNWALL

Some of the best and longest sandy beaches in England are to be found in Cornwall, the southwestern peninsula of the country. It's a bit too far for a day trip, but a lovely place to visit for longer. Here you can visit the quaintly named fishing town of **Mousehole**, the town of **St. Ives** famous for its artistic community and stroll Britain's most southerly point at **Land's End**.

THE NORTH OF ENGLAND

The North of England's two national parks, **The Peak District** and **The Lake District**, offer miles of beautiful and dramatic countryside, popular with hikers and climbers. If you're more interested in industrial heritage and urban landscapes, then a visit to one of Britain's northern cities is recommended. **Manchester** has an award-winning Museum of Science and Technology, and also is home to the country's second biggest gay community, with shops, bars, and lively nightlife centred on the Canal Street area of the city. **Liverpool** has a branch of the Tate Gallery in its Albert Dock development. The city also has a heritage industry devoted to The Beatles. Among the attractions, the Cavern Club where merseybeat began, and the terraced house in which Paul McCartney grew up (now owned by the National Trust). Trains go to Manchester and Liverpool from Euston station.

SCOTLAND

Scotland can be reached by rail, road, and air. The city of **Edinburgh** is perfect for a weekend break at any time. Among its many attractions are Edinburgh Castle, the new and impressively designed Museum of Scotland, and the grand Victorian architecture of the Royal Mile. In August, during the annual Edinburgh Festival, visitors arrive in hordes to take part in one the world's premier cultural celebrations. This raucous event hosts street performers on every corner and even the tiniest spaces are requisitioned to put on plays.

The **Scottish Highlands** are the largest wilderness area in Europe and the spectacular scenery with its mountains and glens attracts many visitors. There are possibilities for mountain climbing, hiking, and skiing in the central area around Aviemore. On the sparsely populated west coast there is abundant wildlife and endless possibilities for hiking. And on the north-easterly Moray Firth coast there are picturesque fishing villages, beautiful beaches, and golf courses. **Inverness** on Loch Ness is the most popular tourist destination for obvious monster-related reasons. Trains for Edinburgh, Aberdeen, and Inverness go from King's Cross, and from Euston to Glasgow and the west coast. There is a road bridge from Kyle of Lochalsh to Skye and ferry services depart from Mallaig and Ullapool to the islands. For more information visit the **Scottish Tourist Board** at 19 Cockspur Street, London SW1; 0131 332 2433 or brochure hotline, 0990 511511.

TRAVELLING EUROPE

RAIL

Many people travel through Europe by buying an all-in-one rail, which allows them the freedom of rail travel on the continent. Special deals are available for families and young people. Visit the **Rail Europe** web site at www.raileurope.com, to find out about these tickets as well as timetables and fares; to speak to someone in person call 0990 848848. **Eurotunnel** allows you to take your car to France or Belgium. Cars and lorries are loaded up onto special trains that travel through the tunnel. Call Eurotunnel Customer Services, 01303 273300 for more information. **Eurostar** runs rail passenger services through the Channel Tunnel to destinations in France and Belgium from Waterloo Station. There are frequently special offers on, for more information call 0990 186186.

FERRIES

You can travel to destinations in France, Belgium and Holland by ferry or hovercraft, either with or without your car.
- **Brittany Ferries**, 01752 227941, www.brittany-ferries.com
- **Hoverspeed**, 08705 240241, www.hoverspeed.com
- **P&O Stena Line**, 0990 980980, www.stenaline.co.uk

AIR

Airlines offer inexpensive flights to cities within the UK and on the continent: Belfast, Dublin, Edinburgh, Glasgow, Inverness, Paris, Frankfurt, Zurich, Lisbon, Barcelona, Venice, Rome, Athens and many others. Flights can cost as little as £70 for a roundtrip flight to Scottish cities, or between £80 and £150 for a return to European cities. There may be special offers running at any given time, and there are sometimes especially cheap deals for internet booking, so check online for details. Other inexpensive flights are advertised in travel agents' windows, *Time Out*, the travel sections of newspapers, and in the freesheet magazines you can pick up from stands in the street. When booking a discount flight check that all extras such as airport tax are included in the price quoted, and that you are aware of any applicable terms and conditions.
- **British Midland**, 0870 6060 360, www.britishmidland.com
- **Buzz**, 0870 240 7070, www.buzzaway.com
- **EasyJet**, 0870 6 000 000, www.easyjet.com
- **Go**, 0845 60 54321, www.go-fly.com
- **KLM**, 08705 074 074, www.klm.com

LONDON'S YEAR IS CHOCK-FULL WITH ANNUAL FIXTURES, FESTIVALS, and celebrations, many of which embrace cultural traditions. New excuses for a party are dreamt up every year making the calendar ever more full. Here are some of the more established highlights.

JANUARY

- **London International Boat Show**, Earl's Court Exhibition Centre, SW5, 01784 223600
- **London International Mime Festival**, various venues, 020 7637 5661, www.mimefest.co.uk

FEBRUARY

- **Chinese New Year**, Chinatown, near Leicester Square in the West End, celebrates with music, parades and fireworks.
- **London Fashion Week**, various venues; the top names in international fashion descend on London.

MARCH

- **Lesbian & Gay Film Festival**, National Film Theatre, The South Bank, SE1, information and tickets, 020 7928 3232, www.llgff.org.uk
- **Ideal Home Exhibition**, Earl's Court Exhibition Centre, Warwick Road, SW5; tickets on 020 7385 1200
- **Oxford and Cambridge Boat Race**, historic annual from Putney to Mortlake—can be watched from the banks of the Thames.
- **Battersea Contemporary Art Fair**, held at the Battersea Arts Centre, 176 Lavender Hill, SW11, on the last weekend in March.

APRIL

- **Easter Parade**, Battersea Park, SW11
- **Flora London Marathon**, Greenwich Park to Westminster, 020 7620 4117
- **Queen's Birthday**, 21st April, marked by a gun salute in Hyde Park and at the Tower of London.
- **The Word: The London Festival of Literature**, various venues; go to www.theword.org.uk.

MAY

- **Chelsea Flower Show**, The Royal Hospital, SW3, spectacular annual display of garden design and plants and flowers from all over the globe, 020 7834 4333, www.rhs.org.uk.
- **Canalway Cavalcade**, Little Venice, W9, 020 8674 3724; Inland Waterways Association trade show with processions of boats, kids' activities and craft stalls.

JUNE

- **London International Festival of Theatre**, www.lift-info.co.uk
- **Islington International Festival**, 020 7689 9891, local arts and community festival
- **Fleadh**, one-day pop music festival with an Irish theme, Finsbury Park; entrance fee.
- **Spitalfields Festival**, Christ Church, Commercial Street, E1, 020 7377 1362; highly rated season of classical music concerts.
- **The Hackney Show**, local community one-day fair and festival
- **Stoke Newington Midsummer Festival**, 020 7923 1599, week-long local arts festival culminating in a jamboree on Stoke Newington Church Street.
- **Trooping the Colour**, Horse Guards Parade, celebrating the Queen's "official" birthday, 020 7414 2497.
- **Lesbian & Gay Pride**, parade and festival held traditionally on the last Saturday in June, occasionally on the first Saturday in July. See gay press for details.
- **Wimbledon Lawn Tennis Championships**, All England Club, SW19, takes place last week of June and first week of July, 020 8944 1066.

JULY

- **International Henley Royal Regatta**, Henley on Thames, 01491 572153
- **Kenwood Open Air Concerts**, Kenwood House, Hampstead Lane, NW3, lasting until September these Saturday night concerts, which each finish with a firework display, are set in the glorious surroundings of Hampstead Heath. For tickets ring 020 7413 1443.
- **Henry Wood Promenade Concerts**, Royal Albert Hall, programme of classical concerts known to everyone as "The Proms." These too go on into September. These are ticketed events and booking in advance is recommended, 020 7589 8212.
- **Greenwich and Docklands International Festival**, festival of arts events.
- **Royal Tournament**, Earl's Court, SW5, 020 7385 1200
- **Blitz**, Royal Festival Hall, South Bank Centre, SE1, dance festival with dozens of free participatory events and performances, 020 7960 4242.

AUGUST

- **Notting Hill Carnival**, held over the Bank Holiday Weekend (last weekend in the month) in and around the Notting Hill area, attracts up to a million revellers.

SEPTEMBER

- **Brick Lane Festival**, celebrates the varied worlds of Spitalfields, with street entertainment, art exhibitions, fashion shows, plus food and music from all over the world.
- **Thames Festival**, a celebration devoted to the river, includes a spectacular torchlight procession and fireworks on the water, 020 7928 8998.
- **Horse of the Year Show**, Wembley Arena, Empire Way, Wembley, 020 8900 9282

OCTOBER

- **Dance Umbrella**, international dance festival stretching through October and November, www.danceumbrella.co.uk.
- **Costermongers' Pearly Harvest Festival**, Church of St. Martin-in-the-Fields, Trafalgar Square, first Sunday in October; pearly Kings and Queens, the emblems of cockney London, attend the service in their traditional garb of suits covered in pearly buttons.

NOVEMBER

- **Guy Fawkes Night**, 5th November, the anniversary of Guy Fawkes' foiled plot to blow up Parliament is celebrated every year by bonfires and firework displays. Many local authorities put on spectacular displays in local parks so check out local press and listings magazines.
- **London Film Festival**, takes place at various venues, this film festival is growing in stature and importance every year, 020 7815 1323.
- **London to Brighton Veteran Car Run**, a chance to see a feast of collectors' cars and motoring oddities as they set off from Hyde Park to trundle down to the south coast, 01753 681736.
- **Lord Mayor's Show**, starting at Guildhall this is the City of London's annual parade with lots of odd costumes on display, 020 7606 3030.
- **State Opening of Parliament**, Westminster, W1; convoluted rituals at the mother of all parliaments.
- **Christmas Lights**, the festive lights on Oxford Street and Regent's Street are switched on by a celebrity.

DECEMBER

- **Olympia International Show Jumping Championships**, top international show-jumping at Olympia Grand Hall and Olympia 2, W14, 020 7313 3113.
- **Great Christmas Pudding Race**, Covent Garden Plaza, includes live music and magic shows before the relay. Costumed runners race with Christmas puddings on a tray in around the market. Benefits cancer research; viewing is free. Call 020 7404 8760.

I T'S TEMPTING TO SAY THAT MORE WORDS HAVE BEEN WRITTEN about London than any other city. Certainly the number of books available runs into the thousands. Many of the English-speaking world's most famous authors, from Geoffrey Chaucer to Virginia Woolf, have had more than a few bon mots to say on the subject. Most bookshops have a London section with racks of books covering the range of the capital's history, architecture, cultures, and people. For the most extensive selections of non-fiction about London, from the Stone Age to present day, visit the bookshop in the Guildhall Library, EC2, or the shop attached to the Museum of London, London Wall, EC2. Below are just a few recommendations to help you on your way.

FICTION

- ***Absolute Beginners***, Colin MacInnes; not to be confused with the appalling film adaptation, this novel is the definitive account of hip and happening 1950s London.
- ***The Buddha of Suburbia***, Hanif Kureishi; an entertaining and satirical look at cultural clashes as an Asian boy comes of age in a London suburb during the 1970s.
- ***Sexing The Cherry***, Jeanette Winterson; a magical jaunt through London down the ages in the company of a giantess and a curious boy.
- ***White Teeth***, Zadie Smith; the sparkling debut of one of London's most exciting young writers, this is a yarn of cultures, lives, and loves lost and found on the Willesden High Road.
- ***Wise Children***, Angela Carter; a bawdy and poignant tale; rooted firmly in south London it chronicles the different generations of one family and its love affair with show-business.

GUIDES, HISTORICAL ACCOUNTS

- **The Buildings of England: London Series (four volumes)**, Nikolaus Pevsner; an incredibly detailed account of London's buildings for serious architecture enthusiasts.
- **The Diary of Samuel Pepys**, Samuel Pepys; a fascinating insight into everyday life in 17th century London. Anecdote, gossip and plenty of laughs as well as eye-witness reports of those apocryphal events in the city's history—the Great Fire of London and the Plague.
- **Fever Pitch** and **High Fidelity**, Nick Hornby; books that launched genres: *Fever Pitch* is the account of one man's life long love affair with Arsenal Football Club; *High Fidelity* describes the north London world of maudlin middle class thirty-somethings.
- **A Guide to the Architecture of London**, Edward Jones and Christopher Woodward; a good general guide to buildings of note from all eras, with diagrams and pictures.
- **A Literary Guide to London**, Ed Glinert; an enjoyably lively account of the haunts and exploits of London's literary figures—large and small, fictional and actual. It includes a great guide to secondhand bookshops.
- **London: The Biography**, Peter Ackroyd; this richly detailed book is massive in scope and takes in all manner of myth, history, and anecdote. Ackroyd has been described as "our age's greatest London imagination".
- **London: A Social History**, Roy Porter; this kaleidoscopic overview of the history of London's peoples is packed with social comment and fascinating detail about how Londoners have lived through the centuries.
- **The London Encyclopaedia**, Ben Weinreb and Christopher Hibbert, editors; a gold mine of information listing alphabetically the buildings, people, places, and events which make up the extraordinary history of the capital.
- **London Fields** and **Money**, Martin Amis; London in the rapacious 1980s, unflinching and apocalyptic satires on the morals of the Thatcherite era.
- **The New London Property Guide**, Carrie Segrave, editor; an excellent and detailed guide to buying, selling and renting in the capital.
- **Time Out Book of London Walks**; from the Thames Barrier in the east to Richmond in the west, thirty writers and personalities choose and narrate walks exploring some very different parts and aspects of London.

TELEPHONE LINES WHICH ARE OPEN 24 HOURS A DAY ARE SO INDI-cated, the rest operate during office hours, usually 9 a.m. to 5 p.m., or at restricted times which will be stated on answering machines.

ALCOHOL AND DRUG DEPENDENCY

- Alcoholics Anonymous Helpline, 08457 697555
- Drinkline, 0800 917 8282
- National Drugs Helpline, 0800 776600 (24 hour)
- Release, 020 7729 9904 (24 hour)

ANIMALS

- RSPCA National Linkline, 08705 555999, www.rspca.org.uk
- Battersea Dogs Home, 020 7622 3626
- Cats' Protection League, 020 7272 6048
- Blue Cross Animal Hospital, 020 7834 4224 between 9 a.m. and 5 p.m.; 020 7233 6479 for emergencies between 5 p.m. and 9 a.m.

BEREAVEMENT

- Child Death Helpline, 0800 282986
- Cruse Bereavement Line, 0208 332 7227

BIRTHS, DEATHS AND MARRIAGES

Contact your local council switchboard, numbers given under the **Borough Profiles**.

BUSINESSES AND SERVICES

- *Talking Pages*, 0800 600900, www.yell.com
- *Scoot*, 0800 192192, www.scoot.com

CHILD ABUSE AND FAMILY VIOLENCE

- Childline, 0800 1111 (24 hour), www.childline.org.uk
- NSPCC (National Society for the Prevention of Cruelty to Children) Child Protection Helpline, 0808 800 5000 (24 hour), www.nspcc.org.uk
- Women's Aid National Helpline, 08457 023468

CONSUMER COMPLAINTS AND SERVICES

- Consumers' Association, 0800 252100, www.which.net
- National Association of Citizens Advice Bureau, 020 7833 2181, www.nacab.org.uk
- Office of Fair Trading, 0845 722 4499, www.oft.gov.uk

COUNCIL SERVICES

For queries regarding all services such as refuse collection, street cleaning and recycling contact the local council switchboard listed under the **Borough Profiles**.

CRIME

- Crime in progress, 999
- Crimestoppers, anonymous tips, 0800 555555
- Neighbourhood Watch, 020 7772 3348
- Victim Support, 0845 303 0900
- West End Central Police, 020 7437 1212
- For local police stations, see the **Borough Profiles**.

CRISIS HOTLINES

- National Missing Persons Helpline, 0500 700700
- Rape and Abuse Line, 0808 800 0123
- Rape Crisis Centre, 020 7837 1600
- Samaritans (crisis line), 0845 790 9090, minicom: 0845 790 9192, www.samaritans.org.uk

DISCRIMINATION

- Campaign for Racial Equality, 020 7828 7022, www.cre.gov.uk
- DIAL UK, the Disability Helpline, 01302 310123
- Disability Information and Services, 08457 622633, minicom: 08457 622644, www.disability.gov.uk
- Equal Opportunities Commission, 0161 833 9244, www.eoc.org.uk
- Gay & Lesbian Legal Advice Line, 020 7831 3535
- Lesbian and Gay Employment Rights, 020 7704 8066 (lesbians), 020 7704 6066 (gay men)

ELECTED OFFICIALS

LOCAL AUTHORITY
To contact local councillors, go to the borough web site or phone number given under the **Borough Profiles**.

CITY
- Greater London Authority (and Mayor's Office), 020 7983 4000, minicom: 020 7983 4458, www.london.gov.uk

NATIONAL
- House of Commons, 020 7219 4272, www.parliament.uk
- For links to all government departments, go to www.open.gov.uk

EMERGENCY

- Fire, Police, Ambulance, 999
- Floodcall, 0845 988 1188

ENTERTAINMENT

INFORMATION
- *Scoot*, 0800 192192; www.scoot.com
- www.thisislondon.com
- www.timeout.com

TICKETS
- First Call, 0870 906 3700 / 020 7420 1000, www.firstcalltickets.com
- Odeon Cinemas, 0870 5050 007, www.odeon.co.uk
- Stargreen Ticket Agency, 020 7734 8932
- TicketMaster, 020 7344 4444

HEALTH & MEDICAL CARE

- Cancerlink, 0800 132905
- Health Information Service, 0800 665544
- Medical Emergency, 999
- MIND (National Association for Mental Health), 0345 660163
- Saneline, 0345 67 8000
- National AIDS Helpline, 0800 567123 (24 hour)
- NHS Direct, 0845 4647, www.nhsdirect.nhs.uk (24 hour, for immediate and confidential health advice)
- Smokers Quitline, 0800 002200

HOUSING

- Shelter London Line, 0800 446 441 (24 hour), www.shelter.org.uk, emergency help, advice and referrals for the homeless

LIBRARIES

- See **Borough Profiles** for library numbers.

LONDON ONLINE

- www.citystreetz.com, for clubs, bars, pubs, and restaurants
- www.londontown.com; the London Tourist Board's official internet site for London with everything from tourist attractions and accommodation to financial services and travel.
- www.thisislondon.com; *Evening Standard's* web site with particularly strong entertainment listings.
- www.timeout.com, *Time Out's* web site.
- www.london-calling.co.uk, current listings of entertainment and culture in the capital.
- www.walks.com; London Walks tour company

MARRIAGE GUIDANCE

- Relate, 020 8427 8694

OLDER PERSONS

- Age Concern, 0800 009966
- Help the Aged Seniorline, 0800 650065, minicom, 0800 269626

PARKING

- NCP Infoline, 020 7404 3777

POLICE

- 999 in emergency
- See **Borough Profiles** for local station numbers.

POST OFFICE

- Customer Helpline, 0345 223344
- Postcode information, 0345 111222
- See **Borough Profiles** for addresses of local post office branches.

SCHOOLS

- Department of Education and Employment, 0870 001 2345, www.dfee.gov.uk
- Ofsted, 020 7510 0180, www.ofsted.gov.uk

SHIPPING SERVICES

- ParcelForce, 0800 224466, www.parcelforce.com
- DHL, 0345 100300, www.dhl.com
- FedEx, 0800 123800, www.fedex.com/gb
- UPS, 0345 877877, www.ups.com

SPORTS

- Sportsline, 020 7222 8000
- www.bbc.co.uk/sport, for results and sports news

TAXES

- Inland Revenue enquiry line, 020 7667 4001, www.inlandrevenue.gov.uk

TAXIS

- Black Cabs, 020 7272 0272 / 020 7253 5000
- Computer Cab, 020 7432 1432 (to book using a credit card)

TELEPHONE

- Operator, 100
- International Operator, 155
- Directory Enquiries, 192
- International Directory Enquiries, 153
- Nuisance Calls Adviceline, 0800 666700

TIME

- Speaking Clock, 123

TOURISM AND TRAVEL

- London Tourist Information Service, 0990 887711
- Tourist Information Centre, 020 7278 8787, www.londontown.com

TRAFFIC INFORMATION

- www.bbc.co.uk/londonlive

TRANSPORT

AIRPORTS
- Heathrow, 0870 000 0123
- Gatwick, 01293 535353
- Luton, 01582 405100
- London City, 020 7646 0000
- Stansted, 01279 680500

BUSES, TUBE, & RAIL WITHIN LONDON
- London Travel Information, 020 7222 1234; for disabled passengers, 020 7918 3312; minicom, 020 7918 3015; www.transportforlondon.gov.uk

COACHES – NATIONAL
- National Express Coaches, 0990 808080

TRAINS – NATIONAL AND INTERNATIONAL
- National Rail Enquiries, 08457 484950
- Rail Europe, 0990 848848
- Eurostar, 0990 186186, www.eurostar.com
- Eurotunnel, 0870 535 3535

FERRIES
- Brittany Ferries, 01752 227941, www.brittanyferries.co.uk
- Hoverspeed, 08705 240241, www.hoverspeed.com
- P&O Stena Line, 0990 980980, www.stenaline.co.uk

UTILITY EMERGENCIES
- Gas emergency, 0800 111999
- Electricity emergency: London Electricity, 0800 096 9000; Southern Electric, 0345 708090; Eastern Electricity, 01268 785566
- Water Emergency: Thames Water, 0845 920 0800; Three Valleys Water, 0845 782 3333

WEATHER

- www.bbc.co.uk/weather

W

Y-Z

JANETTA WILLIS was born in Belfast, Northern Ireland, and spent the first years of her life in Edinburgh, Scotland before arriving in London aged four. Brought up in suburban west London, and having also lived in east London and Brighton, Janetta is now a confirmed north Londoner. She divides her time between working part-time as a charity administrator and writing. This is Janetta's first book and it is for Lucy, whose enthusiasm, support and spirit of adventure made it possible.

We would appreciate your comments regarding this first edition of the *Newcomer's Handbook® for Moving to London.* If you've found any mistakes or omissions or if you would just like to express your opinion about the guide, please let us know. We will consider any suggestions for possible inclusion in our next edition, and if we use your comments, we'll send you a *free* copy of our next edition. Please send this response form to:

Reader Response Department
First Books
3000 Market Street NE, Suite 527
Salem, OR 97301 USA

Comments:

_____
_____
_____
_____
_____
_____
_____
_____

Name: _____
Address _____
_____
_____
Telephone (   ) _____

3000 Market Street NE, Suite 527
Salem, OR 97301 USA
503-588-2224
www.firstbooks.com

FIRST BOOKS

NEWCOMER'S
ORDER FORM
HANDBOOK ®

THE ORIGINAL, ALWAYS UPDATED, ABSOLUTELY INVALUABLE GUIDES FOR PEOPLE MOVING TO A CITY!

Find out about neigborhoods, apartment and house hunting, money matters, deposits/leases, getting settled, helpful services, shopping for the home, places of worship, cultural life, sports/recreation, vounteering, green space, schools and education, transportation, temporary lodgings and useful telephone numbers!

	# COPIES	TOTAL
Newcomer's Handbook® for Atlanta	_____ x $17.95	$_____
Newcomer's Handbook® for Boston	_____ x $18.95	$_____
Newcomer's Handbook® for Chicago	_____ x $18.95	$_____
Newcomer's Handbook® for London	_____ x $20.95	$_____
Newcomer's Handbook® for Los Angeles	_____ x $17.95	$_____
Newcomer's Handbook® for Minneapolis-St. Paul	_____ x $20.95	$_____
Newcomer's Handbook® for New York City	_____ x $19.95	$_____
Newcomer's Handbook® for San Francisco	_____ x $20.95	$_____
Newcomer's Handbook® for Seattle	_____ x $18.95	$_____
Newcomer's Handbook® for Washington D.C.	_____ x $18.95	$_____
	SUBTOTAL	$_____
POSTAGE & HANDLING (*$7.00 first book, $1.00 each add'l.*)		$_____
	TOTAL	$_____

SHIP TO:

Name _____

Title _____

Company _____

Address _____

City _____ State _____ Zip _____

Phone Number (_____) _____

Send this order form and a check or money order payable to:
First Books

First Books, Mail Order Department
3000 Market Street NE, Suite 527, Salem, OR 97301 USA

Allow 1-2 weeks for delivery

THE NEWCOMER'S HANDBOOK® SERIES

NOTES

NOTES

NOTES